Dedicated to all submarine heroes, past and present.

The great majority of the author's thirty-six years' service in the Royal Navy was either aboard submarines or in their direct support. He enjoyed command appointments in two diesel-electric patrol boats (SSK), in a hunter-killer (SSN), and then in two nuclear deterrent boats (SSBN). Sea appointments were interspersed with key operational roles in Faslane, as the Submarine Operations Officer in Northwood, in SHAPE, and in the Ministry of Defence. As a Captain, he was responsible for all UK submarine training ashore and afloat. His lived experience and innate understanding of submarine function, warfare and strategy informs his writing. This is his first novel.

Cover Pictures

A modified photo of HMS *E8* with radio mast raised. Reproduced under the Open Government Licence, courtesy of the National Museum of the Royal Navy.

Satellite photograph of the Sea of Marmara and the Dardanelles by kind permission of NASA Earth Observatory. The different salinities are shown by the different water colours. In addition, the various and unpredictable whorls and currents across the whole area are amply displayed, as is the out-flowing current from the Dardanelles.

Cover Design by averyandbrown.com

Hellespont

A Tradesmen novel by
Byrne Avery

HELLESPONT

List of Contents

List of Maps

Photograph

HELLESPONT

Foreword

This story starts at the beginning of the 20th century at a time when the Victorian Royal Navy is undergoing fundamental change. Competition with the Kaiser's burgeoning fleet is encouraging ever-more radical technology. In parallel, the hero of this story, Ted Crockford, is transported from a rural retreat to the nascent Submarine Service. With so-called 'boats' introduced only in 1901, concepts for the operational deployment of these revolutionary submersible craft had to evolve rapidly within a Navy still bound to the fighting traditions of sailing ships.

The single word "Gallipoli" conjures up grotesque images of military folly and carnage on that distant peninsular. Nonetheless, few people know that an awe-inspiring feat by a submarine committed the whole military enterprise to continue after the most disastrous start. Similarly, the story is seldom told of the singular success of a handful of diminutive submersibles that disrupted the Ottoman lines of communication and reinforcement routes to the fighting front. These submarines rampaged unsupported throughout the Sea of Marmara – the enemy's backyard – but getting there was the problem.

The Dardanelles – called *Hellespont* in ancient times – has been regarded since pre-history as a most treacherous waterway. In 480 BC, it was there that Xerxes tried to bring his Persian armies across from Asia to invade Europe, only for his bridge to be washed away by the fast and unrelenting outward flow. Shakespeare's Othello rages:

". . . Like to the Pontic [Black] *Sea*
Whose icy currents and compulsive course,
Ne'er feels retiring ebb, but keeps due on
To the Propontic [Sea of Marmara] *and the Hellespont . . ."*

These vignettes identify the issue exactly: how could these rudimentary craft with limited dived range overcome the continual counter-current to complete the long transit of the Dardanelles? That was even before the perils of widespread minefields, legions of shore guns, and flotillas of defending warships. From a standing start, a small cadre of enthusiasts brought 'The Trade' to notable success, but with little recognition of their strategic contribution or the tragic costs involved.

So, here is an adventure story featuring a fictitious submarine manned by an entirely make-believe crew. Be assured, however, the episodes described are rooted in history. The key players ashore – Churchill, Fisher, Wilson, Carden, de Robeck, Keyes, Somerville and others – appear as they did at the time, with any additions and alterations to their actions or speech only as essential to support the story. Mostly, real events have been retold, giving the author's interpretation of how they might have unfolded. The epilogue details who did what and when, providing the true chronology aided by a full bibliography, for anyone wishing to investigate further. In essence, a few rogue yarns have been spun through the tapestry of this history and then the whole has been shrunk into a single patrol to honour *all* the submariners – British, Australian and French – who acted as one team to emerge triumphant.

Technical note. Steering orders in this story comply with the conventions of the time. "Helm to port or starboard" cause the ship's head to go in the opposite direction, following the centuries-old practice when tillers were in use. It was not until 1st January 1933 that the Merchant Shipping Act 1932 and associated Admiralty Fleet Order brought the 'direct' system of helm orders into use on all British vessels.

HELLESPONT

HELLESPONT

Chapter 1 – Come Cheer Up, My Lads

1

Ted was sauntering on his way home from the forge, head down, arms hanging, and deep in his own thoughts. He turned into Neville Lane, which led down to the ford and then on to Hurlstone Point overlooking the bay.

"You, there! Come here, please."

Looking up, Ted saw young Lady Margaret, the estate owner's daughter. She was red-cheeked and flustered, standing by her father's automobile. Dutifully, the boy picked up his pace and hurried on towards her.

Lady Margaret wracked her brains. She was sure she recognised him. "Oh! It's you . . . er . . . Crockford, isn't it?" Looking down from the family pew in the church, she remembered the rector telling the congregation of the sad demise of his father whilst serving abroad.

"Yes, Miss," Ted confirmed, touching his forehead but not raising his eyes from the ground.

"I have a problem with this damned contraption and want you to go to Hunnicutt House. Tell them where I am and to send out a carriage to collect me," she commanded. "And Parsons, our chauffeur, will have to come out too, I presume, to arrange the return of the vehicle," she added as an afterthought. "You can come back in the carriage, and if you're quick, I'll give you tuppence for your trouble."

The boy now looked at the car, sprayed with mud and with water dripping off the bonnet. This was not the sparklingly clean machine Mr. Parsons spent hours polishing and fussing over.

Ted had to pluck up his courage even to speak directly to this personage within the community, and his cheeks reddened. "Is it just the engine, Miss, after you came through the ford?"

Taken aback, she looked at him grim-faced. Still, she answered, "Yes, it just spluttered to a halt, confounded machine, and I cannot possibly get it started again myself."

"I think I know what to do, Miss," Ted ventured. "Mr. Parsons has shown me, and I think I can fix it."

"What?" she responded, straightening up in apparent disbelief. "How old are you . . . thirteen . . . fourteen? How could you possibly know about such apparatus – it's certainly the only one around here." She was shaking her head. "Do you have any appreciation of how expensive this vehicle is and how angry Lord Arscott would be if you break anything? But," she conceded after a pause, "if you *really* think you could effect a repair, it would certainly save me a lot of time and probably a row too."

"It shouldn't take five minutes or so, Miss, and I think it's worth a go. I'll run all the way to the house if it doesn't work," Ted promised.

Without waiting for further permission, he went over to the car, undid the leather straps, and folded back the right-hand side of the engine cover. Going round to the back, he located the tool roll and some rags where Mr. Parsons always kept them. Lady Margaret was certainly surprised that he should feel so at home with the machine and its layout. This allayed her fears – at least to some extent – about his ability to fix the car.

Despite the autumn chill, Ted took off his light jacket and placed it carefully to protect the automobile's paintwork as he leaned over to peer into the machine. Already tall, he could reach into the engine compartment easily. As he did so, the young aristocratic lady could see his slight frame, with protruding bones shaping his too-small, heavily-darned shirt. Dark hair and eyebrows framed his handsome, if gaunt, face. Setting to work and talking more to himself than to her, Ted opined, "I expect water has splashed up onto the sparking plugs and leads. I'll just dry them off and see how it goes."

Good to his word, he was no more than a few minutes before he turned to her and proposed, "If you'd like to get back in, please, Miss, select the neutral gear and switch on the ignition. I'll turn the engine over and see if she fires." Unused to receiving such directions from *anyone*, let alone a child, Lady Margaret smiled to herself. She complied whilst he lined up the starting handle. Ready to go, Ted looked back over the bonnet to see if the lady was too. "Yes, it's switched on," she confirmed. He jerked the handle round, once, twice, and the engine burbled into life. He resecured the engine cover and replaced the tools exactly whence they came.

"Well, I must admit I had my doubts, Crockford, but you've done me a huge favour. Wait," Lady Margaret ordered, rummaging around in her handbag. "Here's sixpence – with my thanks."

With eyes still focused on the ground but feeling proud and with a satisfied grin, Ted replied politely, "Thank you very much, Miss. You're welcome, Miss."

With that, Lady Margaret selected a gear, released the handbrake, and continued up the road towards the village and to Hunnicutt House.

Edward Crockford – known to everyone as Ted – had got to know Mr. Parsons well over the last couple of years since his father had died. After lessons, he started hanging around by the forge next door to the school

3

gate. Even at some distance, Ted could feel the glowing coals tingling his cheeks and bringing warmth to his bones. He wished he could soak it up and take it home with him. Everyone knew who he was, of course, and felt sorry for him and his mother. Still, even within such a small community, they were nonetheless outsiders. Everyone else over the northern part of Exmoor worked for Lord Arscott and the estate. Ted and his mother lived in a tiny cottage overlooking the sea, nestled under Hurlstone Point and thus protected a little from the biting north-easterly winds. By some ancient anachronism and historically owned by a fisherman's family, their small plot had remained as freehold land, surrounded as it was by the Hunnicutt Estate. Doubtless, some were envious of their privileged position without rent and other obligations to the landlord. It should have been so for a family of even modest means, but, isolated from the direct support of the estate and with a meagre income, life for the Crockfords was always a struggle.

It had not been so, of course, when his father was alive. Although absent for years at a time, his successful career in the Royal Navy had ensured a regular income and, indeed, had allowed them to purchase the property in the first place. In those now-distant days, their home had always been warm and welcoming, with sufficient to eat and always with meat on Sundays. Even so, they had kept to themselves, with few close friends to visit or play with. There had been time for leisurely walks up onto Selworthy Beacon or, during less clement weather, to cuddle up with his mother in an armchair. At the same time, she read to him from one of their few books. But now that all seemed so long ago. A one-sided, officious and perfunctory note informed his mother of his father's death on active duty, providing extraordinarily little detail of the when and how. Despite her husband's long years of service, her widow's pension was minimal – and even that arrived only after the intervention of the kindly vicar. Within a single season, their life had become one of survival. Fortunately, his mother was a talented seamstress and earned a little money by repairing and altering clothes for the folk in the village. However, this was an unsophisticated, rural community, and there was infrequent demand for her services. Otherwise, she scratched away at the hard ground of their small plot to grow whatever vegetables she could or to gather those few the rabbits left for her. So now, their clothes were thin, if not threadbare, and precious fuel was reserved for cooking rather than heating the house.

But the village people were kind and supported them in whatever manner they could. It was not long before the blacksmiths invited Ted further into the forge and started offering the young lad little jobs, tidying and sweeping up. Occasionally, he earned the odd penny or two in return. There too, he had met Mr. Parsons, often bringing down his lordship's motor car for this or that repair. To the boy, this machine of flawless red and black paint with shining chrome and gleaming brass was a thing of wonder. Ted would often sit, hugging his knees and feeling utterly content simply by looking at this marvellous invention. All the men would grin and shake their heads. Even Parsons – that character known to be gruff and on occasion prone to take on the airs and graces of his employers – mellowed and warmed to the lad. He started to show the boy inside the engine compartment, where the spare wheel was kept and how the fabric roof folded back. In time, he allowed Ted to help clean the car, pump up the tyres, help him change the oil, and carry out other servicing of the vehicle. It became noticeable he was a very bright lad with an aptitude – even love – for mechanics. More important than that, especially to Parsons and the others, Ted was a likeable boy who remained ever-respectful and polite. This applied even when being told by less intelligent adults the same thing for the seventh time when he had understood perfectly after the first!

Having watched the car and Lady Margaret disappear around the corner, Ted continued down the lane and crossed the stream via the stepping stones. His house was about a mile further along the slightly rising track, just as the path came out of the shadow of the overhanging trees. At such a young age, all he saw as he approached was his home and all that was familiar. He took no notice of the peeling paint and the missing shingles along the ridge of the low roof. His mother turned from the stove as he entered the front door. She held him as parents do, in a hug for that fraction of a second too long that makes young adults uncomfortable and want to squirm and pull away. When she released him, Ted put his bag of schoolbooks on the table and mirrored his mother's wide smile with his own. She had a cup of tea ready for them both, with a single slice of bread and blackberry jam for him but with nothing for herself. As usual, she listened intently across the table as he told her what he had done in school that day, occasionally interrupting to add her own comments about his studies. Despite being outdoors most of the time, his mother's complexion remained pale, almost grey. Her cheeks were hollow and the lines across her forehead deep. As November was drawing on, even the fading autumn light was gone by five o'clock, and his mother routinely retired to her bedroom early. He remained awake a little longer, reading by the light of a candle the books the teacher had lent him.

2

The reason for his mother's exhaustion became all too clear about a month later. She had been disguising her symptoms well, hiding the racking cough that troubled her all day by drinking lots of hot, boiled water in the afternoon before Ted came home. This eased her condition for an hour or so before she retreated to her bed. He never saw the specks of blood she coughed onto her handkerchiefs. But, coming home one afternoon, he found her slouched in her chair and unable to get up even for their ritual greeting. He helped her to bed and made her comfortable. Then, despite her protests about the cost, Ted set off at pace on the three-mile journey to the local town to find the only doctor in the area. To waste no time, he cut down straight to the sea and followed the curve of the bay to the town. The shoreline comprised of large pebbles and boulders, being extremely uncomfortable through the thin soles of his boots, and the boy had to take great care not to turn an ankle in the fading light. Fortunately, he found the doctor at home, having thought he had finished for the day. Nevertheless, he responded to Ted's pleadings by preparing his horse and setting off along the road back to their house. The boy retraced his previous route, now in almost complete darkness.

By the time Ted arrived back at home, the doctor was already packing his bag and preparing to depart.

Without any preamble or acknowledgement of Ted's tender years, the physician stated directly, "I'm afraid your mother is quite seriously ill. She has consumption of the lungs, and I will arrange for her to be admitted to the isolation hospital, which is about five miles away. It's only opened recently, so she should receive the best care available. It's not too far, so you should be able to visit your mother whilst she's there." Turning to leave the boy to manage entirely on his own, he concluded, "Your mother's situation is not totally beyond hope, but I must say she is fragile indeed and has not been looking after herself." Ted made his mother a hot drink, helped her to sip it, and then sat by the bed in the dark, holding her hand.

The following morning a pony and trap duly arrived, and Ted helped his mother up into the back. Next to her, he placed a small bag of clothes and other effects, which he had packed under her direction. He climbed briefly into the back of the cart with her and held her close. "It'll be all right, Mother. I can look after myself. You just get better." With their eyes locked together, he stepped down and waved to her continuously until the trap disappeared.

3

Ted's mother died three days later. Being in the school week and with short autumn days, he had had no opportunity to make the half-day return trip to the hospital. After school on Friday, the vicar, Stephen, and Ted's teacher, Mrs. Hunt, knocked on his door to deliver the sad news. Ted was bereft and couldn't understand what had happened, continually repeating, "But I was going to see her tomorrow." There was little these kindly adults could do for the boy but leave him alone with his thoughts.

The stark reality was that Ted had no relations and was now alone in the world. He managed very little sleep that night as a million depressing imaginings swirled around in his brain. The weather next morning was dry, so he set off for some fresh air and to get away from the house with its constant reminders of his mother all around.

If you didn't cross the ford into the village, the track from his home continued along the edge of the woods crowding down from the hill above. These ancient oaks leaned right over the path. Their lower boughs rested in the fields opposite, like elbows, allowing the trees to look up across the vale to the heather-covered heights beyond. Clear of this dark tunnel, the path climbed back into the light and towards the next village. Just beyond and standing proudly above was the parish church, which all communities from that part of Exmoor attended. Ted knew this route particularly well because he was a member of the troop of bell ringers and passed this way for fortnightly practices and on most Sundays.

The white-painted church on the hillside provided superb views, both up to Dunkery Beacon, the highest point of Exmoor, and across the valley which led down to the bay whence he had come. Ted stopped momentarily to gather his breath before deciding to take a different route home. His chosen path would appear more direct if you drew it on a map. Rather than skirt around the hill, it climbed steeply up its side – no route for the unfit – and over the top before descending perilously. Ted crossed the manicured green surrounded by the thatched alms houses. These had been provided by the benevolent Hunnicutt estate for widows, the infirm, or those lucky few who lived long enough to retire from working in the fields and forests. Over the stream, he followed the zigzag path directly upwards, out of the trees to the multivallate Iron Age 'castle' and over the remaining earthworks of mounds and ditches of this ancient hill fort.

Here he spent whole days during his holidays, sometimes with friends but often alone, pretending to be a fierce native warrior protecting his homestead. He would hide in the bracken on the steep side of the fort, looking down into the combe and watching for the enemy approaching. One day a party of ladies and gentlemen with their attendants appeared on the path below, walking with three or four spaniels. The animals were off the lead, and, giggling at their antics, Ted watched the dogs rushing hither and thither. Their noses were to the ground, with tails wagging wildly, following the scents of deer, foxes, badgers and squirrels. Suddenly, the animals started to run rapidly up the slope directly toward him. Terrified that they should catch his scent, he sat stock-still while the dogs came nearer and nearer; if he were caught spying on these gentlefolk, there would be hell to pay. There were now two dogs less than five yards away from him. Then, with a frantic clucking and fluttering, a pheasant suddenly broke cover and took off, chased down the hill by the dogs excitedly barking with pride at their achievement. After that, Ted always kept a couple of fir cones in his pocket to distract anyone getting too close.

These all seemed like ancient memories to him, and such days of play had passed. Leaving a golden wake of broken, dying bracken behind him, he steamed on further up the hill. A solitary copse of silver birch trees was ahead, standing in open moorland. The twigs atop were devoid of all leaves in this exposed place, creating a purple mist and leaving the trunks as vertical white lines in this otherwise horizontal landscape. Ted reached the popular viewpoint at the top and, breathing deeply and with his mind elsewhere, hardly paused to take in the magnificence of the vistas all around. Precipitous cliffs towered over the sea to the west. To the north, the swirling mud and grey waters of the Bristol Channel ran in full ebb. The beacon on the highest spot was now clearly in view to the east. A whole hemisphere of beautiful Exmoor filled all points towards the south. Ted started his descent through a gate and back among the trees.

He came to the clearing containing a huge cross not a hundred yards further on. Erected by some ancestor of the estate owner, the structure towered twenty feet into the air, commanding a view of the whole bay to the west. Decades of differently-coloured lichens had rendered the oak structure to look more like stone. Ted sat down at its base, looking at the pedestal. He didn't truly understand what most of the inscription meant, but he found it somehow comforting and knew it by heart.

"Praise the Lord from the earth, ye dragons and all deeps;
Fire and hail; snow and vapours; stormy wind fulfilling His Word;
Mountains and all hills; fruitful trees and all cedars.
Let them praise the name of the Lord, for His name alone is excellent.
Happy is he that hath God for his help, whose hope is in the Lord."

This was the place Ted came to when he needed to be alone or to think things through. He was sure others came here occasionally, but his solitude had never been disturbed during many visits. The trees surrounding the site shielded it from winds from all quarters, and even the birds sang less loudly here, respecting its tranquillity. Only the buzzards broke the silence with their high-pitched "Eeeeah!" as they glided motionless on the strong winds. They hoped their spectral scream would cause their prey to break cover and run into the open, where they could be caught. Here, Ted felt whole and secure, at one with the surroundings he had always known. Here, he could be at peace and just *be*, free from the turmoil in his brain as he tried to process all the thoughts whizzing around. He sat motionless, just staring – unseeing – at the sea below. Fog was forming out in the bay, as it often did, and fingers of low cloud were starting to drift up the valley. Slowly the wraithlike hands reached further inland, grasping and digging into the earth, heaving the huge grey body ashore until all nature's beauty was obscured by this malevolent creature. He could not express it, but Ted's mood reflected much the same, feeling darkness closing over his life, with his entire future being hidden from him. The thought made him shiver, so he rose and continued down the hill.

4

"Please come in." Lord Arscott was on his feet and welcomed the two visitors into his study. "Mrs. Hunt, if you would like to sit here, please and, Rector, here." Settling back into his leather-padded chair behind the desk, he invited the vicar to start the conversation, "Now Stephen, I believe you want to talk about young Crockford."

Of habit, the parish priest took off his spectacles and started polishing them, looking myopically around the room. "Thank you, Lord Arscott." Clearing his throat and replacing his glasses, he continued, "Strictly speaking, Edward Crockford is almost a senior and would in any case have finished school next year. But how he is to live in the interim is of immediate concern."

"If he could muddle through for the year to earn his education certificate," responded the landowner, "I'm sure we could find someone in the village to provide him with a hot meal every day." With a shrug, he added matter-of-factly, "Or he could even complete his education now, as many do at his age, and we'd put him to work on the estate . . . even though I'm under no obligation to do so," he wanted to make clear. "But I am under pressure from my daughter, Lady Margaret," he continued with a smile. "Having heard of his mother's passing, she came clean about a little incident concerning my car at the ford and how young Crockford had ridden to her rescue! Clearly, I was the last to be told this widely-known tale." He allowed himself a chuckle whilst shaking his head. "Nonetheless, it does seem a truly remarkable story and surprising that he should prove so practical at his age, clearly with an aptitude for mechanics. He might be an ideal candidate for an apprenticeship as a blacksmith or chauffeur."

A disgruntled cough from the lady sitting opposite was the vicar's cue. "We have here a very able and intelligent boy, Sir, who – with no disrespect to those in such worthy trades – would frankly be wasted as a blacksmith or chauffeur."

He resumed quickly. "You will remember that Edward's father, William Crockford served in the Royal Navy for many years until being killed on active service. Starting as a boy seaman and rising to be a senior rating, he was eventually recommended to be commissioned from the lower deck, which is no mean achievement. But further to that, he played a key role in the relief of Ladysmith by the Naval Brigade, in which the whole Nation takes much pride. That gave me the idea that a career in the Royal Navy might be just the thing for his son too."

Lord Arscott could see the suggestion's merit and nodded in agreement.

"It might *seem* farfetched," admitted the vicar, "but I harbour the idea that Edward might even be worthy of seeking a commission from the outset. For example, I asked our bell tower captain to take him on. I thought this might be a way of improving his financial plight slightly – from the gratuities received from special services and such," he explained. "But his progress was prodigious, learning the routines in a fraction of the time others take."

"That might be the case, Stephen, but there is a world of difference between being a tower captain and a ship's captain!" interjected Lord Arscott, delighted at his own wit.

"You are right, of course, My Lord," countered the vicar, "but that is why I have asked Mrs. Hunt to come here today, to provide a fuller appraisal of the boy."

Mrs. Hunt was an esteemed lady who had taught at the village school for more than thirty years. Tightly packaged in a tweed jacket and long wool skirt, she sat perfectly upright with shoulders back. Her grey hair was scraped away from her face, disappearing under a sensible, frill-less bonnet. Seated across the desk separating her from the landowner, she peered straight into his face, seeming to be taking his measure. Her reputation for no-nonsense was confirmed immediately as she pulled out a notebook from the bag in her lap before looking up. "Lord Arscott, Edward Crockford is one of the brightest and most pleasant pupils it has been my pleasure ever to teach."

"I have made some notes," she announced, opening her book and sanctioning no interruption. "In arithmetic, and particularly in geometry, Edward always grasps the key principles quickly. I have routinely had to give him additional work to allow the other pupils time to catch up. His vocabulary is still improving, as is his grammar, but his spelling is always accurate. He has neat enough writing, despite the disadvantage of being left-handed. He is eager to learn in other subjects, such as geography and history, and I have taken it upon myself to lend him additional books to study to broaden his appreciation further. Were he to have come from a more comfortably-off family with greater opportunity . . . " She let her words hang, " . . . I do not doubt that he would have succeeded at public school and possibly university too.

"But I would like to comment principally on Edward's character. Despite his academic prowess, he has no arrogance whatever and understates his achievements. In return, the other students show no envy or malice whatsoever towards him on account of his abilities – which in my wide experience is extremely unusual in such circumstances. Indeed, he appears to be universally liked and is often seen playing in the school yard with all the other groups of children – boys and girls – and enjoying himself greatly. They, in return, seek his company. I believe he is capable of great things and would probably enjoy being stretched, both academically and in all manner of practical pursuits." She closed her book as she raised her head. "I think that covers everything. Do you have any questions?"

Lord Arscott had been concentrating on the ink marks in his blotter rather than risk catching the teacher's eye, "No, I don't think so, Mrs. Hunt. Thank you so much for taking the trouble to come here today and providing such a comprehensive report."

Lord Arscott rested his chin on his hand to think. "His situation is indeed interesting, but let's be practical. Firstly, let's assume the Navy might be prepared to take him. But after that, how on earth could he support himself through training and face the inevitable expenses of wardroom life?" he asked rhetorically. Looking out of the window and thinking out loud, he answered his own question, "I could probably make use of his cottage for some of my forestry workers. He would retain the freehold, of course, and the rental from the property could provide a minimal income. But that wouldn't be enough to live on, so what more could be done?"

"After his father died," the rector interrupted his thoughts, "I investigated payment of the pension due. My brother in London also put me in touch with various charities that undertake to support the widows and orphans of Royal Navy people. Since Mrs. Crockford was taken ill, I've asked my brother to make further inquiries. It seems that all manner of help is possible, from accommodation, uniforms and civilian clothing, as well as some funding, particularly if this involved Edward joining the Service. I don't pretend that it would be easy for him. Still, with your generous offer too, Sir, I honestly believe that we could develop a workable regime."

Lord Arscott sat back in his chair and sighed, weighing matters up. At last, he sat up, "Well done, Rector; you certainly seem to have been thorough in your research. This young man must possess praiseworthy attributes to attract such loyalty from you and Mrs. Hunt. Thank you, both." Standing up and pushing back his chair, he brought the meeting to a close. "I'm prepared to give my blessing to the scheme and hope the Navy might want to take him on. I'll leave it to you, Rector, to talk to the boy. If neither he nor the Navy wants to take the matter further, he'll remain here and doubtless become an asset to the estate."

5

The next day at the cottage, the rector climbed onto his horse and set off down the lane, leaving Ted at his front door. The boy didn't know what to think; nothing in his life had prepared him to make such decisions. He had no yardstick to measure the pros and cons, even if he could perceive them. Reverend Stephen had been very patient in explaining matters and seemed most positive. However, the idea of setting off alone into the wide world – to who knows what and away from everything he knew – was truly terrifying to this country boy.

He knew so little about the Navy. When his father had last been at home, Ted was too small to understand many of his naval expressions or question this larger-than-life character. Ted loved his father's fuss over him and his mother, bringing them exotic gifts. His presence and love just filled their lives for those all-too-brief periods. Nothing else mattered then, but Ted so wished he had his father with him to answer the thousand questions that now occurred to him.

About eighteen months previously, he remembered clearly when they had been visited by two midshipmen who had served with his father in HMS *Powerful*. The ship was in the Southern Atlantic when it was called upon to break the siege of the British garrison in Ladysmith during the Boer War. These fresh-faced young officers seldom referred to his father by his proper name and always called him 'The Bosun'. They held Ted and his mother enthralled as they took turns to regale them with heroic tales of transporting massive five-inch naval guns over mountains and the most challenging terrain. These were to be employed as field guns against the Boers, eventually breaking the siege after one hundred and twenty days. They had to use ropes, blocks and tackles to transport the separate parts of the guns over the deepest gorges and valleys. Ted's father provided the expertise to design the rigs and carry out the various procedures, directing all the others on what they had to do. As such, he was always at the centre of activity, which was how he was injured. Having seemingly met every challenge facing the guns' passage, they were just approaching Ladysmith and were no more than half a day's march from the garrison. Then one of the oxen they were using to haul the guns lost its footing on scree and fell sideways, trapping Ted's father underneath. Having managed to get him clear of the animal, they found his right leg was severely mangled and had to place him on a stretcher for the rest of the journey. The Naval Brigade had no doctor with it, only a sickbay attendant, and the wounds had festered by the time they got him back to the ship. The surgeon had amputated the limb, but it was too late, and Ted's father died of the gangrene that had infested his entire body by then. The midshipmen were full of praise for the Bosun and said he had taught them so much about seamanship and naval life in general.

The young officers had come directly from London where, in celebration of their success, the Naval Brigade – hailed as 'The Heroes of Ladysmith' – had paraded their guns. Later, they were reviewed by the Prince of Wales in Horse Guards Parade. The midshipmen painted an exciting, colourful image of the Capital's streets, crowded with marching sailors and marines, led by a military band, and cheering spectators, all craning to get a view and waving Union flags. "It wasn't right that your father wasn't there, Edward," said one of the midshipmen to him. "He did more than any of us to get those guns through. However, I have a small consolation for you. A special medal was cast to commemorate the event and . ." reaching into his jacket pocket and presenting the contents to Ted, " . . . here is your father's. I'm afraid the Navy's administration is so appalling that they don't seem to have recorded that the Bosun died out there! You should be enormously proud of what he accomplished."

Ted remembered those two confident young gentlemen distinctly with their fascinating stories and cheery demeanour long after departing to continue their journey towards Plymouth. Could he ever be anything like them? He went to the box by his bed and took out the medal. Holding this most precious memory of his father in the flat of his hand, his fingers delicately ran over the engraved face of Queen Victoria, and over the red and dark-blue and orange-striped ribbon, with its "Defence of Ladysmith" bar across it. Ted then gripped it tightly as the tears for both his father and mother started flowing freely. He was crying for himself too, realising his boyhood was now over. But he had made up his mind.

6

Events moved quickly thereafter, almost too fast for Ted to remember them clearly. His mother's passing had ripped a vast part of him from his very centre, and he remained shocked by all that had happened. Most villagers attended the funeral service at the parish church, and the rector spoke kindly of the whole family. Afterwards, standing alone over the malevolent pit containing the simple wooden box, he took in the panorama of the countryside ahead of him. It had been transformed by long shadows of a disappearing wintry sun, with gusts of a south-westerly beginning to deliver spits and spots of rain. He hardly noticed the half-muffled bells still striking behind him like a peal followed by a far-distant echo. This pattern seemed mournful yet, at the same time, triumphant. Ever practical, Mrs. Hunt came up and – unusually – took his hand to lead him away from the grave, "Come on, Edward. You're getting cold, and there's no more to be done here."

Lord Arscott had better connections than the rector in military circles and made inquiries. He found out that interviews for the Royal Navy took place in all the county towns in the early spring, ready for the main entrance into training after Easter. The landowner persuaded his close friend Captain Luttrell that William Crockford's son was a suitable candidate. Ted was duly nominated, and a date was set for his assessment board. Mrs. Hunt set him additional work to be completed every evening, with more at weekends. He had to concentrate on aspects of geography and history which were thought would be of the most help during his examination.

Arriving home the evening before the big day, Ted found a newly-laundered set of clothes waiting for him: a warm wool jacket, corduroy trousers and polished brown boots. Getting up early to travel into Taunton, he dressed in his relative finery. Ted set off, intending to pick up the post-chaise as it passed the pack-horse bridge in the village. Approaching the forge, he saw Lord Arscott's automobile and wondered what misfortune had befallen it this time. Just as he reached the car, however, Mr. Parsons appeared.

"Good morning, young man! Cook has given me a long list of items she needs for a special dinner," he said with a wink. "I'll need to go into Taunton to get them and was wondering if you would like a ride?" Despite having helped the chauffeur with all sorts of jobs with the machine, Ted had never actually ridden in the car. His face lit up.

Remembering his etiquette lessons, Ted replied with mock formality, "Thank you, Sir. I am greatly obliged to you."

"Come on then. Get in beside me here, put your bag down by your feet and let's be off."

What a ride! Parsons provided a running commentary on how he was controlling the vehicle, encouraging Ted to join in, calling out the actions as they happened. Hesitant at first, in case he made an error, Ted was soon able to make the correct calls. The chauffeur then teasingly waited to be told what to do by Ted before changing gear as they sped up and slowed down. They laughed together long and hard as they bounced along the tracks, being jolted from side to side, on their way to the county town. The young man was in his element.

Arriving in Taunton, Ted had no idea a town could be so large, with crowds of people bustling around the market square. He was examined over three days, with various interviews, papers to write about general knowledge, mathematical problems to solve, physical tasks and medical examinations. All this took place in an environment totally foreign to him. Ted had to sleep in a dormitory with a dozen or so other candidates, all except him with their smart slippers and warm dressing gowns. But everyone sitting these tests was just as nervous as him, and his simple dress and ways passed without comment. At least he wasn't one of those who whimpered in their beds during the night.

It was already dark by the time the carriage pulled up by the village at the end of the third day. Ted was exhausted by the examination process and the driver had to poke him roughly with the handle of his whip to wake him up. Having endured the long journey on top and at the back of the carriage, he was frozen to the core and stamped his feet as he set off for home.

More than a month passed before a letter was sent from the Admiralty, addressed to Lord Arscott as Ted's sponsor. A message was sent down to the school, and the boy was summoned to Hunnicutt House. The footman held open the door into his lordship's study. Ted waited.

"Yes, come in, Crockford. I'll be with you directly," came from inside.

Lord Arscott continued studying the papers before him, allowing the young man to take in his surroundings. The room was warm and cosy, with a fire in the hearth and lingering smells of wood, cigar smoke and leather. Three walls were covered in floor-to-ceiling shelves, crammed with more books than Ted had ever seen or could imagine. In the centre of the room, the wealthy landowner was working at a large desk covered by untidy piles of papers. At last, his host picked up a pen and, with a flourish, signed the letter in front of him. "Good. That's done."

"Now, I have some particularly good news for you, young man. Now, where is it . . . yes, here," Lord Arscott said, picking up a cream-coloured letter with a red embossed motif at its head. "In its wisdom, the Royal Navy believes you to be suitable for officer training. Here's the letter, which I'll let you keep because it tells you where you need to be and when, and what to have with you." Ted was beaming, but the gentleman cautioned the boy, "You need to study carefully all the various conditions upon which the continuity of your training will depend. You'll have to work extremely hard – and keep your nose clean – if you are eventually to win a King's commission. It takes many years to be promoted to lieutenant. Nonetheless, when I was in Taunton on business I happened to bump into Captain Haversham, your examining officer. He's confident you have the potential to succeed, provided you come out of your shell more and speak up! Don't worry about that though; I'm sure more self-confidence will come in time with the Navy's training behind you."

Not rising nor inviting any response, Lord Arscott dismissed the lad, "So, you are to be congratulated! I wish you every success. Go and see the rector, show him the letter and he will put some other arrangements in place to smooth your passage. Well done again; now off you go!"

7

The chill of winter kept a tighter grip in Exmoor that year, and it was late February before the first snowdrops started poking their fresh green noses out of the soil at the sides of the tracks and lanes. Ted agreed that a forester and his wife would move into the house with him because they would remain as tenants after his departure. Keeping his old room, the key benefit was that they invited him to join them for a meal in the evening. Because of the man's trade, there was now a plentiful supply of logs for the fire. Ted had met up with the rector on several occasions to have future arrangements explained to him. Now, he was excited and wanted to get on with the adventure. Unusually, it was hard for him to concentrate on his schoolwork, as he found his thoughts often drifting off towards what might be. This was not helped by focusing his reading more on naval history and the organisation he was about to join. He turned fifteen in the middle of March, and the last two weeks before setting off dragged by interminably.

At last, the day of his departure arrived. He would make his way to Taunton and then, for the first time in his life, journey onward by railway. He picked up his chest of belongings, gathered strictly following the list the Admiralty had provided, took one final look back at his home, and then turned down the track. As he had suspected might be the case from unsubtle hints and winks, Mr. Parsons was waiting with the car at the forge.

"Would you believe it?" the chauffeur asked, beaming widely. "Cook needs *more* stuff from Taunton and his Lordship has agreed that I may take you too." Returning his smile, Ted reached for the handle of the front passenger door. "No," said Parsons firmly, stepping in front of him. "You are to be an officer and officers ride in the back!" He held the rear door wide open, and Ted climbed in self-consciously and sat in the very corner of the wide seat.

Chapter 2 – The Sons of the Waves

1

Ted stood expectantly on the platform until, precisely on time, the train appeared from behind trees at the side of the track not fifty yards to the north. The morning sun was still low, shining directly through windows spaced at intervals along the side of the platform, causing the engine to be repeatedly lit up and then darkened again. As the locomotive slowed down, this play of flashing light reduced the scene to slow motion. Ted stood open-mouthed, transfixed by this fantastic Great Western machine of a size he could scarcely believe. Steel, brass, chrome and copper. Huge wheels turning, pistons pumping, water dripping, funnel wheezing. Smells of soot, hot oils and coal. With the train braking noisily, Ted walked alongside the engine, still trying to take in this seemingly bizarre contraption and discover how it might function. Doors slammed behind him, and a general hubbub ensued from many shouts and much chatter, accompanied by wheeled trolleys and luggage clattered about.

The driver looked down at him from the footplate, "Not seen one of these before, young sir? Pretty, isn't she?" He chuckled to himself and tilted his head to engage the fireman, as it seemed that the boy had been rendered mute and could only nod a response. Gesturing back along the train, the smiling railwayman advised, "If you want to ride on this train, son, you'd better act lively – look!"

Ted turned to see the platform now nearly empty. The remaining people were backing away from the carriages, and the last few doors were being slammed shut. The guard passed a green flag into his other hand and was looking down carefully at his fob watch. Snapping out of his reverie, Ted picked up his chest and ran pell-mell along the platform, looking frantically where to board. The doors of the first two carriages were clearly marked second class, so not his; the next two were first class; only at the very back of the train was third class. The guard finally lifted his head from his watch and raised a whistle to his mouth but paused just long enough to see Ted's dishevelled approach.

"Come along. Come along, lad!" he shouted testily.

Ted jerked open the first door marked 'Third Class' and tumbled in. The door had hardly slammed behind him before there was a loud whistle blast and the train jerked into motion. The journey to Newton Abbott was all too short for Ted, who spent most of the time carefully leaning out of the windows. To the annoyance of the other passengers, he swapped from side to side as the track curved, first this way and then that, as he tried to catch sight of the locomotive at the head of the train.

Following the guard's shouted instructions, he climbed down onto the platform at Newton Abbott, needing to catch another train to reach his eventual destination. For the first time, he saw those he suspected would be his companions for the coming months, their new clothes and nervous demeanours announcing them to be other fresh cadets. No one else appeared from the third-class carriages, only him, with about equal numbers exiting from first and second class. He estimated that there were forty or fifty of them altogether. With a long blast on its whistle, the train chugged away, returning the station to quietness, save for the chattering from groups of boys. Many had first met at Paddington and had had hours to chat and get to know one another. Many seemed already to have formed some allegiances – according to the class of their train ticket. Ted was alone at the end of the platform, looking rather unkempt from his untimely haste to get onto the train, and – unbeknown to him – with smuts all around his eyes and nose. A smaller engine had been waiting in a siding just short of the station with a train of just two carriages. This now rumbled into life, pulling up at the platform. Ted had no option but to join the others as they, with trunks and cases too, all started piling into the limited space in the carriages. He sat next to the window of the last compartment, not speaking, as excited chatter filled the air all around him.

The train pulled up at the terminus in Kingswear, directly opposite the *Britannia*, moored on the other side of the river. All talk ceased as the batch of new cadets looked in awe at this historic, three-decked ship-of-the-line that would now be their home. Launched in 1860 as HMS *Prince of Wales*, she was a wooden propeller-driven ship ordered during the then-arms race between Britain and France. But only a year later, the Royal Navy's first armoured battleship – HMS *Warrior* – was commissioned, and other functions had to be found for the surplus of wooden ships. Accordingly, only nine years after launch, HMS *Prince of Wales* arrived in the River Dart to replace the 1820's hulk *Britannia*, taking her name as well as her role in officer training. The current vessel had been rigged originally like many others as a fine three-masted sailing ship with a complete set of sails, but now only the foremast remained. Her hundred and twenty-one guns had all been transferred ashore to make room for additional accommodation mess decks. In addition, her engines had been requisitioned to be fitted to one of the new ironclads. Ahead of her, berthed bow-to-bow, was the *Hindostan*, an eighty-gun two-decked hulk with all masts removed. Two decades older than *Prince of Wales*, she had arrived on the Dart a year later.

"D'yer hear there!" yelled out a young man in a dark blue uniform with a brass button over a buttonhole on his lapels. Rather menacingly, he also carried a short length of rope with a sizeable knot at its end, which he was beating gently against the side of his leg. "All new cadets are to collect their gear and muster at the north end of the platform! When I call out your name, you are to answer 'Here' and proceed with your baggage through that picket gate and down to the quay just below."

So, consulting his list, he shouted out each name in turn, receiving the correct response in most cases. Still, the occasional "Yes" slipped in, occasioning a withering stare from the Senior Cadet. When "Crockford" was called, Ted responded as ordered. Certain of his companions looked sideways at him and at one another as if some mistake had been made. They had assumed he just happened to be making the same journey as them to Kingswear, but not to *Britannia*. Judging by his scruffy appearance, how could he possibly be a prospective Royal Navy cadet like them? One or two even giggled. Feeling his cheeks redden, Ted kept his eyes on the ground, picked up his trunk and set off down the path indicated.

A steam launch and flatboat ferried them all over the river, and they were soon alongside the towering hulk. Once divided into groups of twelve, they were led away to whichever messdeck they had been allocated. They were told to place their baggage onto the bunks bearing their name and directed to a large dining area. Set out ready for their arrival were cheese rolls and large mugs of tea, which were most welcome after the long journey that most had suffered. Given just ten minutes for this impromptu snack, they next had to queue up outside a dimly-lit store in the depths of the ship. They were called forward one at a time to a long counter behind which a row of sailors waited. As the cadets passed, each of these ratings provided them with a different item of clothing, a pair of boots, a belt or stockings, after the most cursory look to see what size they might require. So, having accumulated a towering pile of garments and miscellaneous objects over which they could hardly see, they were taken back to their mess deck. They were then told what clothes to change into. The cadets were instructed that their civilian clothing and *everything* else not specified had to be placed in their luggage, which would be stowed elsewhere.

2

From the outset, Ted welcomed the 'uniform' way of life, with everyone wearing and being treated the same, by providing a disguise for his modest circumstances. With *Britannia's* complement comprising people from all over the Country, there was nothing more remarkable about Ted's rough West Somerset burr than those from, say, Yorkshire, Northumberland or Cornwall. He deliberately remained in the background and watched the others intently. Soon, Ted could identify those who had already spent two years at the naval college at Osborne on the Isle of Wight. They were the ones who knew the routines and expected behaviour better than new boys like him. Emulating them, he was generally found at the right place at the right time. Most importantly, he discovered, was to be in the specified outfit of clothes, which he must now call 'rig'. Attracting little attention to himself, he could concentrate on all the lessons facing him if he were to settle into this extraordinary new life. The other first-term cadets had much the same personal challenges and paid little attention either to him or the other messmates. Their days were busy and tiring, both physically and intellectually. Still, with regular hot meals – a relatively unknown situation to Ted – the routine was undeniably bearable, becoming increasingly enjoyable as they learned the ropes of a naval existence.

Cadets remained in *Britannia* without home leave for the first year, that is, the first three terms. But that did not mean they were confined to the ship throughout that time. Their training naturally included boatwork and other outside seamanship evolutions. This is where Ted met 'The Boatswain' – pronounced as 'Bosun' – and for the first time began to understand the duties his father had performed. Although lieutenants or schoolmasters taught the theory associated with each subject or practice, the boatswain showed the cadets what to do. He led them through each process time and time again until they became experts. Some aristocratic and higher-class cadets initially took umbrage at being ordered about by a warrant officer. They made this clear by the haughty manner in which they spoke to him and by being somewhat slow in responding to his directions. He handled even these proud fellows with exemplary patience. It took only one occasion, when a spar fell or an anchor slipped unintentionally because of their delayed action, for them to recognise his competence, deserving of respect.

Soon Ted and his colleagues, all aged fourteen or fifteen, were no longer first-termers, or 'Cheeky New Fellows' as was their traditional nickname. They became 'Three Monthers' and then 'Six Monthers'. The cadets became ever-more proficient in the esoteric subjects of navigation, nautical astronomy, plane and spherical trigonometry that were crammed into them. Their advances were rewarded with greater privileges, with shore leave being granted one evening each week until ten o'clock. Without the finances to 'waste' – as he saw it – on beer, Ted didn't join his messmates in the local public house. Instead, as was his habit at home on Exmoor, he climbed up the hill above Dartmouth. From there, Ted had a clear view of the harbour entrance and the sea beyond. He was happy to sit, enjoy the stillness and allow the fresh air to clear his head. Of course, on their return, Ted became the subject of much light-hearted ribbing from his alcohol-cheered messmates. Nonetheless, it was always companionable with never any malice.

It was the same with all his ship-wide term-mates. Succeeding in his studies had earned Ted their respect, and many times others would come to him for help when facing one academic challenge or another. Indeed, there was only one other cadet of his entry, Rupert Hardacre, a fellow messmate, who challenged his intellectual prowess. The two would vie with one another in a friendly manner about who would come top in any tests they were set. In this competitive spirit, Rupert came to Ted with a dare; would he climb up and stand on the truck of the foremast? The truck is a circular piece of wood at the very top of the mast and is about the size of a dinner plate. This feat had been a long tradition of the Service and had become a rite of passage to qualify as an upper yardman, the most skilled seaman. But that had been in the days of sail when many had long experience of being high aloft in windy conditions at sea before accepting such a challenge.

Believing it to be a practical joke, Ted replied smiling, "I will – if you do it first!"

"Very well then," was the response. Neither of the two could back down now.

3

Being an exhibition in such public view, the commander had to be informed of their intentions. His opinion was that such activities, reflecting the past glories of the Royal Navy whilst also challenging the new generations, were to be encouraged. Permission was thus granted. Ted had been up the mast previously, but only as far as the top yardarm that would have supported the fore topgallant sail. He had suffered no symptoms of vertigo at that height and felt confident he could keep his head that little bit higher. Nonetheless, the final, precarious part of climbing safely onto the truck – and the reverse process – gave him the most concern. He went to talk to the boatswain about the matter, and, as usual, the latter gave his time freely so that they could talk through the necessary procedure at length.

The commander and instructors had joined all the cadets on the upper deck to observe this feat. Ted and Rupert appeared before him, each wearing light trousers and a simple shirt.

"Now, you two," started the commander. "I don't want any undue heroics with someone hurting himself. The paperwork would be horrific," he added as an aside to the officers behind him. "It's good that you're going to make an attempt and we won't feel less of you if it proves to be too much."

"Thank you for your concern, Sir," Rupert replied, half smiling towards his competitor, "but I have done it before when I was at Osborne College."

This was news to Ted as it had never been mentioned before. It did little to calm the wild flutterings occurring in his stomach.

"With your permission, I'll proceed, Sir," requested Rupert formally, standing to attention.

"Make it so."

Rupert rubbed his hands together and then against his trousers as he made his way to the ratlines on the port side. Climbing steadily, he soon reached the small platform called 'The Top', which is at the head of the lower mast. Rupert pulled himself up into the top by passing through the 'Lubbers Hole', a trap door at its centre, next to the mast. Pausing only to take a single deep breath, he continued his climb and was able initially to use the shrouds to help his progress. When these came to their securing points on the mast, Rupert had to climb rope-like up the final, uppermost section of the mast. Reaching the overhanging truck, he stretched over and grabbed the lightning conductor. This rod stood vertically and rose two feet from the truck's centre, an additional component of the mast that is not visible from below. Careful to keep his balance, Rupert pulled himself up into a crouching position on the truck, placing his feet on either side of the copper post, which he now held between his knees. Slowly, slowly he stood up with arms outstretched to keep his balance and then, fully erect, brought his arms smartly to his side and threw out his chest, standing at attention. A great roar came from below as everyone on deck cheered his success. Reversing his contortions, he regained his position on the upper mast, lowering himself with alacrity to the top and then down to the deck.

"Well done, Hardacre. The captain will no doubt write to your father to inform him of your brave adventure aloft. Now, remembering what I said about being sensible, Crockford – carry on!" ordered the commander.

Ted came to attention, performed a smart about-turn, strode towards the ratlines and started his ascent. He didn't go through the lubber's hole but instead grasped the bottom of the futtock shrouds. For the top to be strong enough to take the strain of the topmast rigging, additional ratlines are necessary. These futtock shrouds are attached to the bottom edges of the top and then secured to the lower mast a few feet beneath. Ascending these, the climber must scramble outwards away from the mast in an upside-down posture, with his back facing down towards the deck. With muscles straining, Ted repeated to himself the mantra taught him by the boatswain, "Never let go of one rope until you have hold of another." Reaching the outside of the top, he was able to heave himself up level with the topmast shrouds. In welcome of this additional degree of difficulty, cheering and applause broke out below, which allowed him just a few seconds more to catch his breath and shake out the muscles of his arms. He continued up following the route and manner Rupert had taken. Reaching the truck, the muscles in his arms screamed at him, causing Ted to worry if he had over-exerted himself with his earlier showmanship. Gritting his teeth, he reached over, grasped the lightning conductor, and pulled himself up. Ted could feel his muscles starting to tremble in rebellion, but he managed to maintain his composure until the task was finished. With huge hurrahs rising from below, he eventually stood there, elated but vowing never to attempt it again. Knowing this was the most dangerous manoeuvre in the whole procedure, he crouched with infinite care. He swung his legs down to encircle the topmast before letting go of the conductor, first with one hand and then the other.

Ted lowered himself slowly back to the deck, this time passing through the lubber's hole rather than adding more theatrics.

As he walked up to the commander, he received many congratulatory pats on the back from the spectating cadets, and the swelling pride in his achievement dispelled any discomfort in his limbs.

"Very well done, Crockford; that was a gutsy refinement to the normal procedure," the senior officer complimented. "Please carry on. Master-at-Arms, this pantomime is over – get everyone back to their proper duties."

Ted went up to his challenger smiling and offered his hand, "Well done, Rupert, and thank you for showing me the route!"

Ted's hand was left hovering in mid-air. "That was a cheap trick and not fair play," Hardacre sneered. "I could have gone over the futtock shrouds too, but that isn't how it's done. Your antics have made me look both foolish and second-rate." With that, Hardacre turned on his heel and stomped away.

4

With the mast climb taking place near the end of term, home leave was fast approaching, and Ted hoped that the less-friendly atmosphere being created by Hardacre in the messdeck might dissipate during the break. As other cadets collected their luggage and resumed their civilian attire, Ted could only watch and try to join in the jolly banter as his messmates prepared to depart. Of course, he was not the only one to remain behind because amongst *Britannia's* complement were the sons of diplomats and military officers serving abroad. This situation made a visit home by their children quite impossible in the short three weeks available. Those cadets, like Ted, now simply wanted the others to leave rather than be reminded of their situation.

Without formal instruction or other arranged activities, the daily routine aboard was much more relaxed during this leave period, and the remaining cadets were left pretty much to their own devices. 'Call the hands' was delayed by half an hour during weekdays and a luxurious hour at weekends. Attendance at Sunday service was still expected, and remaining in one's messdeck for long periods was discouraged. This suited Ted just fine; he would much rather be out and about in the fresh air than remain in the confines of the old ship. If you gave advance warning, it was possible to collect a picnic at breakfast to take away with you for lunch. Ted took advantage of this on many occasions. Sometimes, he and a couple of other cadets would sail a whaler out of the mouth of the estuary by Dartmouth Castle. During clement weather, light on-shore winds allowed them to forge ahead into the open sea and continue, on a broad reach in both directions, around the corner to Slapton Sands. There was just time for them to enjoy their snack on the beach before setting back. Preferably, Ted relished taking away a light dinghy that could be sailed single-handed. He explored the higher reaches of the River Dart and spent time learning the ways of the stream with its changing whorls and eddies as the tide ebbed and flowed. If not out in boats, Ted took himself off down the cliff paths, west from Dartmouth or east from Kingswear, appreciating the views in both directions. He could also assess how the passing vessels were being handled according to his recently acquired knowledge.

When the weather precluded these activities, he would offer his services to the shipwright, sailmaker and ropemaker to maintain the fabric of *Britannia* and its accumulation of smaller vessels. They responded to him warmly and were pleased with his interest, being prepared to show him what to do and praising his inexpert attempts. In this way, he learned much of the finer detail of these historical arts, skills the modern Navy of metal and machines was rapidly losing. With sailors never passing up the opportunity to regale a listener with their tall tales of derring-do, discussion with these hugely experienced petty officers also educated him more widely about many aspects and traditions of the Senior Service. He spent time too with the engineer who maintained the boats' engines, both petrol- and steam-driven, advancing his rudimentary knowledge of such machines. The only disadvantage was that, no matter how hard he scrubbed, he could never remove all the black grease from around his fingernails. As a result, he could pursue these activities only during a leave period. Otherwise, during term time, he would fail the routine inspection before supper. Such activities and the sailors' stories consolidated all he had learned during the previous year. Ted felt relaxed and refreshed for the rigours of his final terms and became more confident of earning promotion to midshipman on leaving *Britannia*.

5

The Sunday before the start of the new term came around quickly enough. From about two o'clock onwards, the ship's complement of cadets returned in dribs and drabs throughout the late afternoon and evening. Stories of exploits at home – some good, some bad – were exchanged, and the reaction to their return onboard was similarly mixed, with some reluctant to have left their homes. Rupert Hardacre was one of the last to arrive, catching the last train available. He said little to anyone as he unpacked and stowed away his gear.

As a term of 'Nine Monthers', they were awarded broader privileges, but, in return, they gained more responsibilities. They were required to perform duties, sometimes overseeing the more junior cadets or standing night watches acting as the 'Boatswain's Mate'. This role required the manning of the gangway to *Britannia* and, from there, running the ship's routine, scrutinising returning libertymen, and carrying out any 'shakes' required overnight for replacement watchkeepers. This was not a particularly arduous duty, other than it kept cadets from their warm cots after a long and tiring day. The 'middle watch' – from midnight to four o'clock – was, of course, the worst. The cadet had hardly got warm and fallen asleep before a shake was given twenty minutes before the duty commenced. This provided little time to freshen the face with water, get dressed and receive a handover from their predecessor. On completion of the watch, the cadet had to pass on all relevant information to their relief, sign the ship's log, return to their messdeck and undress. The bed was now cold, and there was little chance of sleep before 'Call the Hands'.

One evening, shore leave had been granted and the messdeck emptied as usual. Ted took himself off for a walk whilst the others retired to the public house. It was the birthday of one of the cadets, and the ensuing celebrations caused more alcohol to be enjoyed than was usual. So, a lively – almost rowdy – crowd returned to the mess later that evening. Ted was already in his bunk, reading. The laughter and banter continued unabated until one cadet, Jackson, yawning widely, said he must turn in, bemoaning that he had the middle watch the next night. He wasn't among the brightest students on the best of days, and tonight it was clear that beer had dulled his senses further.

"Look," piped up Hardacre, "If you don't want to do your watch, Jackson, why don't we cut for it?"

"What do you mean?" enquired Jackson.

"It's simple," explained Hardacre. "I have the middle watch the following night. If we cut for it and *you* win, I'll do your watch for you. It's perfectly acceptable and common practice to change duties provided we inform the Master-at-Arms and properly amend the watchbill. But – of course – if *I* win, you will do your own watch and mine too. It would be down to a simple game of chance."

Jackson was interested but bemused, "How do we 'cut' for it?"

"It's easy," said Hardacre, reaching up to take a fat volume from a shelf. "We take any book of text – like this one – declare 'right' or 'left' and then two numbers. You open the book at any page. If you have declared 'right', say, you go to the right-hand page." He opened the book and pointed to demonstrate. "You count down the lines according to the first number, and then you count the letters across to the second number. So, if you choose 'fourteen–six', you count down fourteen lines and then six letters across. Taking turns, we compare the letters identified. 'A' is considered high and 'Z' low, and the highest letter wins."

The whole mess was now interested and gathered around. Ted put aside his book and sat up to observe.

"Are you on for it?" asked Hardacre. "We'll make it the best of three: how about that?"

"It's worth a shot," said his colleague, seeing that it might now look like poor form in front of his messmates were he to back down. "All right, but I want to go first," he insisted. "So, I declare 'Left ten–twelve'." Taking the book from Hardacre, he opened it and turned to the left-hand side and counted out loud as he moved his finger down the page. " . . . eight, nine, ten. Now twelve letters in . . . ten, eleven, twelve. The letter is 'M'. Your turn."

Hardacre took the offered book and observed, "Umm, right in the middle of the alphabet. I hope you're feeling lucky! I declare 'Right fifteen–three'." He now opened the book himself and followed the same procedure. "Oh, you *are* lucky, Jackson. My letter is 'R'. You win! I still have two more chances, but you must win only once more and I'll have to stand your watch."

He handed the book back to his excited opponent. "I declare 'Right five–seven'. The letter is 'F'," he determined.

Hardacre took his second turn. "I will choose the opposite. I declare 'Left seven–five' and my letter is . . . 'D'. Marvellous! We're all square – one each – and it's down to this last go."

"All right, now concentrate," said Jackson to no one in particular, holding the book tightly to his head as if this might influence his choice. "Now, I declare 'Right six–eight'. The letter is 'D'!" he announced triumphantly. "Now beat that!"

Hardacre took the book for the final time. "I declare 'Left three–three'. He opened the book with a flourish and counted out loud to find the required letter. "My letter is 'B' – I win! Hard luck, old chap," he said, closing the book and placing it back on the shelf. "I'll delete my name from the watchbill and insert yours."

Jackson groaned at the thought of consecutive middle watches. The other messmates congratulated Hardacre on his good fortune, all starting to prepare for bed.

"That cannot be right," Ted thought to himself, but out loud and at a greater volume than he ever intended.

Everyone stopped and turned towards him. "No one else has seen the letters you called, Hardacre," he explained the logic. "Surely a third party should be involved to identify – or at least be shown the page to verify – what letters had been selected? Otherwise, we have only your word for it."

"Yes, I suppose that's true," mused the unfortunate loser of the bet.

Hardacre turned, his cheeks burning red, eyes ablaze, and mouth tight-lipped. "How dare you!" he shouted. He approached Ted menacingly, putting his face close to his, "Are you calling me a cheat?"

"No," explained Ted as calmly as he could, quite taken aback by this explosion of anger but looking straight back into his eye. "It just seems to me that it would be more proper if someone other than the two gamblers determined the chosen letters. Why not do it again, and I'll look up the letters for you both?"

"You *are* – you're calling me a cheat!" Hardacre almost spat out at him. "You cannot – *will not* – call a gentleman a cheat! But what could *you* be expected to know about that? I will meet you in the woods, *Sir*," he said with a sneer. "I'll teach you and give you a damned good hiding!"

6

The atmosphere in the messdeck changed totally after that. The once-jolly company broke up into three ill-defined groups: those who supported Hardacre and believed a matter of 'honour' had been raised; those who agreed with Ted's logical stance and who, in any case, were beginning to find Hardacre's increasingly arrogant behaviour hard to bear; and the majority who thought the whole situation was unfortunate and an unnecessary distraction.

A time and place were set for the 'big fight'. Shore leave had been granted, and the senior terms made their way into the sprawling woods above the town. On arrival, they formed themselves into smaller groups, hoping to avoid the attention of the authorities. When Ted arrived, he estimated that a hundred cadets were gathered in the clearing on the far side of the woods, as distant from *Britannia* as possible. As he approached, Ted thought he saw a separate figure standing alone over to one side; but whoever it was had gone when he looked again in that direction.

Ted was alone and scared. He wasn't worried about any physical pain he might have to endure, so he didn't feel *cowardly*. Ever logical, he accepted the situation and realised there was no option other than to go through this trial. In retrospect, he appreciated too that he *might* have impugned Hardacre's good name. If he had, it was completely unintentional. All he had done was simply assess the scene that had played out in front of him. With hindsight, he could see that he had just needed to think through how his observations might be received. If it could have ended the matter, Ted would have asked for his opponent's pardon. However, from the outset, Hardacre's whole manner made it unlikely that such an apology would have been accepted. If Ted had tried to express regret, no doubt it would have been interpreted by others as being spineless and a simple ruse to avoid the challenge laid down. He had no option other than to go through with the contest.

But Ted had never been in a fight before, which was the real cause of his anxiety. Throughout his life, he had seemed able to get on with most people, preferring to avoid confrontation, not that he had experienced many instances of that.   As a boy, he had never actually punched anyone. Even now, Ted did not feel such deep animosity towards Hardacre that would cause him to strike his messmate. He didn't know how to get himself ready to fight or his own reaction to being hit. His unease was because of facing an experience he just could not imagine.

The chatter died down as Ted made his way into the clearing. As they jostled for a good view, the spectators moved back to form a rough circle about ten yards across. Seeing that Hardacre had already stripped down to a shirt, Ted removed his jacket too and tossed it to one side before walking into the ring. His adversary stood in the very middle and raised his fists. Hardacre's eyes burned into Ted and, with the minutest lifting of his chin, invited his rival to join him.

Having received training in the noble art, Hardacre took a wide, aggressive stance, ready to drive at the other contestant. His left hand was forward, and he lowered his head so his eyes were on the same level as his fists. Knowing no better, Ted copied his opponent's pose, but once he was in range, Hardacre jabbed twice with his leading left hand before landing a heavy blow on Ted's left cheek with his right. A great cheer rose from the crowd as Ted retreated a couple of steps, shaking his head to restore his senses. Hardacre came at him again immediately, and Ted's hands automatically went up to either side of his face to defend himself from the next onslaught. But now Hardacre landed a clean punch into Ted's undefended stomach, driving the wind from him. Another roar and now some laughter at Ted's poor showing.

Hardacre walked confidently back to the centre of the ring. Nodding in acknowledgement of the audience's support, he indicated with his fingers for the opposition to come to him again. Undeterred, Ted came forward once more but, by instinct, this time adopted a more defensive, sideways-on posture. Unknowingly, he also took up the stance more usual for a left-hander, with his right side leading instead of his left as before, but still with his hands held high by his head. His opponent then let off a flurry of blows. First, jabs towards the head struck Ted's protective right hand. Then, the powerful follow-up with the right would have landed square on Ted's nose if his new stance hadn't allowed him to lean back and put it just out of reach. Repeated left and right blows hit Ted's upper arms in trying to sap the energy from them. Finally, rapid left and right punches into Ted's sides made contact with the elbows and not the soft flesh that was the target.

Both antagonists were now tiring, and the pace of the fight was slowing rapidly. Ted still had no real idea how to cope with the situation, and his whole body was exhausted. Of concern, his left eye was swelling and closing from that early blow, and he could feel the hot blood running down his left cheek. Hardacre was unmarked, but he, too, was blowing hard from his exertions. They faced one another again. Hardacre launched another frenetic attack, looking for the deciding, knock-out blow. But Ted still had the strength – and now the posture – to keep up his defence. Indeed, as Hardacre wearied and his fists dropped a little, Ted was able to land some blows of his own with his leading right fist. These were not forceful, but enough to demonstrate to Hardacre that he was not prepared to let his opponent have it all his own way. Wanting a proper fight, the crowd roared their approval of Ted's revised fortunes and lifted his spirits.

In this manner, the fight continued, back and forth, but still with Hardacre delivering most of the punishment.

Not knowing how to fight, Ted was beginning to realise that he didn't know how to give up either, and his senses were still clear enough to observe the processes going on here. He realised he didn't have to hate his enemy to win through; he just needed to be clever. Now a battle of attrition, both fighters with arms too tired to lift them fully to defend themselves properly, the contest continued. Ted was beginning to feel light-headed, with everything happening in slow motion. It seemed as if a mist was closing in around him. Nonetheless, with his southpaw stance, he was beginning to score against Hardacre, whose left-leading posture removed the protection from Ted's more powerful left fist. Swaying on his feet, Ted waited until Hardacre, expecting to land the killer blow, came towards him. Using his last ounce of energy, Ted put everything into a left-handed punch aimed at his adversary's chin. But this manoeuvre rendered his own head defenceless, and Hardacre's left hand slammed into his right temple at the same instant.

Neither contestant heard the thunderous roar that turned heads in Dartmouth, Kingswear and beyond.

With support on both sides, Ted and Hardacre were frog-marched back to a position just short of *Britannia's* jetty. They were given time to collect themselves, just enough to make the walk up the gangway unaided. Boarding in groups with the battered fighters at their centre, they successfully avoided any adverse attention from the boatswain's mate – one of their own, of course. He had been forewarned and discovered some matter of vital import that required his attention elsewhere at the appropriate moment. After a bath and a most uncomfortable night's rest, Ted and Hardacre still managed to rise and attend the next day's lectures and events as scheduled. Somewhat strangely, their evident lumps and bumps attracted little comment.

Disappointingly for Ted, the fight had settled nothing, with Hardacre continuing to display enmity towards him. Each attempted to steer clear of the other as the confines of the ship and their instruction allowed. Their penultimate term continued without further incident: all cadets had to study hard to pass out as midshipmen within a few months. An additional week's home leave was granted before the final term in which they would face the last challenge of examinations, tests and assessments.

7

The shortness of the leave for some, and the requirement for others to start revising subjects early, resulted in more cadets remaining aboard *Britannia* than on previous occasions. Surprisingly, Hardacre was one of these, probably for the first reason, Ted presumed. With cadets left to their own devices, the two saw little of each other during the day. Only when they returned to wash up before dinner did they come into proximity with one another.

One day a sea fog rolled up the estuary after lunch, and anyone venturing outside was quickly soaked by the fine mist. Accordingly, Ted went off to find the ropemaker to offer his help, knowing there was some work to do to reinforce the stays on the mainmast. As usual, he was welcomed into the workshop in one of the holds and set a project to undertake. Having worked for a couple of hours, the ropemaker checked his progress, made one or two suggestions and then left Ted to it whilst he took himself off for a smoke. About ten minutes later, the boatswain appeared looking for the ropemaker who, as usual aboard ships, was under his command. Apparently, the matter was not too important, and the senior rating requested Ted to pass on a message for the ropemaker to contact him. With that, Ted hunched back over his work and soon again became engrossed in what he was doing.

"You know your father would be very proud of you, Mr. Crockford."

Ted had not realised that the boatswain was still there, turning around to find him leaning on the doorway watching him.

"Did you know him, 'Swain? You've never said anything before."

"Indeed, I did. I knew him very well. I shipped out with him on two occasions," remembered the senior rating. "On the first, I was just a young lad under training in the old hulk *Ganges*, moored down at Mylor, and he was already a petty officer instructor. He was a smart fellow, to be sure, and could work out what needed to be done – just like that!" he explained, clicking his fingers. "He taught me a lot then and even more when, years later, he was the boatswain of a first-rater and ran a very tight ship. Did you know your father even had this job in *Britannia*?" He was nodding. "I like to pride myself that they only send the best to train you officers. He was well known and respected around the Home Fleet. There was much talk of William Crockford receiving a commission, which they do on far too few occasions, to my mind. Stories about his exploits in South Africa are rapidly becoming legends. If even only half-true, the Admiralty would have been hard pushed to deny him had he survived.

"You're like him in so many ways; a right chip off the old block!" the boatswain observed. "He'd be *so* proud to see how well you're getting on. Just keep going as you are – don't let them change you too much – and I'm sure you'll do very well."

Ted felt a lump in his throat, and his cheeks reddened. Misinterpreting the signs, the boatswain quickly added, "Please excuse me, Sir. I've probably overstepped the mark . . ."

"No . . . no, 'Swain," Ted stuttered. "Thank you. I'm most grateful because my father died before I really got to know him. You're a good boatswain – all the cadets will testify to that – and it means so much to me that you held my father in such high regard."

The boatswain nodded and was about to go when he stopped and turned back to the cadet.

"You *do* know why you're called Edward, don't you?" The boatswain studied Ted's face. "No? Well, William always said that he'd call any son of his 'Edward' after Admiral Sir Edward Pellew. That marvellous fellow joined his first ship, the *Juno,* as the purser's servant – just a boy and the lowest of the low – but went on to become England's most successful frigate captain. He fought all his life against those privileged but less-able 'Gentlemen Captains' who looked down their noses on those of the 'Tarpaulin Navy'. That's what they called those who had risen through the ranks and won their promotion through service at sea. Pellew took on tasks that others wouldn't dare to because they were considered too dangerous. But, always victorious, Pellew earned his success. He ended up as an Admiral and was ennobled as Lord Exmouth no less! You have a much better start, Mr. Crockford, but I think you will face some of the same prejudices, given your background. Perhaps you can do no better than to keep Edward Pellew in mind, as your father intended."

The boatswain left him alone then, but Ted found it more difficult now to concentrate on the task he had been set. Not wanting to let the ropemaker down, he continued anyway until it was time to clean up. Returning to his mess, Ted took his father's medal from under the corner of his mattress, where he kept it hidden, folded into the bottom sheet. He held it for a few minutes and looked at it before he heard someone coming along the passageway. He then rushed to return it to its safe stowage, hoping he hadn't been spotted.

8

Now 'Passing Out Numbers' in their final term, Ted and his messmates were afforded great respect by the other, more-lowly cadets, being permitted to 'ask names' and make other personal inquiries of their juniors. As a sign both to display and, if necessary, to enforce their new-found authority, members of Ted's term were permitted to carry 'togies'. These were short lengths of cord with a 'Mathew Walker' knot at its end, which the senior cadets had to learn to manufacture themselves. Originally designed to form a knob or 'stopper' to prevent the rope's end from passing through a hole, this knot also prevented a fraying rope from unlaying into its separate strands. But in time, its use had become more a part of ceremonial and 'tiddly' ropework. The purpose of the togies was originally to administer punishment to the juniors, but that regime had long passed. In fact, there was little bullying by the seniors. Instead of being the boatswain's mate, final term members were now required to act as the 'Officer of the Day'. As such, they were in overall charge of *Britannia's* routines from eight o'clock one day until the same time the following morning, answering only to the Duty Lieutenant.

The Officers of the Day conducted the daily ceremonials of morning and evening 'Colours' when the Ensign and Jack were raised and lowered. In addition, they supervised the boatswain's mates and received their routine reports. Their principal activity was to carry out evening rounds of all the mess decks and bathroom areas. Concentrating particularly on the most junior cadets, they ensured that beds had been made up as instructed and shoes and boots were immaculately polished. They checked that lockers were laid out meticulously as detailed, with no missing or added items. The duty Boatswain's Mate preceded the Officer of the Day in a route around the ship, with the single shrill note of a boatswain's call and the shout of 'rounds' alerting all of his approach.

It occurred that Hardacre was the Officer of the Day, and rounds were in progress. As happened every day, Ted and his messmates acknowledged the boatswain's mate's call as he passed along their passageway. But they gave it little regard as their messdeck did not usually receive a visitation by the Officer of the Day, particularly not by one of their own. Surprisingly, Hardacre did enter the mess with the cry of 'rounds'. Despite being considerably bemused, everyone stood up to attention as their previous long training had instilled in them. Their time in *Britannia* had taught them always to lay out their gear as required, but perhaps without the precision expected of the juniors. Accordingly, they were more or less ready for an inspection.

Hardacre headed straight towards Ted's locker and started scrutinising it. Then, turning to the bed, he jerked the bottom sheet out roughly and pulled it all the way to the bottom of the bed. The precious medal dropped onto the deck.

"So, what's this?" Hardacre asked with a hateful smile. "You ought to know by now that *all* private belongings should have been stowed away in the hold. I will have to confiscate this '*trinket*'," he sneered, bending down to pick it up.

"You will not take it!" was Ted's reply. He arrested Hardacre's movement by holding his left hand against the other's shoulder, preventing him from bending down further.

"Get your hands off me!" Hardacre fumed. "You're at *attention*!"

Following his training, Ted stood back up straight. But when Hardacre again went to pick up his most prized – his only – possession, he stopped him again, "You *will not* have it!"

Enraged, Hardacre swung the togie in his right hand towards Ted's face, but the latter grasped it in his right hand and floored his aggressor with a blow from his left fist right onto Hardacre's nose. Everyone in the mess heard the crunch of broken cartilage, and blood immediately started to issue forth.

"You guttersnipe!" Hardacre screamed, staggering to his feet. "I'm the Officer of the Day and I'll have you court-martialled for this. You could never be an officer and I'll have you thrown out of the Navy; you'll see!" With that, he left the mess immediately to report the incident to the Duty Lieutenant.

9

"Crockford!" the Master-at-Arms called out.

"Sir!" Ted responded, coming to attention, taking one step forward and then immediately wheeling around to bring him into the office and towards the commander's

'Table'. This was, in fact, a lectern raised to chest level, over which the senior officer glared at him.

"Left, right, left, right," guided the Master-at-Arms. "Halt! Off . . . caps!"

Ted complied, continuing to stand rigidly to attention.

The charge of striking a superior officer was read out, Hardacre being superior only by virtue of his duty at the time of the offence.

The commander was reading the formal guidance open on the lectern through the *pince-nez* spectacles resting on the end of his nose. Any image this might conjure up of a kind elderly uncle was immediately dispersed by the chiselled chin and stern countenance. Following the prescribed procedure and looking over the top of his glasses to observe Ted, he demanded, "How do you plead? Guilty or Not Guilty?"

"Guilty, Sir," Ted responded meekly.

"Very well." The commander turned to the officer to the right of him. "First Lieutenant, what are the facts of the case?"

Having provided an outline of what occurred, the first lieutenant called Hardacre as the key witness who answered the questions put to him, which described the episode and served to clarify a few points. What Hardacre said was truthful but with one omission. Having completed his evidence, the commander dismissed him but asked him to wait outside in case supplementary information was required.

Of some surprise to Ted, the first lieutenant then called another witness. Jackson, his hapless messmate.

Firstly, Jackson confirmed he had witnessed the whole event. The first lieutenant's interrogation of him simply sought to confirm Hardacre's version. Whenever Jackson tried to express how unexpected it was for rounds to take place in their mess, that Hardacre had singled Ted out, and that Hardacre seemed to know exactly where to look for the forbidden item, he was cut short, becoming more and more tongue-tied.

With mounting irritation, the commander interjected, "Let us be clear about one thing, Jackson: did you see Crockford strike Hardacre?"

"Yes, I did, Sir." Adding very quickly, "But only after Hardacre had tried to hit him with his togie. Crockford parried his blow and punched him just once in self-defence."

Jackson was dismissed.

"Stand over!" announced the commander. "March out the accused."

When the officers and the Master-at-Arms were alone in the room, the commander told them he had to consider the matter carefully and would confer with the captain about how best to proceed.

The investigation was 'stood over' for about two hours, an unusually long time in military disciplinary practices. Ted sat disconsolately in the Master-at-Arms' office whilst Hardacre waited in his mess.

With the commander's 'Table' reconvened, Ted again stood at attention in front of the lectern with his cap held against his body by his left elbow.

"Cadet Crockford, in view of your plea and all that I have heard, I find you '*Guilty*'," declared the commander, stressing the final word.

"'Guilty' recorded, Sir," reported the Master-at-Arms, scribbling onto the charge sheet.

"Do you have anything to say in mitigation, Crockford?" continued the senior officer.

"Nothing, Sir."

"Very well. You must understand by now that proper order and discipline are at the heart of the Royal Navy's ethos. On these, the entire fighting success of the

Service depends," the commander started his summing up. "It is therefore intolerable for any violence to be offered to a superior officer, and all cases must be handled with the utmost severity." He paused. "Yet it is to your credit that you are contrite about what happened, and your plea reflects that. Similarly, I appreciate that extenuating circumstances *might* have been at play here." He concluded matter-of-factly, "Nevertheless, in the normal course, the punishment would be fifteen strokes of the birch followed by expulsion from the Service."

The commander paused to let this sink in. Ted was finding it hard to remain fully upright: the senior officer's words had hit him like a blow to the solar plexus. His arms went limp, and he almost released his cap from under his elbow. Noting the reaction, the arbiter of his fate rapidly continued, "In this case, however, I am prepared to demonstrate a minimum level of leniency. You are to be given the choice: *either* you will receive a severe birching; *or* you can be dismissed from the Navy immediately." In a gentler voice, he added, "It's up to you, Crockford. Do you understand what is being offered?"

"I do, Sir, and appreciate your consideration," Ted somehow managed to utter.

Softening his tone further, the commander pressed him, "You do not need to make your decision now, Crockford. Would you prefer to consider your position overnight?"

Ted's mind was in turmoil, and one thought chased another. This whole situation was so *unfair*. He'd done nothing wrong. He'd worked so hard to get this far. He couldn't let it come to nothing. What was the boatswain's warning about they'd never let someone from his background succeed? He'd be damned if he was going to let Hardacre triumph in his sneaky game.

Hardly able to stop his lower lip from trembling with emotion, he answered in a shaky voice, "Thank you again, Sir, but ... but ... I wish wholeheartedly to remain in the Navy." Pausing to take a deep breath and hardly knowing what he was committing himself to, Ted determined, "I will accept the punishment, Sir. I will accept the birch – that is my decision."

"Very well," said the commander, nodding in understanding. "I sentence you to fifteen strokes with the birch. Master-at-Arms, march out the offender!"

After Ted had been led away by the senior rating, only the officers were left. The commander asked Hardacre to be brought in, inviting the others to remain.

Although he was not marched in formally, Hardacre was left standing in front of the table. The cadet still had his cap on, whilst the others had already relaxed theirs. The commander was not inclined to ease his discomfiture.

"This whole episode confers no credit on you at all, Hardacre," he started, removing his spectacles to look the cadet square in the face. "I believe you contrived the whole affair, having no doubt myself that you have the intellect to plan such a campaign." He paused. "In the first instance, I want to know why you fought with Crockford in the woods?"

Dumbfounded that the commander had any knowledge of the event at all, Hardacre's jaw dropped open, and he was rendered speechless.

"So, you think we didn't know, do you? Why is it that each new generation thinks it is the first to do such things?" he asked of the other officers. Returning to the cadet in front of him, he continued, "We had a corporal watching the whole thing, just to make sure it didn't get out of hand. And there's your first lesson; you can have few secrets in a ship. That's how a ship's company' works together and how any personal weaknesses will always be known. I'll ask you again; what was the cause of the fight?"

"We had a disagreement about 'cutting' in a book, Sir," the cadet answered quietly.

"Oh, so you got caught out in that old trick, did you?" On seeing Hardacre's reddening cheeks, the commander needed no reply. "Can I also presume that you received some boxing lessons while you were attending the naval college at Osborne?" Hardacre nodded before looking down.

"So, having been caught cheating, where is the 'honour' you were wishing to defend by challenging someone you suspected would not have had the benefit of such training?" the commander asked rhetorically. "And what of the outcome? Despite no experience in boxing, he fought you to a standstill." The senior officer was now becoming quite red-cheeked. "I'm interested to know how you feel about that and, with hindsight, how do you now assess Crockford's character?"

"He . . . he . . . he did well, Sir," Hardacre stammered.

"Can I push you further and suggest he might even have been brave?" The commander was now leaning across the lectern to get his face closer to the youngster in front of him.

"Y . . y . . yes, Sir. I think he was brave."

"So, let me get this right," the older man summed up. "It seems we have this brave cadet whom you know is doing well in his studies and you prepare a plan to get him thrown out of the Service?" Becoming quite angry now, the commander's eyes bored into Hardacre's. "Do you *really* think the Navy is just an organisation in which you can scheme away to your own benefit and play out your petty jealousies?" Raising his voice, "Well, do you?" The commander didn't expect a response, and none came. He moved on, "And then finally there was this incident with Crockford's father's medal. It's highly appropriate that this investigation took place today – a Tuesday. What is the traditional toast for today, Hardacre, and what does it mean to you?"

"It's 'Our Men', Sir. It is a toast to our sailors to wish them health and success in battle."

"That's only partly right; there's more to it. This toast should give us a moment to reflect that without our men, their hard work, their skills and their courage, we couldn't do anything. Our ships couldn't even set sail." He explained further, "So, we must be ever-mindful of what their needs are, to earn their respect and get them to respond willingly to our commands. If you are *ever* to follow your father's footsteps and succeed in your own command, you must afford your people every consideration – officers included – and value what is important to *them*; otherwise, they won't fight for you. Do you have any inkling of what I'm talking about, Hardacre?"

The cadet was now visibly pale and trembling under the wrath directed at him.

"In this case, you behaved in precisely the opposite manner," his inquisitor continued. "You might not have known exactly what was hidden, but it was clearly precious to Crockford because he had taken such care to keep it secret from everyone. By trying to take that away from him, you left a brave man no choice other than to confront you; you found out what he cherished and then used it *against* him. But, as I said at the beginning, I suspect you probably knew that and it was part of your plan. Are you *so* devious?" questioned this seasoned officer. "Unlike Crockford, you have enjoyed every advantage. Your father is a much-esteemed admiral and your grandfather the same. If you want to be a great man like them, stop all this pettiness and raise your horizons to the important matters we must *all* address – both personally and as an organisation." He turned to the other officers around him, "Goodness knows we're likely to have a real enemy to face soon enough." Looking back at the cadet with barely disguised contempt, "Now – carry on!"

After Hardacre had left them, the commander turned to the others, "Yes, I believe Crockford *is* a brave lad. An orphan with no means of support outside the Navy, it's probably true that he had little choice – which of course was our intention because we didn't really want to lose him. Nonetheless, I admire the way he conducted himself today," he continued whilst nodding. "He displayed commendable courage in making his decision. But his real test is yet to come."

10

The day of punishment arrived. Rather than trust this routine to the cadets, the Duty Lieutenant took charge personally. He directed the seniors to form up all the cadets four-deep along the centreline of the ship, aft of the foremast and facing outboard to starboard. Without a specially-designed birching pony, the boatswain had arranged for a substitute to be set up in front of the assembled crowd. A table was positioned between two gunports, with a mattress tied over it. The Surgeon and his sickbay attendant were fussing around aft of the table, with their paraphernalia ready for use. The warrant officers, petty officers and other members of the ship's company were fallen in forward of the table, facing aft.

The birching rod was put ready, deliberately in full view, as a deterrent for all to ponder. It comprised four or five willow withes about three feet long, bound together into a handle at their thicker ends. The warrant officers had discussed the situation between themselves. They chose willow rather than the more usual hazel twigs, known to be particularly painful. In addition, they had not soaked the twigs, as was often done, as this would make them more supple and heavier, increasing the damage done. They also reduced the length of the rod from four feet to three to minimise its effect, hopefully without attracting the undue attention of the commander, who now made his entrance.

Taking his place on the raised platform overlooking the packed arena, he indicated he was ready. At that signal, the Master-at-Arms, in company with a ship's corporal, marched Ted up to the table, bringing him to attention facing the commander.

The latter stepped forward and addressed the assembly in clear tones.

"The success of the Royal Navy depends on the discipline enshrined in our rank structure. No instances of challenging the rightful authority of superior officers can *ever* be excused – no matter what the circumstances. Cadet Crockford has admitted that he struck a senior officer and, accordingly, he must bear the consequences. This is the proper, authorised punishment, on completion of which the matter will be finished. No further sanctions are to be directed towards him.

"To the cadets, I would say this. I require every one of you here to engrave this scene on your mind's eye," he commanded, "and to endeavour to avoid such brutality in your own careers. We have left the age of sail behind. The increasingly technical nature of our work should also herald a new era of mutual respect and cohesion of effort amongst all ranks.

"Now, Master-at-Arms, do your duty!"

Ted was brought to the end of the table, facing forward. His ankles were secured to the bottom of the table legs. Then, bending at the waist, he had to lie on the mattress with arms outstretched towards the far corners of the table where his hands were tied too. The defaulter's untucked shirt was pulled up his body to lie around his neck and shoulders, exposing the rest of his back. Ted turned his head to look outboard, away from the assembled company. The corporal was the same one who had witnessed the fight in the woods and remembered Ted's fortitude that night. He picked up the birch, took up his position alongside the table and then looked at the Master-at-Arms, who gave one sharp nod.

With a full swing of his arm, initially turning away and then bringing his hand directly over his head as he turned back – a movement like that of a bowler in cricket – the corporal laid on the first stroke. As the birch landed with a crack, even the most hard-hearted amongst the spectators felt an involuntary shudder. As the corporal continued his duty . . . two . . . three . . . four times, all could see the savage wheals appearing across the white flesh. When examined dispassionately, one realises how strong the thin covering of our skin really is and how hard it tries to keep its contents within. But, failing now after ten . . . eleven strokes, it releases the blood freely, and the scene becomes barbaric. The increasingly pulped mess under the birch becomes unrecognisable as a human form, with the mattress, the table and even the corporal himself becoming splattered with red.

Two cadets fainted, and it was a welcome distraction for their colleagues to lead them away from the horrific scene. After ten strokes, even Hardacre could watch no longer. He tried to shift his eyes away, but as he did so, he noticed that all the warrant officers and the ship's company were staring straight at him with undisguised scorn. All he could do was look down and contemplate the deck in front of him.

At last, it was finished, and the corporal stood back from his task, wiping the sweat off his brow with the back of his right hand. Ted's hands and feet were untied, but he continued to lie there unmoving. The sickbay attendant came forward and emptied the entire contents of his bucket over the mutilated anatomy. Although intended to help the offender by cauterising the wound, this deluge of salt water was like another most terrible stroke of fire across his whole back. Ted, who thought his ordeal was over, started upright and, for the first time, groaned loudly. As instructed, the corporal stepped forward, wrestled down the offender's wet shirt and supported his arm to lead him away. Ted shook him off and followed the Master-at-Arms below decks.

11

There had been no need for the commander to caution the cadets about allowing the offender to rehabilitate back into *Britannia's* regular routine. He should have realised that everyone in the establishment would become aware of what had gone on. As a result, odium was directed only at Hardacre. This once-proud fellow palpably lost all that arrogance and bravado that had been his hallmarks, now seeming content to go quietly about his business and not engage with any other cadets. On the other hand, Ted was afforded great respect as one who had acted honourably and bravely endured a terrible punishment. Nonetheless, he could not easily shake off the shame he felt from such a public spectacle and did not welcome the attention and near-hero worship offered by some of his admirers. All he wanted was to forget the whole incident, merge quickly into the background, and resume his studies, precisely like his antagonist.

His academic efforts were successful, and he scored well in all the set examinations and other tests towards the end of the term. Now all the final-term cadets were waiting for was an interview with their training officer. From him, they would receive their final assessment and discover if they were to pass out of the establishment.

Ted arrived at the appointed hour and knocked on the cabin door. On hearing 'Come' from inside, he walked in.

"Come and sit down, Crockford," started the lieutenant. "I have all your results here and you've done very well; very well indeed. In all examinations, you were in the top half-dozen for your whole term, which is most creditable. Accordingly, I can put you out of your misery straight away," he smiled, "and can tell you that you *will* pass out as a midshipman. My heartiest congratulations!"

The slightest smile crossed Ted's face, but the unrestrained release of pent-up breath demonstrated better the relief this news brought.

"Nevertheless, success in the academic syllabus is only part of what we assess here. In fact, the examination score represents only half of the total points that can be earned by a cadet," continued his divisional officer. "The other half comes from what is termed 'character and leadership'. In other words, that is a measure of how we rate your overall prospects as an officer, and, in this respect, you have more to learn. The officer looked up from his notes, "Perhaps I should stress that this has *absolutely* nothing to do with . . . er . . . certain events. So, overall, I'm happy to inform you that you have been awarded a second-class pass. This will still attract some gains in seniority as and when you pass the exams to become a lieutenant, for which you doubtless have the ability.

"I hope you are not too disappointed. All the staff officers recognise how much effort you have put in to get even this far," confided the lieutenant. "We are optimistic that you have an excellent brain, good aptitude and the possibility of a most successful career ahead of you." In a more fatherly tone, he advised Ted, "As you go on from here, you must capitalise on that potential and concentrate on making your mark. It comes down to the fact that you are so quiet and polite, never pushing yourself to the front. The Navy needs leaders, and you have yet to demonstrate that you have the ability to take charge. Do you understand what I'm saying?"

"I do, Sir, and I've been told the same before," Ted answered. Failing to look up at the officer, he continued, "But it's extremely tough for someone like me to change. Someone like me who has been taught all their life to remain deferential. It's an ingrained habit that's awfully hard to break. But I *will* try." He reflected for just a moment. "I'm happy enough with a second-class pass. It's an achievement I could not have imagined even a few months ago." His divisional officer studied the young man in front of him. "Yes," he thought to himself, "Crockford has a fine understanding of his own character, which should serve him well. He has come such a long way and deserves to succeed, but his background will count against him."

In fact, only a few first-class passes were awarded that term. His colleagues were surprised that Ted hadn't made that grade. But neither had Hardacre, and a second-class pass clearly rankled with him. Everyone suspected that he would have an awkward interview with his father on that account. The grand passing out parade duly took place with much pomp and ceremony, with the successful candidates being introduced to the inspecting admiral. During the previous week, they had all received their onward appointments. So, as soon as the formalities were over, the new midshipmen hurried away from Dartmouth and were released to the fleet.

Chapter 3 – We Always Are Ready

1

Having graduated from Dartmouth, Ted served as a midshipman in a light cruiser in the Home Fleet. Still exceptionally quiet and introverted, he was hardly known by anyone outside the gunroom, which was the austere accommodation and mess for the most junior officers. His tasks aboard were menial and mostly tedious. Highlights were when he was loaned temporarily to more minor vessels to experience as many aspects of naval operations as possible in preparation for his lieutenant's examinations. He discovered he got on so much better and became more involved within these small ships' companies. Here, there was no need to push himself forward or make himself heard within a larger group, being afforded rewarding opportunities to contribute to what was happening. There was less of a 'spit-and-polish' navy in these vessels, with everyone having a specified role.

Ted was ordered by his training officer one afternoon to cross Portsmouth Harbour from Kings Stairs to Haslar Creek to "find out all about submarines". On arrival aboard the depot ship HMS *Thames*, he was perfunctorily detailed off to visit one of the submarines alongside. She was preparing to sail the next day, and he found a buzzing hive of activity as stores were being stowed and final equipment checks completed. He waited for the seemingly endless flow of bodies crossing to and fro to cease momentarily before venturing across the rickety brow. He could hardly conceive that the insignificant bulbous shape below was a sea-going craft. Explaining the purpose of his visit to a distinctly scruffy sailor in a dirty white jumper, he was guided down a ladder taking him vertically into the bowels of the vessel.

Finding himself in the control room, as he was soon to be told was the name of this area, Ted was wide-eyed in wonder. Every inch of space around him was filled with shining brass, copper and steel. There was row upon row of valves, vents, and kingstons pointed out to him without explanation. He was already familiar with the boiler and engine rooms and other machinery spaces of ships, but this was a markedly different environment. Unrecognisable items of equipment were jammed into every conceivable nook and cranny. Ballast, trimming, and hydraulic pumps were squeezed into this constrained volume.

It was not permitted for such junior personnel to join 'boats', so the midshipman in his clean uniform was patently not one of their own. He was paid little attention by the crew. People squeezed past him, none too gently, to complete their many tasks when preparing to sail. A lieutenant spotted his uncomfortable predicament and ushered him to a corner beside the chart table, inviting him to sit on the single fold-down chair available.

"We can talk here," he said. "I was told you were coming but I'm afraid I can only give you five minutes: there's so much to do yet." The officer looked only a few years older than Ted, but his crumpled reefer jacket, with its tarnished stripes and numerous oil stains, spoke of long experience. "But what do you think of her?" he inquired. "Have you seen a boat before? You do know we call submarines 'boats' and not 'ships'?"

"No, Sir, I've not seen . . . er . . . a boat before," Ted was thrilled and wide-eyed at the technology all around him. "I think it's fantastic – magical even! How does it all work?"

"I think that might take more than five minutes, young man!" the officer retorted with a broad, friendly smile. "But I'll have a go." The lieutenant explained the fundamental processes of diving and surfacing, the principle of neutral buoyancy with the concept of 'catching a trim' when dived by matching weight to buoyancy. He demonstrated with his hands the idea of the hydroplanes acting like horizontal rudders to control the pitch angle and depth of the submarine. "If you get all *that* right, you've more or less cracked it," he joked.

Ted had listened intently to every word. Concepts of buoyancy and trim had been understood before, but now he looked puzzled. "I think I understand, Sir. But if you achieve that balance of weight and buoyancy, how do you fire your heavy torpedoes without instantly losing control and floating to the surface?"

"Ha!" The lieutenant's laugh was more like a bark. His face lit up with a massive grin as he punched one hand into the other. "So *that's* where we've been going wrong! Clever of you to spot that," he nodded appreciatively, staring at the lad. "Let's just say it's not as complicated as it might seem."

"But," persisted Ted, "how do you make all this equipment operate together and at the right times? Who knows how it all works?"

"Well, the two officers do and most of the ship's company too," was the response. "That's why those haughty officers in their swanky ships like your cruiser refer to us as 'The Trade'. What's more, some think we shouldn't be in the Navy at all, believing that we're no better than greasy chauffeurs!"

Ted was awestruck and had a thousand more questions, but the officer was getting up and making to leave. The midshipman took his cue, "Thank you very much for your time, Sir. I'm extremely grateful. But could I just ask what your job onboard is?"

"Yes, of course; I should have said – rude of me. I'm the captain," he explained without fanfare. "I've enjoyed our chat, but I must go now. Good luck!" With that, he turned and went off, immediately issuing instructions to his busy crew.

Ted was deeply impressed by all he had seen in such a short time. He was utterly dumbfounded that a *lieutenant* was here in command of his own warship. A single afternoon was insufficient to complete his ordered training task. Nonetheless, it *was* ample time to convince him about which direction he wished his career to follow. Ted determined to volunteer for submarines as soon as it was permitted.

2

Now nineteen and with midshipman's time and the completion of general training behind him, Ted was promoted to Acting Sub Lieutenant. Rather than immediately joining the Fleet in an appointed role, he was sent to the Royal Naval College at Greenwich for yet more courses and examinations. Colleagues found the night-time attractions of nearby London all too alluring, especially after the extensive time they had spent at sea or abroad since leaving Dartmouth. For some, this impaired their studies and regular test results. But others - and they were very few - showed the ability not to let work interfere with their play yet, regardless, prove successful on completion. The final examinations at Greenwich were the most important in a naval officer's career by determining an individual's seniority and standing for the following twelve years.

Nonetheless, it was becoming increasingly clear to Ted that, no matter how good your exam results, what mattered most in the career of a young officer was 'interest'. In other words, influential relatives or sponsors were necessary to ensure appointment to the plum jobs where individuals could impress and get themselves known. Schooled in humility, this mattered not a jot to Ted, giving no thought to any future promotion and concentrating only on the task at hand to build his knowledge and expertise.

Ted had neither the funds nor the family and contacts within the capital whom he could visit to make the very most of his time near London. Nevertheless, occasional outings to experience the city's delights were enjoyed and – with careful planning – need not create a dent of more than five shillings in his tight finances. So, he was occasionally able to join his confreres – many of whom he knew well from his time in *Britannia* – in their forays to the bright lights of the West End. Weekends found him either revising the subjects studied during the week or walking up the hill and into the parks around Blackheath. By contrast, most of his classmates disappeared to their family homes or to spend time with local relatives.

Having been in the same Dartmouth term, Rupert Hardacre was also at the college but propitiously in a different set from Ted. Their paths crossed at mealtimes in the wardroom, at chapel, and on other occasions, but these were fleeting interactions. If their eyes ever met, Hardacre dropped his gaze instantly. Without deliberately avoiding or ignoring one another, there was never any real connection between them. Hardacre was one of the ones who could afford to enjoy the London high life mid-week and was never in college at the weekend. Ted observed his former antagonist from a distance and watched how he reacted to those around him. Hardacre seemed somehow less cocky and not as before, always trying to promote himself as the main attraction. The shame and righteous rage Ted felt from his beating still pricked his consciousness on occasion, particularly here, back amongst his *Britannia* friends. However, past events were never mentioned, and former raw emotions were in retreat. From his privileged background, Hardacre and he were clearly on different career paths. Consequently, Ted resolved not to dwell on previous events nor hold any lasting malice towards his former tormentor. He had his own life to lead.

If this young officer were to have returned home, nobody in his Exmoor village would have immediately recognised him. The boy they had known had grown about six inches in height, not only with longer limbs from a better diet but also on account of his upright stance with back straight and shoulders square. Ted's frame had filled out, and his fresh complexion had been replaced by a swarthy shadow over his chin and cheeks. His West Somerset drawl had almost been replaced by clipped, correct English, portraying his officer status. An often-arcane vocabulary revealed his naval profession. Only his piercing brown eyes were unchanged, but these remained private owing to his abiding habit of failing to make eye contact as he conversed.

Resulting from his self-enforced confinement in the college and as a keen scholar who had lost none of his academic prowess, Ted excelled in the end-of-course examinations. He gained the maximum seniority that could be awarded when eventually promoted to lieutenant.

Once these whole-Navy training trials were eventually over, Ted followed his earlier resolution and immediately requested to be appointed to submarines, being sent to the base at Gosport. From the outset, the Submarine Service was the perfect fit for Ted and proved to be everything he had hoped it would be. Rather than being an unwelcome chore that everyone must undergo, to him, the submarine training courses were exceptionally congenial. Principally addressing the boats' machinery and systems, Ted went back to the workshops in the evenings to revise straight away what he had learned during the day. He relished taking apart and rebuilding the various pieces of equipment to discover intricately how they worked. He wanted to know about every nut and bolt. Eventually released into the submarines alongside, he pestered the technicians to glean as much of their knowledge as possible. Ted's mechanical bent paid dividends, and he could grasp concepts effortlessly and put them immediately into a constructive context. Rapidly, his understanding grew about how men and machines must work together to enable this complex submarine to function safely and effectively. He couldn't wait to turn the theory into practice.

Service in submarines also had an unsought advantage for Ted; an extra six shillings per day was awarded to officer volunteers. At a time when full pay for a sub-lieutenant was just five shillings a day, this was a considerable inducement. Given numerous disasters – the Royal Navy had suffered several fatal submarine accidents in the early years – this extra allowance was mistakenly regarded by most as 'danger money'. In fact, it was a 'hard lying' supplement to account for the abysmal living conditions aboard boats, with the absence of the most rudimentary facilities in the early classes.

For example, there was no toilet, only a communal bucket. As a result, some officers took opium to delay their body's normal bowel functions for the twelve hours or so that they would be at sea. The sailors would not even have a bunk and would lie down on the metal deck wherever they could find a space. This extra cash certainly eased Ted's financial strictures, allowing him to afford one or two creature comforts within his wardroom-confined bachelor existence. Economic realities notwithstanding, his life in the Navy was everything to him, and Ted was distracted by little else.

It was instantly clear that the cadre of submarine officers was similar to him and not attracted to boats simply by the prospect of better pay. It was more their wish to get away from the rigid hierarchies of the big-ship Navy, ruled over by ancient aristocrats who had never seen action. Their outlook was vastly different. The majority genuinely believed that submarines would fundamentally affect maritime operations, particularly as the arms race with Germany was accelerating. They wanted to play their part in the development of this ground-breaking technology. Thought to be gung-ho by the non-cognoscenti, this new breed of submariners sought to push the boundaries, despite the risks, and not be bound by decades-old routines. They cocked a snook at their parent organisation, focussed as it was on the big-gun Dreadnought battleships, by embracing the supposed insult and happily referring to themselves as 'The Trade'. The submarine service wore this title as a badge of honour, marking them as a breed apart. Together they were a merry crowd of young men, many of whom were accomplished athletes and skilled sportsmen. Life in the mess was tremendously enjoyable, with noisy dinners and outlandish entertainment sometimes not ending until the early hours. The extra pay soon became essential to Ted to meet his share of membership costs in this most sociable wardroom.

No matter the high spirits and the fun and games they enjoyed away from work, it was different when it came to knowing their craft and using them to best effect. The submarine officers proved dedicated and professional, prone to talk shop endlessly and boring those outside this nascent elite company. Ted could not have been happier with this state of affairs, and, in the smoking room of the mess, the old hands were prepared to answer his never-ending questions. They quickly came to appreciate his intellect and recognise him as one of their own, despite his withdrawn manner amongst many extroverts.

To provide an escape from wardroom life, invitations came from brother officers to spend this weekend or that with their families. Frequently these were in grand mansions on expansive estates situated within the verdant folds of the Meon Valley. Ted had learned to ride satisfactorily at Dartmouth but was not of a standard to follow the hunt, let alone to engage in polo as some did. His dancing skills – gained from instruction whilst partnering other *Britannia* cadets – were even more elementary. Nonetheless, these sojourns proved to be welcome excursions away from his small cabin in Fort Blockhouse. In truth, however, he never entirely enjoyed them, unable to relax in such a foreign environment. He had no particular talents to display during the evening soirees and found the inevitable small talk uncomfortable. To him, such settings served only to accentuate his humble background. He felt he had nothing to contribute to these proceedings, lacking the self-confidence evident in those around him. Never to be described as dashing, he was nonetheless a handsome sub-lieutenant who seemed to be well-regarded by his fellow officers. Accordingly, a few young ladies to whom he was introduced made no secret of their attraction, only for him to miss the signs and take no action to progress any friendship. His colleagues came to regard their friend as a confirmed bachelor.

Immediately after training ashore was complete, Ted was appointed to an A-Class boat. Following the first experimental Holland boats, these were the first all-British design of submarine, but, for all that, they were rudimentary craft. Being the only officer apart from the captain, Ted found himself with the grand title of 'First Lieutenant' whilst still only a sub-lieutenant! As such, he was responsible for all routines onboard. His role was to present his superior with an efficient crew and well-maintained vessel such that his commanding officer could use her to fight. Fortunately, Ted was a quick learner, but he still needed to rely to a great extent on the coxswain – or cox'n – and the senior engineer.

The former was an experienced petty officer and the senior non-commissioned rating who acted chiefly as the interface between the officers and the ship's crew. As such, the coxswain had a raft of both administrative and operational duties: he composed the watchbills detailing who should fill what role and when; he oversaw victualling arrangements to ensure everyone was fed; he was the medical lead, which entailed him merely reading from a book about how to apply the primitive first aid kit carried; the coxswain was the boat's policeman and administered discipline over the crew; he manned the helm to steer the submarine when entering and leaving harbour; he manned the afterplanes when dived to control the all-important angle and depth of the boat; he also took on numerous other tasks as and when required.

The senior engineer – always called 'Chief' – was responsible for maintaining the boat's structure and every item of equipment carried, and for operating the propulsion and electrical generation systems. He was forever found in overalls, with a rag in his hands, shaking his head mournfully and a grimace on his face, fussing over the temperamental Wolseley petrol engine. This machine propelled the submarine on the surface and charged the batteries, which powered the electric motor when it dived. Its fuel vapours pervaded all living and working spaces onboard, turning the air foul and complexions sickly as soon as the conning tower hatch was shut.

Ted was the youngest man aboard. With a total ship's company of just twelve, including the officers, the crew comprised seasoned sailors who knew their business and got on with it without fuss. Almost before ordering some action, Ted would routinely find the right person in the correct position and ready to comply, having first repeated the order. This was the submarine practice that had been drilled into all the trainees: an order was always to be repeated before taking the requisite action to avoid any possible misunderstanding or mistake. The more complex evolutions of diving, surfacing or starting the engine reminded Ted of his bell-ringing experience, whereby a pattern was followed. An order was given, it was repeated, and action was taken. The following step was anticipated, the order given, repeated and action taken, and so on. Ted managed to get only some of the convoluted processes right the first time. Still, he didn't blame others when it went wrong and – most unusually for an officer – apologised. The ship's company appreciated his conscientious approach and helped him with subtle hints and actions. Indeed, it was in their safety interests to ensure their first lieutenant made no errors! They quickly recognised that he was intelligent, even if a 'by-the-book' officer, not having the self-confidence to stray from established practices. Nevertheless, the crew knew where they stood and caused him no angst.

Ted was in his element and, as was usual, was moved from boat to boat every few months to build his experience of all submarine classes. As he progressed, his captains took more time to teach him the mysterious art of attacking enemy ships. With natural aptitude and a single-minded, totally professional approach, Ted was bound to attract favourable comment, even amongst this group of equally dedicated and capable officers. Not at all extraordinary at the time, in the spring of 1909, when only twenty-two, Ted was appointed in command of a B-Class submarine – the second British submarine design – just eighteen months after qualifying as a submariner.

Ted had found his niche. Being in absolute charge of this complex machine fulfilled his heart's desire. He felt total contentment when in the control room of his own submarine, instructing his skilful crew of experts who would instantly do his bidding. Gone was any reticence or lack of self-confidence in this environment, with no dependence upon rank to be obeyed. Ted's deep knowledge of the craft and its systems was all that was needed. His diligence was rewarded by knowing as much as his operators about how any piece of equipment worked. Woe betide them if they fell short in any regard. At a time when it was all-important to keep these early submersibles safe, his crew appreciated his skill and held him in high regard. Yes, their captain was a stickler for the highest standards, but the sailors understood this was for the common good. As time progressed, Ted felt increasingly comfortable in the leadership role. In this regard, however, he was somewhat handicapped by his own technical expertise, with a tendency to wade in himself rather than allow others to get on with their job.

One success followed another, and a year later, Ted was the captain of a newer C-Class boat and he was comfortable in his ability to control the submarine and her systems in all conditions. This latest design enabled him to explore deeper into its warfighting capabilities and develop his tactical skills. Every submarine was mandated to spend at least two days at sea weekly, often with the commander of the flotilla embarked. Conducting attack after attack, two boats would alternate between being the assailant or the target. Ted drove himself and his crew hard as he pushed the bounds of what their boat and installed equipment might achieve. Another year on, he was reappointed again, this time to a much larger D-Class boat of radical design. He was making a name for himself as an officer of significant ability, not limited only to the technical aspects of his profession, but also with the mythical 'periscope eye' for successful attacking.

3

Equipped with fixed periscopes, poor optics and only a magnetic compass, the original tiny boats were suitable for daylight operations only. Their endurance of a short twelve hours limited the range at which they could operate, requiring them to remain close to land. This situation suited those outsiders who demeaned the whole concept of submarines and relegated their perceived role to one of local harbour defence, acting as a cost-efficient mobile minefield. Early successes against their larger brethren in Fleet exercises were simply pooh-

poohed as irrelevant in wartime or just unimportant. If their antics proved difficult to the Fleet's movements, the boats were merely assigned 'out of action' so they could take no further part in the manoeuvres. Those scruffy submariners were considered beneath contempt and no attempt was made to seek their help in formulating anti-submarine tactics. However, boats were becoming much more capable.

The situation began to change in 1910 with the arrival of Roger Keyes as Inspecting Captain of Submarines. He was tall, slender and energetic: some would describe him as hyperactive. Keyes was neither a torpedo specialist nor qualified in submarines, as might have been expected for this position. Nevertheless, he was very well respected throughout the Fleet. The then-First Sea Lord was Admiral Arthur Wilson, whose antipathy toward boats was well known: sometime earlier, he had proposed that captured submariners should be treated as pirates. Wilson was keen to break up the closed shop of the submarine service, and, in Keyes, he deliberately selected a non-specialist whom he expected to execute his wishes. As matters transpired, Keyes, with a reputation as a 'fire-eater', relished the fighting spirit and professionalism found in these free-thinking submariners. Contrary to Wilson's wishes, he fought against the regulations that required submarine officers to return to ships after five years. By doing so, Keyes strived to protect the expertise he found amongst this specialist cadre.

In 1912, Wilson moved on to be replaced as First Sea Lord by Prince Louis of Battenburg. As a result, Keyes became freer of constraints from on high and found himself with the new rank and title of Commodore (Submarines). He immediately pulled together a committee of the most talented junior officers to examine how this new submarine capability could best be developed. This was typical of the man: always coming up with new ideas for his young commanding officers to try out, he became known by them as 'the Arch Instigator'.

No one had thought harder about associated warfighting issues than Keyes. Wearing his second 'hat' as Captain (Submarines), or Captain(S), of the Eighth Submarine Flotilla based in Harwich and in command of HMS *Maidstone* – its submarine depot ship – he was one of very few with practical experience in submarine operations. Flying his commodore's broad pennant from the destroyer, HMS *Lurcher*, he used to deploy into the North Sea with his charges.

It was in Harwich that Keyes first met Lieutenant Edward Crockford when the latter was still the commanding officer of one of the small C-Class boats and with a growing reputation as a rising star. Demonstrating distinct tactical acumen with an exhaustive grasp of technical issues – the latter being far beyond Keyes' understanding – Ted was understandably commandeered onto his boss's ground-breaking committee. The two got to know one another well, despite differences in age and rank, as well as emerging from opposite ends of the social strata. Between them, they had a single common aim: to make submarines a significant factor in maritime warfare and to take the fight to whatever enemy the Country might face in the future. Keyes had been party to Ted's early re-appointment to a D-Class boat of the larger and much-improved design, accelerating his career prospects. Now it was pay-back time and the commodore nominated Ted for an audacious assignment.

"Steady, Cox'n," ordered Ted, fixed on the eyepiece of the periscope as he scanned left and right across the dived submarine's track.

"Steady, Sir," responded the senior rate. "Course three-three-five."

"Very good. Port helm, steer three-four-zero," came his captain's acknowledgement. "Down periscope."

Ted took the three steps over to the chart table as his navigator moved to one side.

Jabbing his finger at the chart, he briefed his team. "It's pretty misty up there, but I can just make out Craighead right ahead which'll keep us well clear of May Island. I can see two destroyers broad on my starboard bow which appear to be on nor'-nor'-west and sou'-sou'-east patrol lines, so should remain out of the way. We must keep a good lookout for their reliefs coming out of Rosyth." The coxswain on the afterplanes and the second coxswain, a leading hand on the foreplanes, smiled at one another. Their captain's use of '*we* must keep a lookout' always amused them when he was the only one on the periscope who could see anything. "Pilot, tell me when we should turn up harbour by dead reckoning," Ted ordered his navigator. "How are we doing overall for time?"

The navigator was busy with a parallel ruler over his chart and checked his watch. "By DR, we should turn to port to new course two-four-zero in . . . er . . . eight minutes, Sir," he calculated. "Overall, I think we're on track for time and should make our ETA comfortably. I'll have a better idea when we're on the new course and I can assess the tidal stream more accurately."

The submarine made its planned turn into the Firth of Forth, close to the Isle of May, keeping to the southern edge of the main fairway. Two light cruisers appeared in a regimented line ahead, one behind the other, exiting the harbour. They passed just five hundred yards away, blissfully unaware that they were being tracked by an unseen underwater 'enemy'. Now the submarine just had to avoid the vessel shuttling between North and South Queensferry and pass under the northern arch of the railway bridge. Ted was still taking only occasional observations through the periscope but then – yes – there was his target!

Following the long-established routine, Captain (S) and Commander (S) were standing on the bridge wing of the depot ship. Waiting for the submarine's arrival, its accuracy would be compared to the declared ETA. They would also be ready to take the piped salute as the vessel made its final approach. The commander studied his watch. "Well, there are about thirty seconds to go, and Crockford will be *very* late. I cannot see him down the river at all!" Turning around to his Chief Yeoman, he asked, " Have we heard anything about him changing his ETA?" Submariners were ever-aware that calamity could strike at any time.

Before the senior rate could answer, there was a loud clang. "What the devil . . ." started the commander but stopped as he saw the collapsed head of a practice torpedo bobbing alongside the ship, surrounded by the escaping air that had brought it to the surface. Almost instantly, the grey top of a submarine appeared as it surfaced head-on, just four hundred yards from the ship. In equally short time, a sailor appeared on the boat's bridge and piped the still, with an officer racing up behind him from below and snapping into a smart salute. The commander was incandescent and was pacing up and down, thinking about what terrible punishments he could inflict upon this wayward upstart. Then he caught sight of his calm Captain (S), who was even smiling. "You *knew* about this, Sir?"

The more senior officer was nodding. "Yes, I'm sorry. Keyes told me his plan but wanted to keep the matter totally in-house in case we couldn't pull it off," he apologised and shrugged before continuing. "Doubtless, I will now have a rather awkward interview with the port admiral to explain what we've been up to. But it'll be worse for those patrol ships: I certainly wouldn't want to be in *their* shoes. Word will get out – that's the intention – and perhaps everyone will now heed our warnings about the real threat posed by submarines!" Tucking his ceremonial telescope under his arm, he made to leave and return to his desk. "Get young Crockford alongside and I'll see him in my cabin."

Intelligence warnings about the German navy rapidly building up its number of boats seemed to be ignored, and Keyes' demonstration made little difference. The whole concept of submarines and their employment continued to be derided by many in the Senior Service. Matters improved when Admiral Jackie Fisher returned to be the First Sea Lord. In his previous tenure of this high office, he was feted principally for introducing the Dreadnought battleships into service. Still, he had also been instrumental in purchasing new boats and expanding the submarine corps. Of giant intellect, vision and drive, Fisher had made up his mind about submarine warfare as early as 1904. He observed, "I don't think it is even faintly realised – the immense impending revolution which the submarines will effect as offensive weapons of war." Now back in office as the arms race with Germany accelerated to a fever pitch, he continued to stress the changes to maritime warfare that submarines would introduce. Fisher wrote a memo to the civilian First Lord of the Admiralty. Winston

Churchill replied to him in January 1914, "I have read and re-read with the closest attention the brilliant and most valuable paper on submarines . . . There are a few points on which I am not convinced. Of these, the greatest is the question of the use of submarines to sink merchant vessels. I do not believe this would ever be done by a civilised power." These words would return to haunt him all too soon.

After only a year in his D-boat, Keyes recommended Ted to become the instructor of underwater tactics at Fort Blockhouse in Gosport, the *alma mater* of the Submarine Service. Great things were expected of Crockford, and in April 1914, he was appointed in command of *E57*, a newly-constructed submarine of the latest class, still fitting out at Barrow.

5

Peering up from the granite bottom of the dock, Ted stood alongside the project manager for the build, admiring his new command. The E-Class was an upgrade of the D-Class like his previous boat, so the recently-arrived commanding officer was well aware of many of the revolutionary features of the vessel. Principal amongst these – at least those that could be perceived from outside – were streamlined bulges on each side of the hull. So-called saddle tanks were part of the complement of main ballast tanks. Open to the sea at the bottom, the tanks flooded when topside vents were opened, allowing the air inside to escape and the vessel to submerge. The same vents would be shut, and compressed air blown back into the tanks would expel the water and cause the boat to surface. The benefit of saddle tanks was twofold. Firstly, more internal space became available for a larger battery, additional torpedo tubes, more reload weapons, a larger crew and limited creature comforts. Secondly, a greater reserve of positive buoyancy would permit safer operation in a seaway without being swamped by waves. The boat builder pointed out a circle on the nearest saddle tank, which did not feature in Ted's previous command. He explained that this was the outside cap of a beam torpedo tube – one on each side – which the broader beam of this newer class allowed. These were in addition to the two side-by-side torpedo tubes forward and one at the stern.

Internally, the petrol engines of previous classes had been replaced with less-thirsty diesel engines. These machines proved more reliable, didn't intoxicate their operators, and boosted surfaced speed to fifteen knots. These novel designs also included an early version of a gyro compass. Twenty feet longer than the D-Class, the E-Class allowed a crew of thirty, which could be separated into watches, permitting the vessels to be operated for an extended period. Additionally, the much-improved sea-keeping properties and economical engines enabled them to roam at greater ranges. All D-Class and E-Class were based at Harwich. They were described as 'overseas' submarines to define them as separate from, and significantly more capable than, the earlier 'coastal' vessels.

On arrival in Barrow the previous afternoon, *E57*'s crew had been formed up for inspection. The new commanding officer was delighted to discover that Petty Officer Albert Prescott was to be his coxswain. They had served together before, and – different in so many ways – their contrasting characters complemented each other. Prescott was in his late thirties and looking forward to retirement if the threatened war did not intervene. Signing on as a boy sailor, he had been 'round the buoy', being disrated from Leading Hand down to Able Rate after one particularly hedonistic 'run-ashore', before advancement again. With a less-than-perfect disciplinary record, Prescott was lucky to have been accepted into the Submarine Service, but this 'dangerous' profession was short of volunteers in its early years and needs must. Nonetheless, he was the ideal fit for submarines: burly, fit and strong, he could put up with the harsh conditions and was blessed with boundless innate common sense. In appearance, he was now the archetype of the hardened sailor, complete with a 'full set' of a beard. Every scar and wrinkle on his face had its own story, as did the faded tattoos over his hairy forearms and broad chest. He proved to be one of the stalwarts of every crew in which he served.

Prescott was selected for the coxswain's course relatively late, at age thirty-three, the completion of which brought promotion to Petty Officer. The first appointment in his new role had been to a C-Boat with young Lieutenant Crockford in command. His captain wanted everything done by the book, as all the young officers often did, without the experience of getting the best out of the sailors. Coxswain Prescott's 'interpretation' of his superior's wishes rankled on occasion, but, without fail, the ordered task would be completed efficiently to a satisfactory standard. As time passed, Ted learned to trust his coxswain implicitly, and they worked together well with mutual respect. In such a small submarine, the captain had to be involved personally in every aspect of business. The first lieutenant, fresh out of training, just did not possess the nous to act fully as the crucial interface between the commanding officer and crew. *De facto*, the coxswain assumed this role. With officers and sailors living cheek by jowl, the ship's company could assess the strengths and foibles of their superiors with remarkable accuracy. If Great Britain was to go to war, as seemed inevitable, here was a captain, Prescott thought, who would be able to keep him safe and get them through it. Accordingly, when he heard *E57* was being commissioned with Lieutenant Crockford in command, he jumped at the chance to be her coxswain.

The engineering department of fifteen artificers and stokers was headed by the senior engineer, Chief Artificer Harry Bowers. He had turned out smartly in his best uniform to be introduced to his new captain, but his role onboard was given away by the crumpled hat. The cover was clean and white, but the cap's frame had been mangled by having been shoved behind pipework or forced into convenient crannies when busy with his many tasks. Of average height, Bowers had lost the fight with gravity to keep his substantial belly above his belt. His round glasses and distant gaze gave him an academic air: indeed, he had to be of above-average intelligence to perform this role with the latest technology all around. Nonetheless, Bowers' strong Scouse accent betrayed his background as a stevedore's son from an unruly neighbourhood. His stokers crossed him at their peril.

The officers met that evening in their impromptu wardroom mess, the hotel bar where they had been billeted. Lieutenant Walner Hackett-Jones introduced himself confidently as the first lieutenant, shaking Ted's hand vigorously. He had had the role before, he explained, but only in a C-boat, expressing his utmost pleasure at being appointed now to *E57*. His deportment and precise pronunciation suggested he had been a public schoolboy, seeming to be extrovert and with a most sociable demeanour. Ted believed he would make an entertaining colleague in the wardroom, *provided* he proved professionally competent. Only time would tell.

Hackett-Jones' companion was of an entirely different character. Lieutenant Robert Buckle had served in the Royal Navy for only three months and was distinctly reticent under his new commanding officer's examination. This was understandable in the circumstances. A fully qualified deck officer in the merchant navy, he had been transferred to the Royal Naval Reserve and then to *E57*. Buckle was to serve as her navigator after a laughably-short introductory course into submarines and how they operate. Nevertheless, he was expected to take the watch in turn with the first lieutenant and take charge of the boat. Mistakenly, it was considered by the powers that be that enlisted navigators need not be involved in any of the esoteric processes necessary to operate the vessel as a submarine. It was thought they needed to concentrate only on her navigation. Ted found Buckle to be bright and agreeable but training up the third officer onboard from scratch was a job he had not anticipated.

Matters did not start well. *E57* suffered a whole catalogue of machinery accidents and equipment breakdowns even before leaving Barrow. Ted made the most of this additional time with his new ship's company. Either he conducted drills onboard when dockyard activities permitted, or he arranged the loan of key crew members to operational submarines. This would bring them back up to speed and allow them to glean up-to-date tips on how best to operate the E-Class boats. Only after several months' delay did *E57* eventually join the Eighth Submarine Flotilla at Harwich, by which time war with Germany appeared inevitable.

On 4th August 1914, Great Britain issued its ultimatum to Germany, requiring her to withdraw from her attack on Belgium by midnight. That evening, Keyes summoned all his officers to the quarterdeck of HMS *Maidstone* and briefed them on developments. In a stirring speech, he gave his opinion on how the Kaiser had engineered the current situation over many years and how he thought Germany would never back down. Accordingly, every submarine had to be prepared to wage war relentlessly from the very outset. Before finishing, he stoked up the fervour of his audience, "You must go into this seeing red." He then led the commanding officers away to provide them with details of his initial plan. As Keyes had foretold, there was no response to the ultimatum. At eleven o'clock that evening, the Admiralty sent the fateful message, "Commence hostilities against Germany." Without fanfare, *E6* and *E8* slipped from the depot ship before the next dawn, headed for the Heligoland Bight, being the very first Royal Navy units to deploy on war patrol.

In the early days of the war, *E57* was often left alongside nursing one defect or another as her sisters departed on patrol. All too slowly for Ted, the relentless efforts of Chief Bowers and his team brought the boat up to an acceptable level of reliability, at last permitting Keyes to give his permission for her deployment. It was already the beginning of September.

Life on *E57*'s first patrol in the North Sea was far removed from all the hurrahs and singing of nationalist songs during the run-up to conflict and the excitement of at last joining the war. Days of indifferent autumn weather passed. It was constantly overcast, raining, foggy or blowing a storm, and the whole operation became a ceaseless battle with the elements. Fully surfaced at maximum buoyancy, the submarine's bridge would be just a few feet above the water's surface, and there was only a canvas screen 'dodger' to protect the duty officer and lookouts from the worst the weather could throw at them. Consequently, they were on watch for barely a few minutes before they were soaked to the skin. Conditions were no better in the warmer engine room, where stokers suffered burns or sustained other injuries as they were thrown against piping as the boat bucked and bounced. Ted wanted to remain either surfaced or at periscope depth so that no enemy vessel could pass, but he was forced to accept the reality of the situation. Once the batteries had been charged to an acceptable level, he bottomed the boat overnight during the worst conditions to relieve his dog-tired crew. He excused himself because it was doubtful that a darkened warship could be detected passing even a mile away in those long, bleak hours. At the same time, *E57* would be exposed to the possibility of being rammed. Bottoming the submarine in such shallow water was not without its perils and discomfiture. A moderate swell could cause the boat to pump, whereby she would be lifted up before being dumped heavily down again.

When settled on the seabed and most of the ship's company stood down, sailors would crash onto the deck wherever they could find a space, immediately falling into an exhausted sleep. Hackett-Jones, Coxswain Prescott and Chief Bowers then conducted rounds together by torchlight after most lights had been doused to save power. Stepping carefully over bodies, they assessed new and existing defects, checked for leaks, examined remaining stores, and reviewed injuries and the general health of the crew. Within twenty-four hours of taking up station, the insides of the submarine had been running with condensation. Everyone's clothes were soaked, never to dry out again whilst they remained away from harbour. There was no chance of washing, of course, with the quantity of water carried being sufficient only for cooking and drinking. Arrangements for toilets and ablutions remained primitive, and the abhorrent atmosphere was unimaginable. The officials conducting rounds, however, were thankfully unaware of the rank smell to which they had become totally accustomed. The bread had been covered in mould within a single day, and the potatoes had turned black after two or three. The crew's staple diet had become one of 'Hard Tack Hash', being tinned bully beef cooked with crumbled hard ship's biscuits in whatever variety of forms the chef's imagination could conjure up. In short, conditions were squalid.

Buckle had no chance to take sun or star sights to fix their position, relying totally on inaccurate dead reckoning – or DR as it was called. It was essential, and his primary role, to keep the boat clear of neighbouring enemy minefields. However, the Admiralty could only estimate the locations of these areas, so there was no certainty concerning their exact boundaries. Neither could the DR take into account local tidal streams or unknown currents. Before sailing and chatting with colleagues at the bar, Buckle had been informed by returning navigators that they had routinely found themselves miles away from the assumed position. Even worse, they had, on occasion, found themselves in the patrol area of another submarine with the consequent risk of collision with the other British boat. It became established practice to refer jokingly to navigation as "by guess or by God." The mine was the most significant threat, and, in an instant, the submarine's war could be over. This bore more on the officers' minds than the crew, being a cause of constant anxiety, adding to the stresses of inadequate sleep and poor diet.

After receiving the nightly report from his key personnel, it was up to Ted to decide when it was time to return to Harwich. Although it was assessed that a minimum of three days would constitute a practicable patrol, there was no stipulation, leaving the decision entirely to the commanding officers. Without any radio whilst they remained on station, there could be no consultation with, or direction from, operational authorities ashore. Only the boats' captains could assess enemy activity in their assigned areas and know the status of their own submarines. On *E57*'s first patrol, Ted determined to set off for home after seven days when the crew had been on dry rations for four days. Niggling but potentially serious defects were also beginning to appear. There had been no opportunity to fire a torpedo, and only one possible enemy warship had been detected. That had passed five miles away and was too distant for a definite identification. Nonetheless, *E57*'s ship's company had coalesced into a tight team. Despite his frustrations, their commanding officer was more than satisfied with his crew's conduct.

On 17th September, at a conference aboard HMS *Iron Duke*, Admiral Jellicoe agreed with 'the arch instigator', Keyes, on the concept for a force of three E-Class submarines to enter the Baltic. There they could attack the German battleships and battlecruisers known to be exercising in those areas, currently free of risk from attack by Allied forces. Sailing south from the Kattegat, it would be necessary to transit either through the Sound between Copenhagen and Malmo or via the Belts on the western side of Zealand. Either route was treacherous in the extreme. These channels were constrained and congested, and so shallow in some places that it would be impossible for the submarines to dive. If caught by one of the many German destroyers patrolling there, it was intended to blow the submarines up. Otherwise, they might fall into enemy hands or be interred by the neutral countries on either side. Accordingly, Keyes selected what he decided were the best submarines and crews for the job – *E1*, *E9* and *E57*.

E1 set off in October and was the first to attempt to pass through into the Baltic, followed a little later by *E9*. Despite some frighteningly close passes by enemy patrols, both proved successful. After the time by which all three should have completed their transits, *E1* attacked a German cruiser which saw the torpedo tracks and managed to evade. The presence of British submarines in their backyard was now known, and the approaches to the Baltic became a hornets' nest of German patrol boat activity. Unfortunately, *E57* had experienced more engine problems and had to retreat back into harbour. By the time repairs had been effected and she tried to pass south from the Kattegat, the submarine faced significant opposition. Ted tried every ploy imaginable to get past the German patrols. He even pretended to be a small coaster with navigation lights switched on and following another ship, which he later discovered was a German destroyer! After six days of trying unsuccessfully to break through to the Baltic, *E57* had no option but to return to Harwich.

7

In December, Admiral Hipper's battlecruisers bombarded the coastal towns of Hartlepool, Scarborough and Whitby. Having been forewarned by intelligence, fourteen British submarines were deployed across the Heligoland Bight to intercept the returning ships. *E57* was one of them.

The submarine had been on station for two days with no further intelligence concerning the whereabouts of the enemy ships. They could be snuggled up back in Kiel for all the submarine knew. *E57* had surfaced at first light to run the diesel engines and charge the batteries to the maximum extent before diving again, ready for her watchful vigil. It was a grey winter's morning with hardly any distinction between sea and sky. Determined to remain at periscope depth, to lose no opportunity to attack whatever might pass, the submarine was rolling heavily in a north-westerly swell. This only added to the tiredness everyone was already feeling, as their legs and bodies constantly reacted to remain upright. Hackett-Jones was on the periscope, sidestepping in endless circles to maintain an all-around lookout. He also had to wind the field of view up and down as he tried to observe the poor horizon despite the boat's motion.

"I'm washing over, Afterplanes," he admonished the senior operator.

"On depth, Sir! Twenty feet," came the retort.

"Very good. Keep eighteen feet," ordered the periscope watchkeeper. The first lieutenant continued his surveillance and then stopped. "Captain to the periscope!" Hackett-Jones bellowed, taking his eyes from the eyepiece for the briefest moment to look up at the bearing ring.

Ted had been sitting in his chair, reading a book as best he could without nodding off. Instantly, he was fully awake and took the few short steps to the centre of the control room.

"Make your report." The captain demanded.

"Captain, I have smoke on a bearing of red five-zero! No identification and no range, Sir," the first lieutenant announced, moving aside to let his senior take the periscope. "We are steering zero-three-zero and ordered depth is eighteen feet, Sir," he continued.

"Very good. Go to action stations and bring all bow and beam tubes to readiness," the commanding officer directed without lifting his eyes from the periscope.

The cry of "captain to the periscope" had alerted the experienced crew that a game was on. The message filtered around the submarine in seconds, and asleep sailors were shaken, even before 'action stations' was ordered. The inevitable hubbub as key watchkeepers took up their action posts lasted very few minutes.

"Cox'n on the afterplanes, Sir. Course to steer zero-three-zero. Depth to keep eighteen feet," Prescott indicated he was in position and ready.

"Very good, 'Swain," his captain acknowledged. "Starboard twenty, steer three-four-zero. We'll be head to sea but don't let her come any shallower."

Ted made a slow circuit with the periscope to ensure no other contacts before centring up on the smoke trail, now clearly visible. At first, he could make out just the top of a mast and then increasingly the superstructure.

"It's a German destroyer," he declared. "I'm broad on her port bow . . . no, wait . . . she's under helm and travelling at speed. Keep twenty feet! Down periscope!"

The whine of the electric motor as the periscope was lowered was still audible by the time Ted was over the chart table. He needed to check the submarine's position and his navigational freedom of movement. Over his shoulder, he continued the one-way dialogue. "Her range is about two thousand five hundred yards. I will not attack her unless she threatens us directly. We're here for bigger fish!"

"On course three-four-zero, Sir. On depth twenty feet," came the cry from the afterplanes.

"Up periscope!"

Ted clicked the periscope handles down. "Her range is two thousand yards. I'm now abaft her starboard beam and she's passing clear. She must be screening something," Ted mumbled as he scanned across the bearing from which the destroyer had appeared. "Oh, my goodness!" was all he could utter as his brain captured the scene now presented to him.

He explained to his crew that he could identify at least six destroyers zigzagging and coming straight towards *E57*. Judging by the dense billowing smoke, heavy ships were behind this screen: these were their target. Their small boat was directly in the path of these capital warships.

Ted was kept busy on the periscope, popping it up to rapidly appraise each escort in turn to judge its danger to his vessel. He also had to assess the overall force formation as best he could. Ted contented himself that the destroyers were zigging but maintaining an approximately straight line, abeam to one another. If he got under one, he should be clear of them all.

The nearest destroyer was no more than five hundred yards away; everyone could hear the high-pitched whine of her propellors as she closed. The submarine descended to forty feet. The intensity of the thrashing clamour grew unbearably. The knowledge that this ship would pass well clear, even if she went directly overhead, did little to appease the crew's anxiety. At last, it was over, and the tumult lessened as the destroyer moved away.

"Six degrees up," Ted commanded, "Keep twenty feet!"

Immediately the top lens of the periscope cleared, Ted realised he had concentrated too much on the escorts and not enough on the targets behind. There, fine to starboard, was a battle cruiser racing towards him with a bow wave halfway up the stem of the ship, confirming his target was travelling at speed. Ted had no time to manoeuvre into a better firing position and had only seconds to act.

"Standby the starboard beam tube! Open the outer cap!"

The gigantic battle cruiser was only two hundred and fifty yards away and approaching *E57*'s beam.

"Fire!" Just as the order was given, the submarine rolled heavily to starboard, caused by this massive ship passing so close or being suddenly caught by the swell.

Seconds passed, but the expected explosion never came. Even at such a short range, the torpedo might have failed to detonate on striking the hull. Alternatively, the sudden roll caused the fish to pass under the target.

The boat's captain pondered the situation for a fraction too long; other ships were behind this one. Raising the periscope again, the bow of the next battle cruiser in line filled his vision.

"Full ahead together! Full dive on the planes! Flood in whatever you can!" were Ted's immediate orders. "Depth of water, Navigator?"

"Seven or eight fathoms, Sir," came the instant response.

"Very well. We must bottom the boat!" the captain decided. Watching the depth gauge, the log speed and the angle of the submarine, the safety of his command depended on the finest judgement. "Half astern together. Keep one degree bow down," Ted ordered after a few seconds, which seemed like a lifetime. "Pass the word – standby for a heavy landing!"

Luckily, the seabed was quite sandy, but the scraping noises as *E57* struck the bottom and ploughed a furrow before eventually coming to rest was frightening in the extreme. Every member of the ship's company was anticipating the cascade of flooding water as the hull was breached. Before they had time to assess their new situation, a terrible thunder now shook the whole submarine. This new clangour was many times worse than all that had gone before. They could not control the trembling of their own bodies, and they couldn't hear the shouted orders of their officers just a few yards away. Lights were extinguished, and the glass on gauges smashed as twenty thousand tons of speeding warship rushed past, just feet above them.

Of all the submarines off Heligoland, only *E57* saw the hostile ships as they returned, and Ted's chance came to nought. Damage to the boat was superficial, and she returned safely to Harwich. Through all these trials and tribulations, however, Ted never once blamed anyone but himself. "No one can blame my excellent crew," he would say. "They just have an unlucky captain."

The overseas boats endured the ferocious storms, blanketing fogs, incessant enemy destroyer patrols and the ever-present danger of wandering into a minefield during their patrols in the Heligoland Bight. Furthermore, Admiral Wilson's suggestion that submariners should be treated as pirates had become true, with boats regarded as "*enemies of all mankind*". They were just as likely to be attacked by friendly ships and aircraft as by enemy forces, especially when they returned home unescorted.

Away from home waters, events had been developing in the Eastern Mediterranean. On the outbreak of war, British naval authorities had dithered, and local commanders failed to show any initiative. The modern German battlecruiser *Goeben* and light cruiser *Breslau* had evaded superior forces and escaped through the Dardanelle Straits to the safety of the Turkish capital, Constantinople. These ships were then transferred to the host nation as a gift, even though their German crews remained aboard. Although feigning neutrality for as long as convenient, it became increasingly clear that the vast Ottoman Empire had sided with the Axis Powers, closing the Straits to all traffic. It was not until 14th November, however, that the formal declaration of war against the Triple Entente was proclaimed. The Sultan, also the Caliph, Commander of the Faithful, declared *jihad* – a holy war – despite fighting alongside German and Austrian infidels.

Never accepting that these powerful warships were no longer German, the British and French remained concerned they might break out and wreak havoc in the Mediterranean. Accordingly, a powerful Allied force maintained a constant blockade at the entrance to the Straits to intercept them. Their Russian allies then became alarmed by Ottoman preparations to attack them through the Caucasus. If this happened, an already weak Russia would have to fight on two fronts, and the Tsar implored Britain to attack their aggressors from the south as a diversion. As a result, a prodigious armada of warships was being assembled to force the Straits. To succeed, this fleet would have to silence numerous forts, overcome mobile defences and clear untold minefields to gain access to the Sea of Marmara and hold Constantinople at risk.

Within this force were three obsolete British submarines: *B9*, *B10* and *B11*. Together with their French counterparts in *Faraday*, *Le Verrier*, *Coulomb* and *Circé*, they suffered the discomforts and boredom of endless day-time patrols off the entrance to the Dardanelles, searching for an enemy that never appeared. Then, on 13th December 1914, Lieutenant Norman Holbrook in *B11* slipped in the early hours from his depot ship – the ancient *Hindu Kush* – penetrated the approaches to the Straits, dived under the minefields off Kephez and sunk the ancient battleship *Mesûdiye*. The submarine had run aground, come under intense fire, suffered a damaged compass, and returned under the same minefields. *B11* surfaced safely at the entrance to the Dardanelles mid-afternoon. The air was so foul that the engines would not start until the boat had been ventilated. This seemingly insignificant vessel had achieved more than all the rest of the assembled force, and Holbrook was awarded the Victoria Cross for this incredible feat.

The severe limitations of the primitive boats assigned to the Dardanelles theatre had been observed from the outset, and local commanders entreated the Admiralty for more modern and capable boats to be assigned to the force. This appeal was refused time and again on the grounds that duties in the North Sea were more important. Nonetheless, *B11*'s success changed minds, and reinforcements were on their way. The Australian E-Class submarine – *AE3* – built in Britain and then having completed the lengthy voyage out to its home base, was ordered back to the European theatre. Having passed through the Suez Canal, *AE3* made her way to join the Dardanelles submarine force operating from the tender *Hindu Kush* moored at Tenedos. In addition, on 27th March 1915, three British E-Class submarines left Harwich to set out for the Aegean Sea in company with their decrepit depot ship HMS *Adamant*. They were *E14*, *E15* and *E57*.

With *Adamant* leading the way down through the Bay of Biscay, with her charges following in line astern, Ted hoped that operations in the Mediterranean would be a new start. Anything had to be better than those debilitating patrols in the North Sea. Despite being told repeatedly he had so much potential, he had actually achieved *nothing* of significance and had yet to 'score' his first success against an enemy ship. But the young captain's hoped-for change of fortunes did not occur, with *E57*'s mechanical problems continuing as she limped into Malta behind the others. This time it was a cracked drive shaft and low insulation on the armature of one of the electric propulsion motors. He cursed his lousy karma; would his submarine never experience that high level of reliability that successful operations demanded? In fact, his luck was better than he believed. During his unwelcome confinement in Malta, he met individuals who would have a crucial influence on his future.

We Always Are Ready

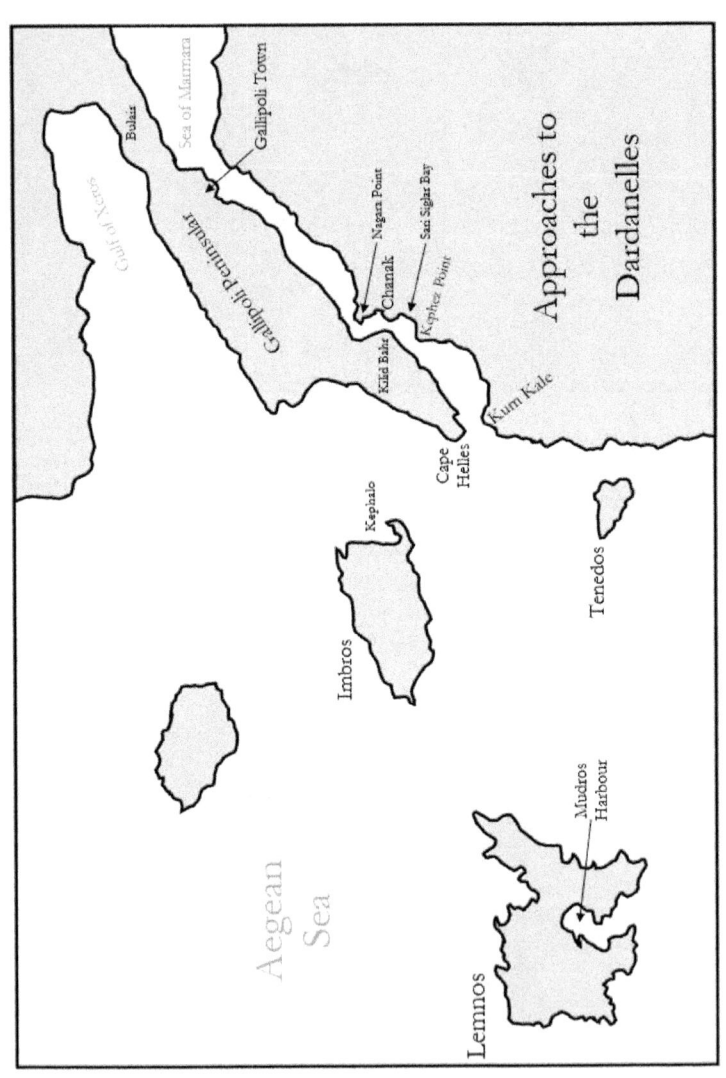

Chapter 4 – To Honour We Call You

1

Lieutenant Ted Crockford was not the only one heading south from Harwich. Habitually assessed as being more of a war-fighter than an intellectual, Roger Keyes had been reappointed to become the Chief of Staff for the naval forces assembled at the Dardanelles. Although he was sad to leave the Eighth Submarine Flotilla, he was content to relinquish the Commodore (Submarines) role with its frustrating interactions with those hopeless pen-pushers at the Admiralty. Unrecognised dyslexia had rendered the endless paperwork even more difficult for Keyes. Whereas in the Mediterranean, there was a realistic chance for front-line action. Furthermore, he had been given the wink that he was needed to help stiffen the spine of the risk-averse commander of the Eastern Mediterranean Squadron. In late 1914, Vice-Admiral Sackville Hamilton Carden had been bundled out of his sinecure in charge of Malta's dockyard. To everyone's surprise – including probably his own – now he was placed in command of an ever-growing armada of warships. Lord Fisher later noted in a letter to Jellicoe, "Who expected Carden to be in command of a big fleet? He was made Admiral Superintendent of Malta to shelve him!"

Churchill had requested him to investigate the possibility of forcing the Dardanelle Straits with a sizeable force into the Sea of Marmara, as the Russians had requested. Carden opined that it might be achieved. This would entail, he advised, a prolonged, combined operation employing naval and military forces to progressively overcome and hold the many forts and ground on both shores. After all, there was no point in fighting their way into the Sea of Marmara unless they could be constantly resupplied by ships passing to and fro through The Narrows. The warships must then be able to depart when the operation is complete without having to run the gauntlet past the forts all over again. Kitchener, however, would not hear of releasing any land forces from the Western Front. Accordingly, Carden, cajoled by the First Lord of the Admiralty, began attempting to edge slowly into the approaches by engaging the big defending guns one by one with his battleships, creeping ever closer towards Chanak and the Narrows. Churchill continuingly supplied him with more and better ships, culminating with the newest and greatest battleship of the time – HMS *Queen Elizabeth* – with her fifteen-inch guns.

At the heart of the problem were the minefields above Kephez, which had to be swept to allow the Allied armada to pass safely. The converted fishing vessels were deployed every night, only to face searchlights and harrowing fire from all directions. Everything was tried. The civilian volunteer crews were replaced by regular sailors, with destroyers and even battleships leading them into the Straits to destroy the searchlights and shore guns. Regardless, all efforts were repulsed, often after minesweeper crews had suffered mortifying casualties.

Carden was under extreme pressure from an impatient London, with signals implying the slow progress was due to his weak leadership. As a result, he ordered his staff to devise a plan marshalling all naval forces under his command into a massive attack on the Straits and the forts above Chanak. Once these had been silenced, the minesweepers could lead the fleet through. As the intended day for the assault approached, Carden's spirit collapsed and, on 16th March, he had to withdraw owing to ill health. His deputy, Rear-Admiral John de Robeck, was appointed as Carden's successor. Having been actively involved in preparing the operation, de Robeck decided to execute it rigorously as designed. Roger Keyes had arrived in Malta on 14th February and travelled on to Lemnos a little while later, so he was on the scene to observe and oversee the next historical event.

Thursday, 18th March 1915, dawned clear as the Allied ships lined up. The plan was simple and provided plenty of flexibility. The commander raised his flag in *Queen Elizabeth* and led the other three modern battleships – *Agamemnon*, *Lord Nelson* and *Inflexible* – into a line fourteen thousand yards from the forts at Chanak. What a magnificent scene this presented, with an awe-inspiring armada of ships manoeuvring with precision in confined waters, more like a sovereign's review than a fleet about to attack! At eleven twenty-five, the flagship opened fire, and within ten minutes, the whole of this 'Line A' of the four capital ships was engaging their targets. *Triumph* was guarding their southern, Asiatic flank and did her best to hold down the fire from the howitzers and field guns on that side. *Prince George* was doing the same on their northern side. Whilst Line A was still firing, the older French ships of the next 'Line B' – *Gaulois*, *Charlemagne*, *Bouvet* and *Suffren* – moved up between and ahead of them to be ten thousand yards from the Narrows to add their more rapid but lower-calibre fire. Their secondary armaments targeted the lighter minefield defences too. The smaller ships of Line B now came easily within the range of the defending forts' guns which only now could join this artillery contest. No longer was this a simple display of maritime power but a real battle!

When fired, the ship's cordite charges are smokeless, but the silk bags which encase the explosive sticks evaporate into a dense light-brown cloud, enshrouding the turret. The eruptive gases do not ignite until they have gone about ten feet from the muzzle when they meet oxygen, and then they flare up in a fraction of a second. So, a vivid burst of lightning is released from this fog, even in full daylight. Trapped by the topography of the Straits, the ear-splitting cacophony of gunfire unleashed from multiple batteries came like physical blows. Clouds of smoke, gun flashes, geysers of salt spray from shots falling short, and detonations as shells found their mark, all disorientated senses in this vicious confrontation. First, *Bouvet* was severely wounded, with her forward turret rendered inactive. Then *Suffren* suffered fourteen direct hits in quick succession, with a giant shell damaging one of her six-inch turrets beyond repair. With a slight lull in the enemy's fire, the admiral recalled the French division to be replaced by British ships *Vengeance*, *Irresistible*, *Albion*, *Ocean*, *Majestic* and *Swiftsure*.

The battle-scarred *Suffren* and *Bouvet* turned back and were almost abeam Line A when an explosion was observed on *Bouvet*'s starboard side. Still at speed, this proud old lady rolled over and disappeared below the waves in less than two minutes; only sixty-six were rescued from a crew of eight hundred. A little later, *Inflexible* reported that she, too, had hit a mine. The admiral now had to contemplate the unpalatable fact that his fleet was within an undiscovered minefield. Noting that *Irresistible* appeared dead in the water and in distress – it transpired that a mine had flooded both her engine rooms – he ordered her to withdraw and alerted

Ocean to start preparations to take her in tow. Even as the second Line B of British ships was signalled to withdraw, *Ocean* herself hit another mine and, coincidentally, a shell struck home and jammed her helm hard to port. She was obviously sinking. Having ensured the crews had been taken off, there was nothing else he could do, and the admiral signalled the general recall.

Before that calamitous day, General Birdwood, in charge of the Australian and New Zealand troops, had signalled Lord Kitchener on 5th March, "I am very doubtful if the Navy can force the passage unassisted." So, it had proved to be. Believing the honour of the Navy had been impugned – this was a task assigned to the Senior Service which must not fail – Roger Keyes was intent on renewing the attack at the first opportunity. But de Robeck assessed that he no longer had the means to carry it out: *Bouvet*, *Irresistible* and *Ocean* had been lost; *Gaulois* had been beached to repair gun damage; *Suffren* required dockyard assistance, and *Inflexible* had to be sent to Malta for extensive repairs. Although the other ships could return to the fray, all were short of ammunition, for which no reserve was available. The theatre commanders faced the grim reality that the Navy could not achieve the objective alone. Instead, the entire military force already building up on Lemnos would have to be deployed. In truth, the whole naval plan had depended on either the enemy being hopelessly inefficient as gunners or their moral fibre would be unable to withstand the terrifying onslaught to be unleashed upon them. There was plenty of prior evidence that neither of these was true. Despite losing more than two hundred men, the defenders had fought on effectively and gallantly under an unbelievably ferocious attack. Sadly, the same lesson continued to be missed in future planning.

2

The open anchorages off Tenedos had resulted in ships repetitively moving north to south and *vice versa* to seek a lee from the strong variable winds. Now, the build-up of naval and military forces necessitated a better and more secure base from which to operate. With their prime minister's agreement, the Greek garrison was withdrawn from Lemnos. They left the defences undisturbed, allowing Allied troops to take over their position on the island on 7th March. Lemnos is about fifty-five miles from the entrance to the Dardanelles, whereas Tenedos is only twelve to fifteen miles and, therefore, more convenient. Nonetheless, the great advantage of Lemnos was that it had a vast natural harbour at Mudros, which could shelter the host of ships and accommodate an army ashore. Tenedos could still act as a staging post, with its airstrip employed by aircraft for spotting and surveillance duties.

When *AE3* arrived in theatre, her energetic captain – Lieutenant Commander Gordon Tucker Royal Navy – was immediately seized by the idea of a dived passage through the Straits into the Sea of Marmara. He studied the detail of the situation with the utmost care and became convinced that it could be done. Nevertheless, he agreed to carry out a regular surveillance patrol off the entrance to the Dardanelles to acclimatise himself and his crew to the local conditions before formally putting forward his plans. Unfortunately, before his subsequent entry into Mudros, he was not informed that one of the lights used as a headmark had been extinguished as a security measure against hostile units.

As a result, *AE3* hit a rock and stuck fast, which was not the most auspicious of circumstances before presenting the admiral with a plan that required meticulous navigation. The submarine was eventually refloated, but not without some underwater damage, the repair of which could be attempted only in a dockyard. Accordingly, *AE3* set off for Malta, and she arrived just before *Adamant* appeared in company with her three charges.

The submarine depot ship, *E14* and *E15* continued their transit to Mudros the day after their arrival, leaving Tucker and Crockford to effect repairs to their submarines. Ted handed over control of the rectification work to his senior engineer and left the submarine's routines in the safe hands of his first lieutenant. He repaired to the wardroom in the castle of St Angelo where he had been assigned a cabin. It was there, in the bar before dinner, that he met Tucker. Their paths had not crossed previously, but they hit it off immediately. Outwardly, they were a most unlikely match. Tucker was sophisticated, outgoing, flamboyant, the star turn at every party, with gay repartee and endless jokes at hand, and the master of all card games and sporting activities. Crockford was quiet and introverted, old beyond his years, bound to service life, and reserved in company. He was happier to recount the latest refinements to his ballast pump rather than face the agony of small talk. However, what fired their ultimate interest was their love of their submarine craft and the investigation of what more this modern innovation could yet achieve. Their minds were simply buzzing with possibilities. In this, they were as one, and the two submarine captains became inseparable. Day and night, they would be found pawing over the charts of their new theatre of operations. Ted was infected by Tucker's enthusiasm for the task, discussing how they might undertake the perilous passage through to the Sea of Marmara.

Without a doubt, the transit through such confined waters required navigational excellence. This would be taxing enough in a ship with all-around visibility, let alone in a submarine with only occasional opportunities at periscope depth to estimate its position. If the periscope were sighted, direct fire from the many forts guarding the Narrows could be expected. Smaller-calibre artillery could hardly miss at such a close range, and damage to the periscope would signal the end of the mission. In addition, lines of moored mines were known to be strung across their intended route, but the location of most was entirely unknown, as the Allied naval force had found to its cost on 18th March. To avoid detonating the buoyant mines, the best option would be to remain deep and hope to steer clear of the mooring wires. But then, accurate navigation would be impossible. Should the submarine attempt to come up to fix its position within a minefield, the risk of collision with a mine would be significant, with the inevitable disastrous result. Neither could the submariners ignore the many gunboats now constantly patrolling the area since B11's surprise attack had scored such a remarkable success. To these two ultra-intelligent men, however, these deadly hazards represented mere operational challenges that would have to be dealt with when encountered.

What really exercised their minds was a simple mathematical conundrum. They could measure on the chart the distance to be covered from the entrance to the Straits to open, deep water in the Sea of Marmara – some thirty-seven miles. They could also assess the approximate range of the submarines' batteries which would be barely sufficient even in still conditions. What was not known, however, was the strength of the current against them throughout this transit. This was thought to be as strong as three knots in the Narrows, whereas the economic dived speed of the E-Class submarine was only five knots. As a result, only two miles would be gained every hour if these adverse conditions confronted them throughout, with the whole passage taking eighteen or nineteen hours. This would be impossible. Even a fully-charged battery would be completely depleted in half that time and surfacing to recharge would be far too risky in such confined waters under Turkish eyes. As *B11* had discovered, this pesky current would swirl in and out of bays, with the inclination to turn the submarine about its own axis, together with the tendency to carry the boat bodily in any direction other than the one desired.

On his third morning in Malta, Ted received a message from Tucker to meet him at the main Mediterranean HQ. He found him at the back of the main operations planning room, surrounded by ceiling-high wall maps. Tucker was deep in discussion with a lady wearing a dark headscarf and, as Ted approached, he realised she was wearing all black clothes. With brilliant manners as ever, Tucker smoothly interrupted their conversation to introduce Ted to Mrs. Kapadoukas. Tucker explained that she had been sent down from the Dardanelles HQ with a team to debrief C-in-C Mediterranean on the recent calamities. Tucker told him Mrs. Kapadoukas was half-Turkish with an English father, and could speak both languages fluently, with some Greek as well. She was employed within the intelligence cell, monitoring events both in theatre and within Constantinople itself as best it could.

She had completed the presentation to the admiral, and Tucker had managed to engage her in their problem.

He already looked disappointed and shook his head at Ted. "Britain had fostered a first-class relationship with the Ottoman Navy over many years and was regarded as their pre-eminent ally concerning naval affairs," Tucker stated. "Despite this, no one seems to have ever bothered to chart the Dardanelles passage properly, let alone collect any useful information about the currents that might be expected. It's an absolute disgrace," he concluded. "What did all the naval attachés think they were there for?"

He had given no thought to what her voice might sound like, but when she spoke, Ted was quite surprised that it was light and melodious. The all-black attire had misled him into assuming she was an older lady. Now able to study her face a little more closely whilst listening to her, Ted realised she was only in her late twenties.

"Yes, the Admiralty charts are quite sparse, as we discovered when planning the attack on the forts, but they are still better than those the Turks themselves use!" she explained. "There is a little more detail shown within the Narrows, but even this cannot be guaranteed to be accurate." With a wistful look, she added, "And, of course, we didn't get far enough the other day to prove matters one way or the other.

"The ships had no need for information about the current out in the approaches, so I'm afraid we just haven't looked into your problem as far as I'm aware," she continued. "In any case, it's not something the intelligence cell would have been involved in directly. But I will ask around when I'm back at Mudros to see if anyone else has any better ideas. I'm sorry I cannot help you more, but I must rejoin the rest of my party directly and get back to Mudros. There is a *lot* going on!" Mrs. Kapadoukas called over her shoulder as she hurried away.

Again, left to their own devices, Ted and Tucker continued to gnaw away at the problem. They were both keen to be the first to force the passage and were hugely frustrated by being forced to wait while the dockyard worked at its own pace. Chief Bowers had been successful in rectifying the motor insulation problem. So, rather than loitering in Malta for the section of propeller shaft *E57* needed, Ted arranged for it to be sent directly from Gibraltar to Mudros. He was confident that the engineers in the support ship would be able to machine it to fit. He took the gamble that he wouldn't have to dive quickly and that the temporary repair that had been made would hold out for the short two-day passage. *E57* sailed from Malta on 12th April, leaving *AE3* and Tucker, who would follow a few days later to join the others at Mudros.

3

E57's two-day passage up into the Aegean Sea proved to be uneventful, with mirror-calm seas and crystal-clear nights, with only the background clamour of the diesel engines disturbing the peace. As pre-arranged, the submarine arrived at Mudros at first light, being met in the outer approaches by a gunboat acting as the guard ship, which then led the submarine into this natural amphitheatre. The spectacle that met the boat in the harbour left the bridge party speechless and looking in all directions, trying to take it in. There were numerous battleships, battle cruisers and light cruisers, destroyers by the dozen, gunboats, merchant traders, troop ships and hospital ships, all joined by a cobweb of wakes from picket boats and lighters busily racing from one to the next. In pride of place in the most protected berth lay the magnificent HMS *Queen Elizabeth*. She was the Royal

Navy's most modern super-dreadnought, now acting as the HQ for the entire maritime and soon-to-begin land operation. *E57* was a dwarf within this great armada, and she was afforded no more attention than a picket boat as she made her final approach alongside HMS *Adamant*. There, waiting in the waists of the ship to meet the submarine, was Commander Somerville, her captain and in charge of the E-class new arrivals. A light aluminium gangway was pushed across from the support ship. Once it had been secured, Ted made his way across, being piped by the Quartermaster as he finally stepped onto his depot ship's deck.

"Welcome to Lemnos!" Somerville greeted Ted after returning his salute. "You'll be pleased to hear that your new half-shaft is expected to arrive here tomorrow and the technical team from the repair ship *Reliance* has already been down to *E14* to check the layout and plan what needs to be done. They'll make a start on the preparations today and clear out any work in way, so they'll be all ready to go as soon as the part arrives. After that it shouldn't take them more than about thirty-six hours' hard graft to get you into tip-top condition."

He continued in the same business-like tones, "I'll let the Leading Steward here show you your cabin and allow you to clean up. There's little time to waste because the Chief of Staff wants you to become familiar with the operational scene here as soon as possible. I've arranged a courtesy call on the admiral for you at eleven o'clock and the tender will be ready for you here at ten forty-five to take you across."

At the appointed hour, Ted crossed the harbour. As he approached the side of the battleship, HMS *Queen Elizabeth* loomed even more huge above him. Ted could see the Officer of the Day at the top of the seemingly endless gangway, fussing around, getting ready for the arrival of this commanding officer. The leading steward had done his best to sponge off and press Ted's uniform, but it remained shabby in comparison to the immaculate fittings of the battleship. Ted self-consciously pulled his reefer jacket down straight as a chorus of bosuns' pipes, flawlessly performed, greeted him over the side. Ted snapped to attention, faced the Quarterdeck and saluted smartly. A kerfuffle along the broad waists of the ship immediately announced the arrival of the Chief of Staff as he hurried along, moving languishing sailors out of his way.

"Thank you, Lieutenant," Keyes dismissed the Officer of the Day. "I'll take Lieutenant Crockford along to the Admiral's day cabin."

Already ushering his charge back in the direction whence he had come, Keyes offered his hand as they walked. "So, you've made it at last," was his welcome, with a wry grin forming because he knew of all the trials Ted had endured. "But it's excellent to have you and the rest of the team here," Keyes raced on, shooting out his words like a machine gun. "You'll like the Admiral. He's an old warrior and would like to get stuck in himself given half a chance! I've provided him with a pen picture of you and your background, so he'll doubtless seek your view about the chances of an E-Boat making the passage to the Marmara. I'd like you to be unequivocal in your support if you'd be so kind. I've persuaded him to let *E15* have a go in a few days' time and I don't want him having any second thoughts."

Ted obviously failed to hide his disappointment. "Oh, I see you'd hoped to be the first – like all the rest of my brave submarine captains!" laughed Keyes. "Never mind, let's get one through and then the rest can follow. There'll be plenty of work for you all if things go well. I'm afraid you'll only get about five minutes with the admiral – he's got much bigger fish to fry currently, as you will find out. I'll get my staff officer, Brodie, to collect you afterwards and brief you on aspects of *our* vital business." With that, Keyes deposited *E57*'s captain with the flag lieutenant and disappeared down the passageway at speed.

Ted didn't get even the five minutes promised with Vice-Admiral John de Robeck before the flag lieutenant apologetically informed the admiral that General Hamilton had urgent business with him. His new commander-in-chief had been very welcoming, nonetheless, making a real effort to listen carefully to all Ted had to say before they were interrupted. However, the admiral was plainly distracted by other matters and never mentioned Keyes' intended transit of the Straits. Lieutenant Commander Charles Brodie was outside waiting for Ted when he emerged; they had been colleagues in Harwich and greeted one another warmly. Brodie led him away to a compact office that served as the submarine cell. Sitting Ted down with a small scotch, he conducted his guest on a *tour de horizon* concerning theatre underwater operations. It was confirmed that *E15* – with Charles' twin brother in command – would make the first attempt to complete the passage through the Narrows in two days' time. Ted told Brodie of his meeting with Mrs. Kapadoukas and asked if it would be possible to seek her out. He wanted to discover if anything had come of her investigations, as these might help the operation.

They found her alone in a similar office, having a snack lunch at her desk. Patting crumbs away from the corners of her mouth and putting her wrapped food to one side, she gestured them in and invited them to sit down. But there was no other information she could offer.

"I'm so sorry," she started. "I have asked around everyone who might have any information about the currents in the Straits, even local Greek fishermen who might have been up there. But with no result, I'm afraid. I'll keep on asking about the problem and let you know if I find out anything at all." Thanking her for trying, the two officers left her and set off for the wardroom for some lunch.

They were enjoying the main course of Ted's first full meal since leaving Malta, when Brodie observed, "She seems to be a most interesting and intelligent lady, that Mrs. Kapadoukas. She's not afraid to speak out if she doesn't agree with what is being said, even within full staff meetings. Accordingly, she hasn't made many friends and even gained a few enemies; that is those whose opinions she has proved publicly to be totally wrong! 'Doesn't suffer fools gladly' hardly comes close!" Brodie stopped to pat away crumbs at the corner of his mouth before continuing. "The only woman of officer class on the ship, the wardroom is hardly a welcoming place for her, so she keeps herself to herself. She arrives in the morning, remains in her office all day, then goes ashore at night. Some refer to her as 'The Black Widow' and I've heard tell that some wag has even offered a case of champagne to any brave lad who overcomes her defences! She certainly has no love for the Ottomans," Brodie concluded, "and has shown herself to be a real asset to us. If there's any information out there that can help us, I can guarantee she'll find it."

They realised they were having increasing difficulty in hearing one another speak. A crowd of junior officers stood by the bar, delighting in ever-noisier banter broken by raucous laughter. Amongst them, Ted could easily spot the slim frame of Hackett-Jones, standing head and shoulders over many of the other officers. He and the rest of the throng stood in an informal circle around a jovial, red-faced character, with everyone enjoying and interrupting his evident story-telling.

"That chap in the centre is the intelligence officer from *Doris* which has just come up from Alexandria to join us," explained Brodie without being asked. "They've been briefing the admiral this morning on their operations off the Syrian coast, just before Christmas. Made quite a stir in Alexandretta, apparently, using that venerable cruiser's eleven six-inch guns to deliver some good, old-fashioned gunboat diplomacy. The captain – Frank Larken – sent his demands ashore and, when they threatened not to comply, landed heavily-armed parties ashore several times to make the point. They damaged the main Constantinople-to-Bagdad railway significantly and destroyed two brand-new engines. All exciting old-Navy derring-do perhaps, but it certainly worked and made any possible Ottoman attack on Alexandria much more difficult!"

After lunch, the two friends returned to the submarine office while Brodie ordered the boat to take Ted back to *Adamant*.

4

Having had a three-course lunch, followed by tea and toast later in the afternoon with all his colleagues in the support ship, Ted felt no need for an evening meal. He decided to take himself off for a walk to investigate his new environs. A fleet tender repeated a round cycle to pick up libertymen from all the ships and return them back onboard later, and Ted jumped on the first one. He was wearing an outfit of just an open-necked shirt, casual trousers and robust brogues that he always carried with him for just this purpose. The tender was nearly empty because – as he soon discovered – there were no bars or similar establishments that sailors would habitually frequent when ashore. Furthermore, the shoreline and the great valley to the north were filled with numerous tented encampments, sheltering the enormous army about to be flung onto the beaches of the Gallipoli Peninsular. Soldiers and sailors ashore are not accustomed to getting on well together, particularly if alcohol is involved. As a result, the granting of shore leave was a rare commodity for ships' companies in these circumstances. West from the harbour, Ted could see a few village houses on a rise away from the tents, with a hill beyond, which he assessed would afford the best all-around view. He took the dusty track that led in that direction.

On reaching the settlement, he realised it was a small town mostly hidden from view from the harbour behind the crest of the hill. The houses looked neglected and tumble-down, with seemingly the minimum infrastructure and without the typical shops and bars that one might expect. A couple of dogs were sniffing around some rubbish but, otherwise, no one was in sight. Ted was tramping through the near-deserted main street when he saw someone coming out of the last house. They were busy locking the door but were hidden in the shadow of the porch overhead. When the person turned, he realised it was a lady but dressed similarly to his own attire. She stopped at the gate post not ten yards ahead of him when he discovered - to his total surprise - that it was Mrs. Kapadoukas. In the same instant, she must have recognised him.

Gone was the all-black garb and all-concealing headscarf, freeing her dark auburn hair, cut in a modern style an inch or two above her shoulders. Her cheeks coloured instantly, and she was clearly embarrassed.

"Oh, Lieutenant Crockford, it's you. You must excuse my appearance but, having been cooped up all day in that ship, I'm always desperate to stretch my legs and get some fresh air in the evenings."

"No apologies are necessary; I'm hardly the image of sartorial elegance myself!" Ted responded, looking down at his own attire. "If you find that enormous ship claustrophobic, imagine what it's like being confined within a submarine for days on end. I love to get out and onto the hills whenever I can and fill my lungs with anything that doesn't smell of diesel," he joked. More formally, he added, "I had my mind on going on to that hill over there, but I would hate to interrupt your relaxation and, if that had been your intended destination, I will alter my route." In truth, Ted would have preferred to continue alone.

"That's where I always go but, no, you must go there too as the views are superb and you'll get a good feel for the whole island. If it wouldn't disturb *your* exercise too much, I would be happy to accompany you and perhaps point out the major landmarks."

"That would be very kind indeed. Thank you."

The two fell quickly into step as they set off up the rough path, with Mrs. Kapadoukas setting a surprisingly rapid pace. They walked in silence but without any feeling of awkwardness, both enjoying the freedom and physical activity. On reaching the rounded summit after about thirty minutes, her words proved to be true, and the panorama that opened up was spectacular. They rested on a couple of large rocks to catch their breath whilst Ted looked around. To the east, he could see the true extent of the harbour, with its many bays and inlets previously hidden by the multitude of shipping. To the north and west lay rolling, arid countryside with pine forests like zigzag scars across the face of the island, delineating deep valleys and coombes. The dark blue Aegean filled the entire southern horizon, with turquoise hues and young-beech green lighting the shallower areas and sandy bottom. The spring sunshine was strong enough to cast shadows of the playful clouds over the sea, adding lively movement to the scene. Breathing this fresh air deeply into his lungs, Ted half closed his eyes. For the first time in many years, he imagined himself back in Exmoor, sitting in his special place under the cross and looking across the Bristol Channel. He felt the same calmness and at peace with himself and the world, visibly relaxing and letting out that unknowingly held-in breath.

"Yes, I feel the same when I come up here," she gently interrupted his reverie, and he found her openly studying his face intently. "It reminds me of my home in Smyrna and of a place I used to go to look out over the harbour."

"It's the same for me," he replied. He didn't know why but for the first time ever since leaving his village to join *Britannia*, he told someone else about his home, school, teacher, father, and mother. He lifted the lid and looked inside a trunk full of mementoes he hadn't taken out for so long. She had magically turned the key to unlock deep memories. As he rifled through these treasured, deeply-personal artefacts, not once did she interrupt him other than to give an occasional nod or murmur of understanding.

Only when the flow of his reminiscences was eventually exhausted did she speak. "So, you're on your own too. But at least you still have a home." She paused for an instant, wondering whether she should continue, but took a sideways look at him and resolved that she would.

"My father was an English merchant captain who sailed all over the Mediterranean, often calling at Smyrna where he met my mother, a Christian originally of Greek descent. They fell in love and, probably against her parents' wishes, they married and set up home in Anatolia. All was well and they were blissfully happy and . . . I arrived! I have such happy memories of a safe and wonderful childhood, especially when Daddy was home. They called me Andrina after a mythical pirate's wife. The story went that, after her husband and his men had been repulsed from an attack on Skopelos, and all killed, she hid their hoard of treasure, burned their ship and dived into the sea, never to be seen again. Daddy said he had chosen my name because I was *his* treasure!" She stopped momentarily and took a second to look up blankly in the direction of the distant horizon, eyes smarting. "When I was ten, he was concerned for my education and we moved lock, stock and barrel to England where I attended a private school which I just loved. But my mother was never genuinely happy there, finding it cold and hating the rain. Her parents needed help as they grew old so, after five years, we went back to Turkey. I married a wonderful man – my Nikolaos – and we rented a little place of our own. I thought life could be no better."

Lost in her own thoughts, Ted was able to scrutinise her face. The absence of the scraped-back hair and tightly-tied scarf softened her features, and the fresh air and mild sunshine brought more colour to her smooth complexion. Dark, full eyebrows matched her brown eyes, which caught the sunlight. For a married woman, she looked remarkably youthful, he thought, and could be only a few years older than Ted himself.

Andrina continued her reminiscences. "That all changed when Enver Pasha and his cronies came to power. Previously Muslims and Christians, Turks and Greeks, all lived side-by-side, inter-mingled, and the occasional inter-religion marriage was not unknown. Almost overnight, everything that went wrong in the country was blamed on the Christians who became second-class citizens and were openly abused in the streets. When the Balkan wars started, most of the young men stepped forward to fight. For about fifty years before that, Christians had always been recognised as 'dhimmi' – protected people, 'People of the Book' – with nearly equal rights as Muslims and permitted to volunteer for military service. However, when it came to war and the Sultan declared '*jihad*'– a deliberate misinterpretation of the word – Muslims were sent into the army and Christians into 'labour battalions'. That's where my Nico was sent, finding these so-called 'battalions' to be no better than slave gangs, expected to complete hard labour for eighteen or more hours a day with insufficient food and no medical attention at all. Nico was fitter than most but . . . he survived for a year before contracting typhus. We had been married for only eighteen months," she added in a faltering whisper.

"Oh, I'm so sorry . . . " Ted started only to be interrupted by Andrina continuing her tale.

"Things were no better back in Smyrna. There were almost daily disturbances, with Christians being attacked by Muslim rioters. I moved back into the family home and, being in the better-off part of town, we weren't affected at first. Then even our neighbours started to act strangely. Daddy made plans for us all to leave and, as soon as we had received word of Nico's death, he sent me to Salonika in the care of a British family we knew well." She continued angrily with gripped fists, fighting back the tears, "I only agreed to go because they *promised* to follow me within a day or two after Daddy had wound up his affairs. But obviously word got out that they planned to escape and a mob broke into the house, ransacked the place looking for money and valuables, and, when they resisted, murdered my parents in cold blood and torched the house. Some of the people that did this had been our *friends*. . . " She left the statement unfinished.

Shaking her head vigorously to bring herself back into consciousness and apparently annoyed with herself for revealing so much, she said, "I'm so sorry. You really must excuse me; I had no intention of burdening you with any of this." She stood up and stepped away, ready to set off for her house.

"Please don't upset yourself. I'm to blame for, er . . . burdening *you* first with *my* story," Ted insisted gallantly, rising himself. "But time is getting on. Would you permit me to accompany you back to your house?" She half-smiled and, with an almost imperceptible shrug, turned to let him catch up.

They retraced their steps down the path, in silence now, with each lost in their own thoughts back in time. At her gate, Ted stopped, "Well, thank you for showing me and sharing your special place. It certainly did seem to work some kind of magic! I'll leave you in peace now and bid you a good evening." Andrina said nothing more and disappeared into the house.

5

The propeller half-shaft arrived as promised at lunchtime the following day. Leaving the engineers to their task and having instructed Hackett-Jones about storing the submarine for an extended patrol, there was little more for Ted to do except go over again and again in his mind how he might conquer the straits. He made his way to *Adamant's* chart house, where he had arranged to meet his navigator, Robert Buckle. Together they sketched out possible routes through the straits, and Ted rehearsed some thoughts that he and Tucker had shared in Malta. Buckle offered one or two refinements that he had picked up from other submarine navigators who had been in theatre for some time. With mounting evidence that even the E-Class boats with the newest batteries had insufficient range to achieve the full transit against the expected currents, their attempts to crack the problem seemed solely academic.

Nonetheless, there was considerable excitement running through the support ship because *E15* was preparing to sail overnight. She would make the first assault on the Narrows, hoping to be on the edge of the minefields at Suandere by first light. Everyone aboard *Adamant* and the submarines alongside her wanted to be involved and do all they could to help. Engineers, pursers, electricians, torpedo handlers, navigators and even the commanding officers fussed around, completing the most menial tasks if it would help *E15*'s crew. The inevitable sailors' banter and jokes were all around; some shouted across from the duty staff on the outboard boats just so they could join in this almost carnival-like event. Rather than the endless boredom of patrolling off Cape Helles and Kum Kale, at last the submarines had been given a worthwhile challenge, and all were eager to succeed. Everyone had a smile on their face, and the atmosphere was electric, with a tangible *esprit de corps* shared by all. Eventually, by mid-afternoon, everything that could be done had been. *E15*'s ship's company was stood down to get some rest and complete personal preparations for the momentous task ahead.

Ted was in two minds about whether he would take himself off again for a walk. The wardroom would likely be in a noisy, party mood that evening, as had become increasingly common as the way to send off colleagues on patrol in style. But, not a great drinker himself, Ted did not really enjoy these excesses and certainly not when it was he who was to sail. He had taken the opportunity at teatime to wish the officers of *E15* good luck, so he felt duty had been done. Accordingly, Ted dressed in his walking clothes and caught the next boat ashore. Again, he was uncertain about his route, but he didn't want to approach any military camps. He was therefore left with no choice other than to climb up through the village along the same path as the previous evening. As before, the road was deserted, and he did not pause as he left the houses behind him.

"Excuse me! Lieutenant Crockford!"

He turned to find Andrina coming out of her gate and hurrying towards him.

"Oh, good evening, Mrs. Kapadoukas. I'm just out for another stroll; would you care to join me?"

"Yes, I'd enjoy that. But I also heard something today that might be pertinent to your problem, so was hoping I might see you." She stopped by him, "We Turks, or rather half-Turks, aren't very formal people and 'Mrs. Kapadoukas' seems very stuffy, particularly outside on a dusty track! Please call me Andrina."

Ted nodded his assent, "Very well . . . Andrina. I'm Edward, but everyone calls me Ted," and offered his hand, which she shook.

This time, they exchanged polite small talk as they walked. He had enjoyed last night's walk; she had too; hadn't it been hot today; is it always this warm in early spring? Those politenesses over, Ted went on to describe the preparations for *E15*'s departure. She paid great attention but replied that the HQ was hardly aware of it, with total focus on the forthcoming land campaign.

"It's only Keyes and Brodie who are at all interested," Andrina explained. "The generals are completely ignorant of *any* maritime business, let alone *submarine* matters. Following the all-out naval assault in March, even the naval officers fail to see what more can be achieved from the sea. Most believe your whole enterprise is a forlorn hope and one that can be virtually discounted."

They had reached the viewpoint and sat on the same rocks as before. Ted took a few minutes to look around again before asking, "You said that you'd heard something?"

"Yes, that's right," she confirmed, "but it's probably nothing. Waiting for the boat out to *Queen Elizabeth* this morning, I was talking to a fisherman sitting by the jetty. Too old to go out in the boats anymore, he was left mending nets for the others. His view was that no one knew what those currents do, no matter how long they fish those waters. They'd be going along with their nets down and would sometimes be pulled off in another direction entirely." She shrugged with arms held wide. "But he did tell me of a well-known – but probably apocryphal – anecdote," Andrina was now pointing upwards with her right index finger to make the point. "*Apparently*, the much-loved wife of the Caliph died many years ago and, with great ceremony, he committed her to the sea at the entrance of the Golden Horn of Constantinople. In view of the strong currents running south through the Bosphorus, he expected her to be carried away into the Sea of Marmara and beyond. But then the body was washed up in the same place two days later!" she exclaimed. "It seems to me that you won't know what the currents do until you experience them yourself and, even then, they are likely to change day-to-day, which will be no good for planning," Andrina concluded.

Ted was nodding his head, "You're probably right, Andrina. If the currents are that strong, they will continuously form, shift and destroy sandbanks, changing all the time. Thanks anyway for trying. We'll just have to see how *E15* gets on and what information she brings back."

With a last look around at the view, they made their way down. Tonight's talk was solely about professional matters, with Andrina answering Ted's questions about Turkey and its people, with nothing more said about their former lives.

6

By the time Ted arose the next morning, *E15* was long gone, and an air of expectation filled the support ship. As part of the plan, Brodie had made the short crossing to Tenedos by destroyer to hitch a ride with one of the planes. These were to harass the forts with crude bombs, intended to disrupt their lookout over the Narrows as *E15* passed. Everyone hoped that he would return later with good news.

Ted went aboard *E57* to check on his own submarine to discover that the repair was progressing well and, as he had assessed in Malta, certainly within the capabilities of this specialist team. He was given the good news that they were 'buttoning up' already and, together with replacing the machinery around the site of the repair, expected to be ready for alongside trials by early evening. Ted crossed to *Adamant* to make this positive report to Somerville. He found the commander in the makeshift operations room with the other submarine captains sitting around, kicking their heels and waiting for news.

"Expecting everything to be fine today," he told Somerville, "what I'd like to do is to sail tomorrow and stay out for, say, four days to test the repair, really get to know the area well and to work up the crew. We've really been only in passage routine since leaving Harwich with hardly any decent time dived at all." He added rather mysteriously, "I'd also like to try something slightly different . . . if we could talk over here by the chart table."

Somerville raised his eyebrows and followed Ted as invited.

"I'd like to remain in this area here," Ted explained, pointing out an area on the chart roughly five miles square, centred to seaward of the entrance to the straits. "There should be lots of Allied traffic but I don't want anyone to be told we're there. I want this to be treated in all respects as a war patrol, to bring up the performance of *E57* as quickly as possible. Onboard, we will treat all contacts as hostile and try to remain undetected throughout. *When* we break through into the Marmara," he stated positively, "we'll have no friends there and I consider such preparations essential. You and Brodie will have full details so you can warn those who need to know of our return, just before we do. If we have any serious problems, we'll of course have the daily recognition codes to identify ourselves."

"Ummm . . . an interesting concept." Somerville contorted his mouth as he thought about the proposal. "I can't think of any *obvious* objections, but I'd still want to run it past the Chief of Staff before giving the green light. It's just in case Keyes thinks it might disrupt our other preparations. In the meantime, Mum's the word," he added with a nod and a smile.

At about three o'clock that afternoon, a messenger was sent to find all the E-boat captains. They were required to muster as soon as possible to cross to *Queen Elizabeth* for a briefing. When Ted arrived at the gangway, he found Somerville and the others already aboard the cutter that would carry them. The commander sounded glum. "I don't know what this is all about, but I don't think it's good news."

Brodie was at the top of the HQ ship's gangway to meet them, saluting Somerville and acknowledging the others with a nod and a forced grin, more of a grimace. He led them along one lengthy corridor, then another, until they arrived at a meeting room with an extended table down its middle and chairs along the sides. The Chief of Staff was already seated at the far end and impatiently flapped his hands, inviting them to take their seats as quickly as possible.

"We've had a setback," was Keyes' introduction. "I'll let Brodie describe the situation."

Charles Brodie explained that he had taken off in an aircraft as planned. At the agreed time, he had attempted to drop a bomb on the fort at Kilid Bahr, more as a distraction rather than expecting any significant damage to be inflicted. Because the available planes possessed no proper aiming device, they used an improvised gadget devised by the pilots. It proved hopelessly inaccurate, and any such ploy would be discounted for future operations, as needlessly putting the aircraft and their pilots at unjustified risk. Nonetheless, one of the pilots thought he had spotted a submarine at the north end of the Narrows, near Nagara, allowing the aircraft to return to Tenedos with their task complete.

At this news, the audience smiled and started to shuffle in their seats.

"But," Brodie silenced them in a louder voice, holding his hands out level with his stern face, "as we returned, I could just make out a grey pencil line at right angles to the beach just southwest of Kephez Point. I shouted at the pilot to get as low and as close as he could, despite the fire we were coming under. We cannot be absolutely certain . . . but I am convinced that *E15* is aground and unable to refloat herself."

There was not a sound. Heads were lowered as they could visualise the fire that the submarine would have come under whilst stuck in that position. Furthermore, this was the twin brother of *E15*'s captain delivering such devastating news.

"We'll be taking every action necessary to prevent *E15* falling into enemy hands," Keyes proclaimed matter-of-factly, indicating Brodie to sit. "I might even be calling on one of you to torpedo her if that's the only way. But that's not why I've called you here.

"You'll be aware the prestige of the Navy has been blemished by the calamities we've experienced in this theatre. Soon our beloved *Senior Service* is to be demoted to a transport role, to deliver the army ashore and act as a mere supporting force thereafter. It serves us right. We thought we could just turn up and bombard the Turks into submission, just as Lord Exmouth did in Algiers. But I need not remind you that was *ninety-nine* years ago! No, we shouldn't forget our glorious history, but so too we must not be burdened by it and forget vital lessons from the past. I believe we have some of the brightest and most forward-looking minds across the Navy in this room." He looked at the young faces around the table. "So, we are going to debate and not leave the room until we have decided – one way or the other – if another attempt to transit the Narrows is a practicable proposition." Breaking the tension, he added, "Gentlemen, please relax your jackets and feel free to smoke if you wish. Now, Brodie, you've studied the problem; perhaps you'll start us off."

Brodie pulled out charts and other papers from behind his chair and spread them over the table so everyone could refer to copies. He talked without a break for about thirty minutes, ticking through the comprehensive list he had prepared of aspects of the operation and matters to be addressed. This issue had occupied the minds of everyone present, and a lively discussion ensued, but with little dissent about the real difficulties. However, there were no solutions. Just as Ted and Tucker had concluded, the overall problem always came back to the need for knowledge about the strength of the out-flowing current running against them. *E15*'s fate – and *B11*'s close shave – demonstrated too that they were wrong to dismiss the clearly-evident swirls and eddies. Many reports from patrols conducted within the approaches had recorded profound changes in the salinity in the body of water. This made it exceedingly challenging to remain in trim, with the danger of exposure in sight of the guns. The other great unknown was how the Turks and Germans had reinforced their defences since the torpedoing of *Mesûdiye*. There was talk of nets strung across the Narrows and of shore-based launch tubes to deliver torpedoes, but nothing had been observed yet.

The debate lasted about two hours, throughout which Keyes had said nothing but instead listened intently, making notes. Ted, too, remained silent, simply acknowledging others' points. Guided by his nature and unlike many egos in that room, he never felt it necessary to repeat what others had already said. The chief of staff eventually broke up the discussion, "Gentlemen, that has all been stimulating but we are now beginning to repeat ourselves endlessly. We will take a five-minute break – and I mean just five please – while we each decide individually if we should make another attempt on the Narrows or not."

Whilst some sought out the 'heads', Ted and a few others were happy to escape that smoke-filled room and get some fresh air on the waists of the ship. When they had reconvened, Keyes said he would go clockwise round the table, asking each one for a single-word response: 'Yes', another transit should be attempted; or 'No', there is little chance of success.

Somerville was first: No. Then Brodie: No. So, it went round clockwise to all of these ultra-keen, courageous men who would give their absolute all and risk everything to make it happen, *if* indeed possible. No. No. No. Ted was sitting on the Commodore's right and was preparing to give his answer in agreement with the others when it was his turn. Then a nagging thought occurred to him, something he couldn't quite put his finger on, and he concentrated hard to give it some shape or form, blocking out everything else. Trying to marshal his thoughts, he wasn't even aware that he might be talking out loud, "Loss of trim . . . changes in salinity . . . bodies going the wrong way. Yes, that's it!"

"Crockford . . . Crockford?" Keyes enquired, a distant voice bringing the young officer back to consciousness. "Is that your answer?"

"Yes, Sir. Yes, it can be done! We've assumed all along that the great rivers running into the Black Sea cause the great out-flowing currents that everyone's experienced. That's probably right, so the water should *all* be fresh. So why is it that some boats have experienced large changes in salinity and loss of trim? There must be at least *some* back-flow of salt water from the Mediterranean and, being denser, is likely to be at an unknown depth *under* the fresh-water surface layers. That would explain why *B11* found herself much further into Sari Siglar Bay than she had reckoned when running deep under the minefields. With many rip currents and eddies, there's bound to be a good deal of mixing of the fresh and salt waters, making it nigh on impossible to maintain a steady trim, of which we must be constantly aware. What is more, that counter-current of salt water probably runs all the way back to the Black Sea, or certainly as far as the Bosporus; that's why the Caliph's wife's body was swept back on the beach!"

To smiles all around the table, Keyes interjected, "I was with you until you got to the Caliph's wife; you need to explain that bit!" Ted did so, and, despite its mythical basis, all agreed that it fitted in with the rest of his thesis.

"Does this change your view?" Keyes challenged his audience to a resoundingly positive response. Jumping to his feet, the Chief of Staff affirmed enthusiastically, "Well, it's got to be tried, and you shall do it, Crockford! Now, everybody, the answer is 'Yes', but we're not finished yet. My next question is 'How?'" With their enthusiasm recharged, the assembly eagerly rehearsed their ideas, with Brodie and Ted making copious notes. All was complete after another thirty minutes before Keyes dismissed them.

Somerville managed to catch the Commodore before he escaped and ushered Ted over to him to discuss his other proposal. Ted explained his plans for a 'war patrol' while Keys listened intently. "I like it," he opined. "Yes, you have my permission to proceed on the basis you've outlined." Looking at Somerville, "You are to hold all the necessary details, Commander, and you are to share them with Brodie. I have only one word of warning for you, Crockford. You must be aware that we're concerned about the possibility of German submarines operating in the area. We believe that Smyrna is probably out of operation as a base for them since Admiral Peirse paid that harbour a visit at the beginning of March. Nonetheless, they might have found a safe refuge somewhere else. People are pretty twitched by any prospect of Fritz U-Boats in our area, and you can expect everyone to act first and ask questions afterwards if they get even a sniff of you!"

Chapter 5 – To Add Something New

1

E57 planned to slip from *Adamant* at eight o'clock, immediately after morning colours. Everyone and everything necessary had been checked aboard by seven-thirty. Ted gathered his officers and key ratings around him in the cramped control room and outlined his plan.

"We will slip as usual on main motors and start the generators as soon as we've passed *Queen Elizabeth* and paid our respects. We will dive as soon as we are out of sight of land and any other shipping and then . . . disappear." Turning to Bowers, he continued, "We must first prove the shaft repair and I'll give you as much time as you need, Chief. But, if you can do most or all of your tests on the surface, so much the better." Swivelling around, he addressed them all, pointing to the chart. "We will remain in this area where there will be *a lot* of Allied movements, but our challenge is to remain undetected by *everyone*. Is that clearly understood?" He caught the eye of every one of these pivotal members of his crew, who responded with a nod or an "Aye, Sir."

Then he delivered his bombshell. "We'll be out for four days and back in here just overnight. Then we're going all the way through to the Sea of Marmara!" Although they tried not to show it, he could see the mixed reactions. The young, single men were excited, clearly relishing the chance of glory. But the older ones - particularly those who had tried to fight *E57* through to the Baltic without success - feared the opposition that would be waiting. Even then, they must first overcome the navigational hazards, with the fate of *E15* all too clear in their minds. "*When* we get into the Marmara," the captain continued positively, "everything *will* be hostile, so you can see why we must get this training right."

Ted picked on the newest crew member, who had joined the submarine just before leaving Malta. "Leading Telegraphist Andrews, when we're in the middle of the Narrows, what don't we want the forts to see?"

"The periscope, Sir?" he answered with a shrug, looking around at the others, hoping for a clue.

"Yes, you're partly right," confirmed his commanding officer, "but it's the *feather* of the periscope – that small white wave and wash behind it – that is easiest to spot. We must keep the size of that to a minimum by going as slowly as possible through the water as the periscope breaks the surface. We're not in the North Sea now, with a perpetual chop on the sea's surface. Here, it's likely to be millpond calm. Just think how difficult it would be to see a small tube sticking out of the water in the middle of a lake a quarter of a mile away if it had no feather. So, what we'll do is emulate a woodpecker." Coxswain Prescott caught the eye of the LTO, the torpedo and explosives specialist, and his eyes went to his forehead. These two were used to their captain's regular recourse to nature to explain matters. "The woodpecker doesn't fly level but in a series of shallow swooping dives," Ted demonstrated with his hands. "At the bottom, he flaps, gets up speed and starts to climb. Then he stops flapping halfway up, and is almost stopped when levelling at the top, before picking up speed again as he glides down under gravity and starts again. We'll try to do the same: propel ourselves upwards; stop the motors at, say, thirty feet; let the boat settle at periscope depth at as slow a speed as possible; raise the periscope; before going deep again, all in one continuous action. This technique should give me just enough time to check our position or see what's around whilst minimising the chance of detection. Over the next four days, I want you to practise this *every* time we go to periscope depth until we have all perfected it." The captain checked his watch, "Number One, it's time. Pipe Harbour Stations!"

Ted tested his crew hard over the next two days. As soon as it was dark enough on the first night, he surfaced and ordered the wireless mast to be raised. As agreed before departure, he assured Somerville that the repair had been successful, he was in his designated area, and all was well. Frustratingly, even that short message took two hours to clear and be acknowledged whilst *E57* remained on tenterhooks, scanning the horizon for any intruder. Without need, he broke the overnight charge early, so the battery had to be nursed through the following day. In daylight, he conducted mock attack after mock attack. He chanced his arm to see how close he could get to his unsuspecting quarry and test his people to the limit.

After the initial cobwebs of their performance had been brushed away, everyone started to settle into the routine and, short of firing torpedoes, accepted the reality of this 'war' patrol. On the surface, they felt exposed and vulnerable, ready to react to that second blast on the klaxon. Not the first one, which could have been made by mistake, but on the second blast, the untutored observer would believe that pandemonium had broken out. The officer of the watch would clear the bridge and be almost on the lookout's fingers as he chased him down the conning tower ladder. The engine room staff dashed hither and thither, swinging off handles, shutting some valves and opening others. They were frantic to shut down the diesel engines before they sucked out all the air from the boat as the conning tower's upper hatch clanged shut. All kingston valves on the bottom and vents on the top of the ballast tanks were opened to lose the boat's tiny reserve of buoyancy. The clutches from the diesel engines were disengaged and propulsion was assumed by the electric motors, which began to hum as they drove the boat underwater at speed. Fore and after planesmen spun their large brass wheels to set their controls to the dive position, watching the bubbles in their inclinometers disappear aft as the bow dipped. Off-watch sailors would race to the fore-ends to deliberately trim the submarine down by the nose and expedite the dive. All control room eyes were clamped on the central depth gauge to measure progress. The entire ship's company reacted as one to this simple, unmistakable signal, the *second* blast of the klaxon.

Before daybreak on the third day, Ted closed the Cape Helles fort and made his first foray into the Straits. He wanted to identify for himself where the searchlights were positioned and other distinguishing navigational marks too that he could use to fix his position. *E57* followed the northern, European shore for about seven miles before cutting diagonally towards the southern, Asian coast. Ted used the cliff edge at Kum Kale as a headmark, with the top of the fort above beginning to be lit by the awakening dawn. No ships were in evidence, so midday found him back in his chosen patrol area, seeking out more targets.

The day had gone well as, indeed, had all the training and Ted believed that *E57* was back on song. With one full day and a night left, there was enough time yet to iron out one or two remaining creases in their performance, so he determined to go easier on his crew overnight. The captain decided the battery would receive a full charge whilst cooking a hot meal, which he'd allow his people to enjoy without interruption. Ted didn't want them to be totally exhausted before the enormous challenges yet to come. He waited until the charge was complete before diving the submarine and bottoming her on a sandbank he'd identified on the northwest edge of the allocated area. With just one of the crew standing watch, the majority could get four or so hours of sleep before surfacing again and completing a top-up charge before daybreak.

Events proceeded to plan, and, just after five o'clock in the morning, *E57* was on the surface with the diesel generators pounding away. Ted was on the bridge and made a final careful look around the whole horizon with his binoculars, took one last deep breath and made to go down the ladder. "You have the ship, Navigator."

"Aye, aye, Sir. I have the ship," came Buckle's reply.

Ted relaxed into his chair with the cup of tea he had summoned; as always, his thoughts returned to his next patrol. As a diversion, he picked up a novel he had found in *Adamant*'s library and flicked through it while he finished his hot drink.

"PRESS THE KLAXON TWICE!"

The shout from the bridge brought Ted immediately back to his senses. The helmsman did as ordered, and the chain of automatic actions cranked into motion. But their captain could see that everyone was reacting that second or two slower, like him still slightly befuddled by sleep. Nonetheless, his years of experience allowed him to scan around automatically, without thinking, and tick off in his mind that list of critical actions that he had experienced so many times before: Kingstons; main vents; diesel engines; clutches; motors; afterplanes;

foreplanes; sailors running; depth gauge; lookout through the hatch. He stopped. Where was the officer of the watch?

The submarine answered her crew's bidding and took on a distinct bow-down angle. The bubble in the inclinometer was moving aft: two degrees, three, four, and picking up speed as the depth gauge needle started its relentless clockwise travel. In very few seconds, the surface would be level with the top of the conning tower, and water would cascade into the submarine.

"Report the upper hatch!" the captain roared. In the absence of any immediate response, he commanded, "Shut main vents! Standby the blows!"

"Shut main vents; main vents are shut, Sir! Standing by to blow," reported the diving panel operator.

A muffled shout came down from the conning tower, "Upper hatch is shut . . . upper hatch is shut and clipped!" But this was followed by a cry as Buckle fell down the ladder, catching himself on the many protuberances on either side. He landed awkwardly on the control room deck with a groan and lay prostrate.

"Open main vents. Keep forty feet. Stand down the blows."

"Open main vents; main vents are open, Sir. Stand down the blows." His orders were again echoed from the panel.

"Keep forty feet. Aye, aye, Sir," repeated the first lieutenant.

Paying no attention whatever to his subordinate's distressed condition, the captain ordered, "Navigator report."

Grimacing through the pain, Buckle answered. "There was a destroyer at green eight-zero, Captain, no more than a thousand yards away. I think he was coming towards us at speed; he might have seen us."

"Very good. Speed for trimming, Number One. Conduct full post-diving checks throughout the boat. Cox'n, get yourself relieved from the afterplanes and attend the navigator." Ted's orders were repeated to his back as he went over to the chart table. He wanted to hide the annoyance with himself for letting down his guard, with others seeming to follow his lead.

With several shouts of pain, the navigator was manhandled out of the control room and forward to the crew's sleeping area. There he was subjected to the tender mercies of Coxswain Prescott, who, besides all his other duties as the senior rating aboard, also acted as the medical orderly. After a ten-minute inspection, the coxswain returned and reported to the first lieutenant. Together, they went to brief the captain.

"Captain, Sir, I'm afraid Lieutenant Buckle is in a pretty bad way," the coxswain was the first to speak. "He's got a couple of deep gashes down the side of his face that require stitches, he's twisted his right arm and wrist, and I think his left ankle is broken. The way he fell, he might even have some internal injuries; he's in considerable pain and I've already administered some morphine."

"Post-diving checks are complete and correct, Sir," joined in the first lieutenant. "But the Aldis signalling lamp became tangled on the bridge and Buckle was unable to free it. That's what slowed him down and I think he panicked a bit. Even if it's still up there, the Aldis will be flooded and useless."

"Umm . . . very well. I have no choice really," Ted surmised after only a few seconds' thought. "We must return directly to Mudros to obtain medical attention for Lieutenant Buckle. The loss of the Aldis is a real tragedy because we won't be able to respond to signal challenges from anyone. We'd better make best speed over there –

but remain dived – so that we can arrive in daylight and be recognised – hopefully – as a *British* submarine!"

2

It did not loiter in the area, so there was no indication that the destroyer had, in fact, detected them. To be safe, however, Ted waited until they had cleared the datum by about five miles before returning to periscope depth. First, he conducted a prolonged search of the horizon before taking three bearings for a navigational fix. Satisfied with *E57*'s position and with no vessels about, Ted ordered the submarine deep. He set course for a position three miles off the outermost navigation mark off Mudros harbour, with revolutions set for five knots. The medical emergency took priority over any exercise requirement to conserve the battery.

When dead reckoning showed that they were thirty minutes from their destination, Ted called together his team. "Our arrival is a day earlier than planned and no one will be expecting us. A submarine popping up in full view just off the harbour is bound to set a few hearts fluttering, so we'd better allay their fears as soon as possible!" He tried to sound light-hearted but understood the perilous situation they were in. If *E57* was attacked, his would not be the first British submarine to be fired on or rammed by friendly forces; far from it! "Look out every white ensign and jack we have, and I want every one of them to be taken up to the bridge as soon as we surface and hoisted where they can best be seen. As soon as that job has been done, I want all hands back down below; only I will stay on the bridge. We will not start the generators and the boat must be ready in every respect to dive again should we face a hostile reception. If that happens, we'll open out again, wait until nightfall and rig the WT mast. But the navigator is quite poorly and I want to avoid that delay if possible."

The preparations were made as ordered and, when in position, the captain ordered the boat to periscope depth. This time he swung around the full three hundred and sixty degrees very quickly to ensure they had not come up close to any other vessel before lowering the periscope. Having assured himself thus, he waited a full minute before ordering the periscope up again to take bearings for a fix to clarify their position; once done, down it went again. Another full minute passed before a hand signal from the captain silently ordered the periscope to rise again for Ted to make a careful scan across the entrance to the harbour. "That bearing!" he shouted. "Green seven-zero!" He snapped up the training handles of the periscope, and it disappeared down into its well.

"That's the guardship," he explained to no one in particular, "at a range of about eight thousand yards, which should be outside the accurate range of her pop-gun, giving us time to rig our flags. Cox'n, come to port by twenty degrees. That will put him directly on our beam to aid his recognition, whilst not causing us to close the range, keeping him at arm's distance. Now, is everybody ready?" He acknowledged the nods all around and climbed up into the confines of the conning tower.

"SURFACE!" came his echoing shout from above.

In that claustrophobic space, Ted heard the blast of the main ballast tank blows. He counted silently to himself whilst immediately removing one securing clip from the hatch. At the count of 'five', he released the second clip and could already hear the burbling water clearing from the top of the conning tower. At 'ten', he swung the hatch open and, ignoring the spray and drips from inside the structure, made his way immediately to the bridge. Already he was aware of others hot on his heels. Once on the platform, he glanced around again to confirm there were no other contacts before bringing his binoculars up on his starboard beam.

There was the guardship, and she was certainly alert! It had been – what? – only twenty seconds since *E57* had surfaced, but a puff of smoke from her funnel indicated she was on her way. A deadly white smile started to form at the base of her bow as she picked up speed, heading directly towards them. His crew had reacted well too. An ensign and a union jack had already been secured to the jumping wires both fore and aft, and another ensign was flying from the bridge. However, these were all of the small variety – the only ones carried in boats. Then Ted saw the spit of flame from the twelve-pounder gun: perhaps this morning's destroyer had in fact detected them and reported their presence. Otherwise, how could they have reacted so fast? He looked again at the flags. To his horror, Ted realised that the fresh north-easterly wind was causing them to fly almost horizontally, away from, and therefore presumably unseen by, the guardship. He managed to order down the voice tube, "Set revolutions for ten knots," just before the first shell landed in the water less than one hundred yards short!

The spray from the first shot would mask *E57* for a little while, but so too would it cover the flags they *wanted* to be seen; his increase in speed was intended to help them fly more fore-and-aft. He had to think quickly. "Starboard twenty-five," he shouted down, to bring the submarine in a retiring turn to port, away from the guardship, thus confounding his fire-control problem and open range ever so slightly, whilst all the while hoping that the fluttering flags might yet be identified. The succeeding shell landed fifty yards on his starboard quarter as he turned. He steadied his course with the guardship now on his port beam, and he could see that she was closing relentlessly. He must be in range now!

"Standby to dive!" he roared as a third shot landed close off the starboard bow, drenching *E57*'s bridge, including the ensign that had been strung up. Straddled by exploding shells, the submarine was now in a most precarious situation: the guardship had found its range, and the next round could prove fatal. As a last-ditch action, Ted unshackled the soaked white ensign and flopped it down to lie flat against the port side of the fin.

Ted shut the voicepipe cock and took a final look around before intending to leap down the conning tower. At the last instant, just before he started his descent, he heard the guardship repeatedly sounding its horn, attracting his attention. Ted saw her coming sharply round to port to parallel *E57*'s track, with her gun training away to point forward. At last, they realised she was friendly, and the guardship indicated the submarine to follow her into the harbour!

Safely alongside *Adamant* late afternoon, *E57* was met by Somerville and Brodie, who were eager to discover the state of the submarine and whether the crew was ready to undertake the transit of the straits as planned. Ted assured them that they were prepared in all respects, stand fast the need of a replacement navigator. Brodie brought word from Keyes that he wanted the operation to get underway as soon as possible. Still, the three submarine officers agreed that the next day should be used to rest, store and make final preparations before sailing in the early hours of the following day. That would also give Somerville time to think about which navigator from one of the other submarines would be best to join *E57* for this momentous voyage. However, he forewarned that none of the other captains would be at all happy to lose one of their own officers.

Ted excused himself and went back aboard *E57*. He had thought of one or two last-minute refinements to his preparations and wanted to speak to his senior engineer and the first lieutenant.

AE3 had arrived at Mudros on 21st April and moored with the other E-boats alongside *Adamant*. Tucker had waited out of sight until *E57*'s arrival formalities were over before asking to see Somerville and Brodie in the chart house. "I don't wish to sound petulant, but how can it be justified for Crockford to make the first attempt through the straits? *AE3* has been on station here the longest and I was the first ever to advocate such an operation. *You* know that, Charles," Tucker turned to accuse the staff officer.

"Yes, I am aware of that," Brodie replied, "but you weren't here for the conference that Keyes chaired – that was just bad luck – and the chief of staff has made his decision."

"Bad luck . . . *my* bad luck! If we're talking about luck, what about Crockford's *bad luck*," Tucker sneered, "when *he* failed to break into the Baltic, whereas *E1* and *E9* got through without difficulty? What about *his* bad luck when his torpedoes passed under a battlecruiser – as *he* claims – at point-blank range? Despite his wonderful reputation, what has he actually contributed to this war so far? I've taken *AE3* across the world and back, as well as been engaged in the battle for German New Guinea. I want to see the chief of staff myself and put this right!"

Somerville had had enough but kept his composure. "I would not deny your right as a commanding officer to call on Commodore Keyes and of course I salute your wish for action." The commander moved closer to the aggrieved officer. "I would, however, point out that currently you are under *my* command, Lieutenant Commander Tucker, and *I* don't support any change in the plan. *E57* is ready to go in the next thirty-six hours and that is how it is going to be. I appreciate your disappointment, but these matters are of strategic importance and I'm sorry to say that your grievances smack of personal jealousies that have no place in this enterprise. I would hope that *every* boat in my flotilla can work for the greater good, each submarine supporting the others, and that is what I expect from you and *AE3*. Is that understood?"

3

Having retired early after his non-stop exertions during the three days of the training patrol, Ted was up with the lark the next morning and down his submarine in time to witness morning 'Colours', formally raising the Jack and Ensign to wish His Majesty, "Good Morning!". With Buckle out of action, he was keen to familiarise himself with all the charts and sailing directions for the area. In addition, he wanted again to run through the notes he had made from the meeting with Keyes and all the other submarine captains so that his own preparations were complete. An hour later, a call came down from the casing that an officer had arrived to see him. Squaring off his books on the chart table, he ascended the main access ladder.

Arriving at the gangway, he squinted up, and an immaculately turned-out officer stood on *Adamant's* deck above him.

"Hardacre?" Ted enquired disbelievingly.

"Yes; I've come to apologise."

"What on earth for?"

"I was the guard officer yesterday who fired on you."

"But you were only doing your job and that was some damned fine shooting! No one was hurt, so there's really no need . . ."

"I should have identified you properly as a British submarine," Hardacre interrupted, "and I felt it was only right to make my apologies in person. But couldn't we have this discussion in your cabin?"

"Well, of course; forgive my manners. Please come aboard." Ted and his quartermaster exchanged grins as the visitor crossed the gangway. "I'll lead the way."

When below, Ted showed his guest the solitary chair opposite the chart table and invited him to sit. "You see, there is my bunk behind you and this is my 'cabin'. The first lieutenant sleeps in the bunk there behind me and the navigator in the bottom chart drawer; so, this is the wardroom too! I'm really lucky to have one of the more modern boats with all this space and creature comforts," the submarine captain added with a wide smile.

"Oh, I see," was the reply as Hardacre wiped the seat of the chair with a white handkerchief before sitting down and looking around disbelievingly. "I really had *no* idea; I'm sorry." He settled himself and, taking a breath, he continued, "When I discovered that you were the commanding officer of *E57*, I thought it was a good opportunity to remake our acquaintance and perhaps apologise for my past conduct when . . . "

"No, no, that really was a long time ago and we were both young lads then," Ted cut him off short. "By the look of us, I think we have both done a lot of growing up since then, Rupert!" This was not the Hardacre that he remembered, and Ted appreciated the courage he was showing by acknowledging his past behaviour.

"That's very generous of you," the visitor responded, seeming to relax slightly. Still looking around, he asked. "Would you permit me to have a quick look around – only if it's no trouble of course."

With that awkward introduction over, Hardacre had inadvertently stumbled on the best way to get on the good side of *any* submariner: just ask him to look around his boat! Ted proudly led the tour of *E57*, pointing out equipment and machinery to the right and left, up and down. He noted that his guest was genuinely interested in all he was shown and – given their personal history – remarkably deferential. Hard to imagine after their experiences in *Britannia*, their conversation was easy and unforced. Still, perhaps this was *because* they had been through the same training together.

They returned to the chart table, and Ted ordered them both a cup of tea which, of course, arrived in a mug without a saucer. Hardacre asked Ted what he had been up to since training and was held enthralled as the latter reeled off the extensive list of his responsible appointments and commands. "I've fired one hundred and four practice torpedoes and quite a few live ones too since the war broke out but have yet to sink *anything*. But you've told me nothing about *your* career?"

Hardacre explained that he had always served in large ships, with nothing smaller than a light cruiser, other than for short interludes. He was a navigation specialist and was currently the 'N2' in the flagship, *Queen Elizabeth*. "N2 is the second navigator," he clarified. "The first navigator is a Commander. It was just my turn to be the guard officer last night," he concluded.

"*Queen Elizabeth* is a magnificent ship!" Ted enthused out of politeness. "I suppose you were involved in the attack on the forts; that must have been some day!"

"It was the scene we had all imagined a naval battle would be when we joined up, with ships lined up and giving their all. My ears are still ringing with the sounds and memory of it! So magnificent, so stirring, with such bravery on display . . . yet, ultimately, proving to be so pointless, with such unnecessary loss of life. In a battleship everything is so formal, so impersonal, with the enemy unseen; it's difficult to feel any *reality* to what's going on."

"There's plenty of reality here, let me tell you!" With that, an absurd thought crossed Ted's mind. He was quiet for a second or two before leaning forward and, very unlike him, looking at Hardacre square in the eyes. "Look, you're a navigation specialist and I need a navigator; why not join *E57*? I'll be shot if you tell anyone else, but we sail in the small hours tomorrow morning for a patrol inside the Sea of Marmara. Are you up for it; to go to sea under my command – for the greatest challenge of your life?"

4

Hardacre was keen for the adventure but, thrown into this alien world, he had severe misgivings about being aboard this most technical of vessels whilst knowing nothing of its workings. He was assured that Buckle, from a merchant navy background, was borne for navigation duties only but had picked things up quickly enough. The captain opined it should be easier for a full-time RN officer. Furthermore, Ted assured him that *E57*'s crew knew how to operate the submarine. At least initially, all he required of his potential recruit would be his constant presence at the chart table, guiding the boat through the Straits. Nothing else.

When approached, Commander Somerville had reservations too, his principal concern being the loss of a submarine-experienced officer to support the watchbill when on station and unsupported for a protracted period. Nevertheless, he could perceive distinct advantages as well with this solution. Firstly, he wouldn't have to disrupt other crews to fill *E57*'s gap. More importantly, the presence of a senior navigational expert could only enhance the submarine's chances of success in fighting through the Narrows which, after all, was the principal challenge. As the flotilla commander, he decided that he could sanction the proposal himself: crewing the submarines ready for patrol was *his* responsibility. Nonetheless, he saw the benefit in seeking Keyes' endorsement. The chief of staff could bear down on *Queen Elizabeth's* executive officer about the importance of the mission and the need to release Hardacre. Somerville instructed the two lieutenants in front of him to assume that permission would be forthcoming and to make the necessary preparations. The commander next called for the cutter to be made ready to take him over to the HQ ship.

Utilising Adamant's more spacious chart house, *E57*'s captain and new navigator spread out the charts, and Ted walked through the plan. Hardacre had already studied the outer approaches to the Narrows *ad nauseam* in preparation for the attack on the forts. He already appreciated that, beyond Kephez Point, few deviations were possible from a track right up the middle of the tight channel. Ted encouraged his protégé, "I believe this will work out very well indeed. I will be right beside you most of the time and we'll battle this through together. Having someone of your experience, beavering away constantly at the navigation, will help me enormously." After a pause, he added, "I'll take you back down the boat now, to familiarise you with the layout of the chart table and associated equipment. None of it will be entirely new to you; it's just so you can arrange everything to *your* satisfaction. Before that, I suggest we get one of *Adamant's* stewards to go and collect your kit, ready for the off. He'll also need to find you a berth here for the night."

It was already early afternoon and, returning to the submarine, they found *E57* looking vastly different, with a not-so-pleased first lieutenant on the casing to greet them.

"I hope this meets your requirements, Sir?" enquired Hackett-Jones, rather flatly.

Rather than the uniformly grey-painted submarine, with natty blacks and reds picking out details on the casing, with polished brasses and tiddly ropework, *E57* had been transformed. The submarine was now camouflaged with random areas of black, greens, blues and greys of different hues, covering *everything* above the waterline.

"That will do very nicely; thank you, Number One. Now, meet our new navigator," Ted introduced Rupert Hardacre. "You'll need to settle him in and show him where to stow his kit when it arrives."

"Of course, Sir. All the stores are secured aboard and we're ready for the off. With your permission, I'd now like to pipe 'Secure'. All the hands will be required back aboard by midnight."

"Well done! Yes, please; make it so."

After another half-hour, Ted left Hardacre to arrange the chart table as he wanted and made his way back to his cabin in the support ship. He lay down on his bed and tried to close his eyes for a nap, but his mind was buzzing. Sleep would not come. Accepting the inevitable, he swung his legs off the bunk and dressed in his walking clothes.

He trudged up the road, through the village and onto the viewpoint, eyes on the path ahead, seeing nothing and lost in his thoughts. He sat at the summit, closed his eyes, took a deep breath and let it out slowly, letting his shoulders relax. After sitting there for about ten minutes, he recognised Andrina coming up the way towards him.

"Hello, Ted," she welcomed him, her cheeks red from the exertion of her climb. "I haven't seen you here for a few days."

He described all that had happened in the intervening period, adding, "You know what you told me about the Caliph's wife? That was the key to solving the problem – or at least we *hope* it will be!" He explained his theory about the existence of a lower salt-water counter-current.

"Well, far be it from me to comment – I'm certainly no maritime expert! – but your supposition all seems quite logical." Andrina was nodding her head. "I just hope my story hasn't misled you at all. Surely, it's all academic now? After what happened to *E15*, I don't suppose another submarine will try again."

"No, it's important that we get through. I'm sailing tomorrow morning for the next attempt."

"Oh!" is all she said, looking down at her feet. That day, the Constantinople newspapers had reported that *E15*'s captain had been killed by the first shell that hit the submarine. Most of his crew had been taken off safely and made prisoners of war. Many attempts had been made to destroy the boat and stop it from falling into Turkish hands. Long-range gunfire from battleships had failed, and a foray by *B6* almost stranded a second submarine in precisely the same position. *E15* had ultimately been destroyed by torpedoes during a daring attack by the picket boats from *Triumph* and *Majestic*. Andrina couldn't be sure that Ted knew any of this, so she kept her own counsel.

"I must try to get an early night," he stated, getting up. "You've just arrived, so I suppose you'll be staying here a while longer?"

"No, I'd like to accompany you down the hill. If you don't mind, I'm eager to hear more of your adventures in the wilds of Exmoor!"

They chatted freely as they strolled back to the village, not at the fast pace as before but taking their time. Both at their ease, they laughed at each other's stories. Arriving at Andrina's gate, he shook her hand with awkward formality and thanked her for her company. But they continued to stand there in silence, not quite facing one another, with arms limply by their sides. Neither seemed willing to turn away for possibly their final parting. He couldn't say what possessed him, but Ted stepped forward and went to kiss her. Their lips met for a microsecond – if at all – before she pulled her head sharply down and away from him.

"Wha . . . what ?" she exclaimed querulously. "No . . . *No!*" She was becoming angry now, and her eyes burned into him. "What do you think you are doing? Is this part of a bet? Yes, do you think I'm unaware of those schoolboy sniggerings behind my back in the wardroom? I thought you were different from the rest of them, but obviously I was wrong!"

She spun away from him and went directly into the house, leaving him to mutter a confused, "I'm sorry . . . !" to her disappearing back.

Back in his cabin in the support ship, Ted had two tasks to perform before turning in. Before a war patrol, every crew member was required to prepare a will. After little thought, that chore was efficiently completed, also including a farewell note to accompany it. Now the more arduous duty. He took out his notepad again to write.

HMS Adamant
24th April 1915

Dear Mrs. Kapadoukas,

I write to apologise unreservedly for my indefensible behaviour this evening. My attentions were clearly not welcome, and it is my most earnest wish that my clumsy approach causes you no lasting harm. Wedded to my profession for many years, I have no experience at all in matters of the heart. But already, this is beginning to sound like an excuse and I must offer none.

My mind, however, is in considerable turmoil as I write. An apology is in order if any action is dishonourable or deceitful – on which grounds you accused me – and I wish only to assure you that this is not the case. So why, I ask myself, should I say sorry for a sentiment well-meant, no matter how poorly expressed? I genuinely enjoyed our conversations and have felt closer to you than anyone in the world since leaving my rural refuge. Indeed, I have never divulged so much about my life and lowly beginnings to anyone else. You were brave enough to relate your recent tragedies, which only strengthened our rapport. I might have been wholly deluded but believed that a friendship was blossoming. It pains me so much that my unpremeditated and thoughtless actions have probably damaged irreversibly what might have been. My own feelings are nevertheless unimportant here.

To Add Something New

I expect you to consign this note immediately to the waste bin, as you are right to do. My sole wish is to make a full apology, with the assurance that my contrition is total.

Yours sincerely,
Edward Crockford

Putting down his pen, he sat back in his chair and involuntarily let out a huge sigh. He looked at the letter and wanted to write more. But what was the point? A sadness enveloped him, one that was so deep and unlike anything he had felt since seeing his mother being driven away to hospital that day. As he thought about his situation, Ted realised he didn't really have any close friends with whom he could confide on whatever subject it was that troubled him. In fact, he had no one in the world. He had ignored learning any social skills – he'd certainly had plenty of opportunities – always believing that his Service career would be enough to sustain him. But his friendship with Andrina had developed so quickly without him appreciating the depth of it. Now – too late – he realised it could have been so much more . . . perhaps something for which he'd unknowingly been searching. His stupid, unthinking behaviour had destroyed that possibility for ever, leaving him – once again – all alone. At war or not, he steered his boat towards danger on every occasion they left port. If the worst were to happen, who would mourn his passing? Who would grieve for him?

Naturally optimistic, he had never paid any heed to the hazards when he set off on war patrol. His current gloominess had changed his perspective this time. He'd faced countless challenges before, but this undertaking was of a totally different order; was this whole enterprise no more than a 'forlorn hope' as many people thought?

He would be taking *his* submarine and *his* people into extreme danger, the like of which was nothing they had faced thus far. Could he be risking the sacrifice of his courageous crew on the altar of his arrogance or the Navy's reputation?

It wasn't in his character to feel self-pity or to become maudlin, and he shook his head to clear his brain. He folded the letter into an envelope, addressed it and put it to one side for his steward to despatch after he had departed. He needed to be at the top of his game for this next adventure. He shifted his thoughts toward preparations for tomorrow.

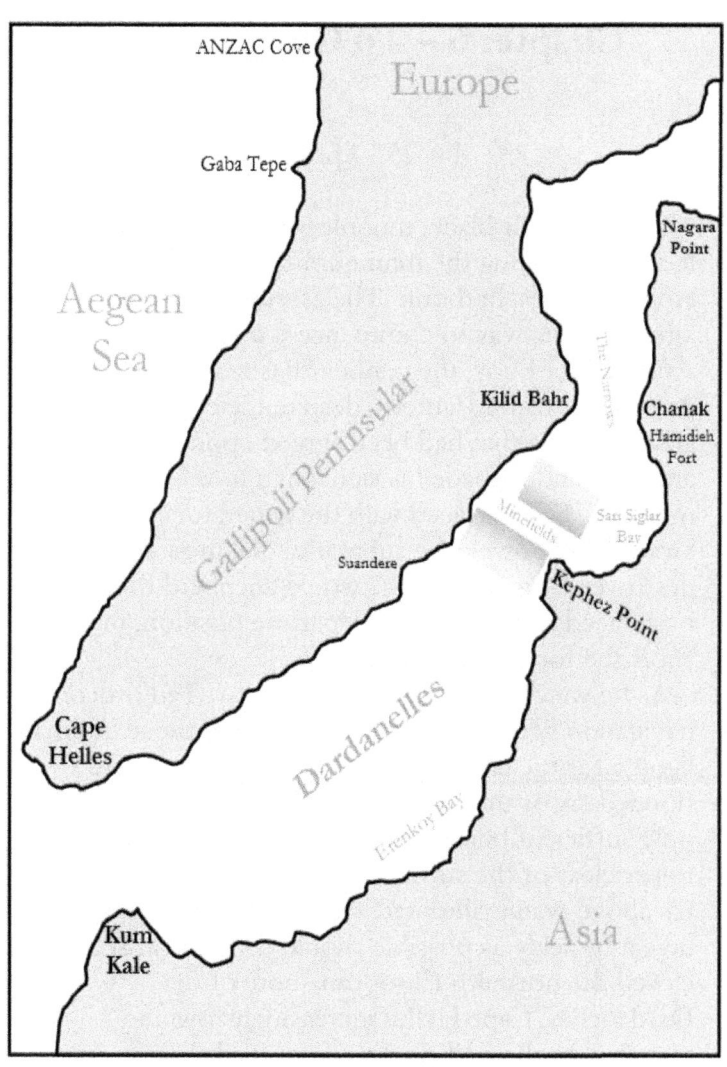

The Dardanelles and the Narrows

Chapter 6 – To Glory We Steer

1 – 25th April 1915

It was a pitch-black, moonless night as the guardship led *E57*, showing the minimum lighting, out of a near-empty Mudros harbour. The assembled armada was already on its way to commence the sea-borne attack. At the outer buoy, the gunboat flashed "good luck" on its Aldis signalling lantern, despite the covert arrangements that had been agreed upon. Ted was annoyed and forbade his signalman to acknowledge the message. Still surfaced with the generators throbbing away at full power, the submarine fell in astern of the destroyer *Grasshopper*. She would shepherd them at the best speed to the planned departure position, making short the forty-mile transit.

As he watched his escort wheel away, Ted ordered all navigation lights to be extinguished and those internal lights near the conning tower to be dimmed. He flooded six of the eight main ballast tanks, maintaining only sufficient buoyancy to keep the top of the conning tower clear of the surface. The captain thus minimised his above-water silhouette whilst also being ready to dive as quickly as possible should the need arise. As he closed the northern European shore of the Dardanelles, Cape Helles increasingly towered menacingly above the submarine. Ted shut down the port diesel to diminish the noise on that side closest to possible lookouts. As if on cue to help this objective, a cacophony of warships' heavy guns rent the peaceful night, and bright flashes floodlight the northern horizon. Ted looked at his watch: it was five-fifteen exactly, and the eastern horizon already hinted at the coming dawn. With seven or eight miles yet to cover before diving just short of the minefields at Suandere, Ted couldn't dispense with his generators if *E57* was to dive with a full battery. Ahead, he could see searchlights from both sides – five on the northern shore and three to the south. They swept up and down the channel, principally on the lookout for the fishing vessels being used as minesweepers. Still, they could not be discounted: *B11* and *E15* had provided graphic warnings of the submarine threat. Then, as had been observed previously, all the searchlights were extinguished simultaneously. It was six o'clock on the dot. Ted smiled. "Thank goodness for good German efficiency – timed to the second!" he muttered to himself.

Down below in the control room, Hackett-Jones had been taking occasional bearings through the periscope enabling Hardacre to continually update their position. The latter was still coming to terms with the cramped conditions under which he was expected to perform, together with the minimum available lighting by which to read the chart. The positions of the searchlights had been located accurately over many months of Allied effort and, like lighthouses, provided good navigational marks. Now they were switched off, the first lieutenant strained to make out the blurred edges of land in the semi-darkness, exacerbated by the light loss through the periscope.

"Captain, Sir – Navigator," Hardacre called up in hushed tones. "The submarine is five cables from the diving position marked on the chart."

"Very good. Shut down and secure the starboard diesel. Standby to dive." Ted had a few more minutes to study the scene through his binoculars, repeatedly scanning for any hostile contacts far ahead in the channel. He heard the diesel cut out and wheeze to a standstill before climbing down and shutting the upper hatch, then making his way directly to the chart table. Happy with their position, he took a last all-round look on the periscope before snapping the handles up.

"First Lieutenant . . . dive the submarine!" the captain commanded.

"Dive the submarine. Aye, aye, Sir," came the response, with the order invariably repeated in standard submarine practice to ensure the correct actions. "Open Number Three and Number Four Main Vents!"

Rather than the pell-mell race to complete all necessary actions when the klaxon sounded, this procedure was controlled step-by-step from the control room. It avoided the straining of equipment or the risk of damage to machinery or people. With the experienced coxswain on the afterplanes controlling the angle and the second coxswain on the foreplanes watching the depth, *E57* glided on a steady path down to sixty feet and back up to forty feet. 'Running the bubble' in this way, first aft and then forward, ensured all air had been expelled from the ballast tanks and from under the casing. Having shut the main vents and observed no untoward behaviour of the boat, "Group down. Speed for trimming" was ordered. This was the first lieutenant's cue to progressively slow the submarine whilst adjusting the bodily weight of the boat by pumping out or flooding in, and moving water fore or aft to attain a level keel.

"Less than one knot, Sir. Happy with the trim," Hackett-Jones reported after a further five minutes.

"Very good. Half ahead together. Six up. Keep twenty feet." Watching the bubble run forward to the six-degree mark, the captain wanted one final check at periscope depth – or 'PD' as they abbreviated it – before committing the submarine to the minefields. Although the sun had yet to appear over the horizon, dawn had nearly arrived, and Ted could discern slightly more detail on the northern shoreline. "That bearing," he called before the periscope hissed down to the boat's keel. "Six down. Keep eighty feet. Revolutions for five knots."

The captain then went over to confer again with his navigator. He pointed out his latest fixing point by Kephez so that it could be drawn on the chart, trying to assess the strength of the current they had experienced so far.

"It's been only one-and-a-half knots against us so far, Captain, but of course will increase as we get closer to Chanak," Hardacre ventured.

"Yes," Ted agreed, "but we hope a counter-current might help us on our way while we're deep." He was leaning on the chart table and trying to remember everything suggested by the other captains at the meeting with Keyes. "Keep estimating our actual position using that strength of current we've experienced, but also calculate for a stronger stream of, say, two knots against us. That should be our slowest speed which we can use to check we're through the minefields." The captain was nodding as he remembered what he must do. "Having done that, work it out all over again, but this time with two knots' current behind us. That should conceivably be the fastest speed across the ground, to ensure we don't progress too far and run aground on Chanak beach." As an after-thought, he added, "Although we're as near as we dare go to the north side of the channel, I'm still concerned about the cross-current that carried both

B11 and *E15* towards the southern shore. I will adjust ship's head ten degrees to port to counteract that."

The submarine had hardly settled at eighty feet before a thump at the bow, followed by a screeching sound, caused everyone to stop what they were doing and listen. A cable securing a buoyant mine was scraping down the side of the boat. Heads twitched from side to side, trying to guess exactly where the sound was coming from: it was as if they might neutralise it if they could just see where it was. Speed was immediately reduced to three knots to give this blind visitor time to tap its way past the submarine without becoming caught up on anything and bringing the mine down towards them. Sensibly, whilst they could still hear the high-pitched squeal, the cable must be continuing its journey safely aft. In these situations, logic plays no part, and this devil's own tune gnawed at the crew's anxieties, with them wishing it were gone. Past the first one, the sailors relaxed and, in typical style, laughed it off with a quiet joke until, four minutes later, there was another. Rappings and scrapings of a different note and throbbing of a mismatched rhythm immediately brought back all their fears and silenced their banter. Their captain stopped the shaft on the side of each mine so the mooring wire would not become entangled with the propellor.

Over the next forty minutes, they encountered the cables of five mines before all became quiet. No one could tell if they were through the minefields or just on a lucky course that was missing all the obstructions, with still more deadly 'eggs' ahead. Ted went over to the chart table to review their progress.

"I've worked out those two situations you wanted, Captain," Hardacre reported. "It is assumed that the minefields extend about one-and-a-half miles, which, at three knots and with a two-knot current *against*, would take us ninety minutes to transit. On the other hand, it is only three-and-a-half miles from where we went deep to the shoal waters right ahead of us south of Chanak. With a two-knot current *behind us*, that'd take only forty-two minutes – which has just about passed. We need a fix, Sir! Otherwise, I have no other information by which to advise you."

"I understand," confirmed the captain. "First, we'll come to a course of – what's that heading . . . " he manoeuvred the parallel ruler on the chart, ". . . north – to parallel the shore ahead and then come to PD for a fix."

On the order, the helmsman put the helm over to starboard, and the gyro clicked around the forty degrees until they were steady on the new course. "Now's the time to show me your perfect 'woodpecker' drill," Ted smiled at this ship control team. "Six up – keep twenty feet!"

The coxswain called out the submarine's depth, "fifty feet . . . forty feet . . . thirty feet . . . twenty-five feet . ." The periscope whooshed up as the captain ordered. The training handles were clicked down into position. ". . . twenty-four . . twenty-three . . twenty-two . . . twenty feet, Sir!"

Ted was scanning the periscope across the bow and waiting for the top lens to clear of water before rapidly conducting an all-round look. "No contacts in sight," he reported before steadying the periscope. "That bearing – right-hand edge Kilid Bahr . . . and . . . that – right-hand edge Kephez Point. Down periscope. Keep thirty feet."

Ted hurried to the chart table to find his navigator plotting the second bearing. "Not a very good fix, I'm afraid." Hardacre showed his captain the result. "The bearings were nearly parallel without any crossover, but we seem to be in clear water off Sari Siglar Bay."

"That last bearing on Kephez Point is the more accurate; I'm guessing it's only about half-a-mile away," the captain explained. "But that does seem to put us past the minefields." Ted was annoyed with himself, "When we slowed down for the mines, I should have steered even more to port to counter the cross current. Never mind, we're safe here, on a good course and I can make out the Narrows ahead." Then a thought occurred to him, "What current did we experience at eighty feet?"

Hardacre measured the distance they had travelled and noted the time taken. "I cannot be accurate, but it seems like nothing at all. We've made good about three knots as set. The strength of the stream does seem to be reduced by going deep."

"Right, we'll get another fix and then head straight for the Narrows. Three up! Keep twenty feet!"

The second fix was no more conclusive but, at least, was consistent with the first. More worryingly, Ted could tell the submarine was hardly holding its own, fighting against a much stronger current. They were being washed down into the bay and towards Kephez Point. The captain decided to go deep again at seven knots and run for fifteen minutes. This should bring them to a position just short of the entrance to the Narrows, where they'd likely achieve a more accurate fix.

Not ten minutes later, the bow started to come up rapidly, accompanied by a loud "sssssssshhh . . ." They were running aground at speed. "fifty feet . . forty feet . . thirty feet, Captain!" the coxswain announced in strident tones.

"Stop together! Full astern together!" Ted shouted above the noise coming from outside.

". . twenty feet . . fifteen feet . . . steady at eleven feet, Sir."

Never mind being careful not to expose the periscope, all the crew knew that now most of the bridge structure and conning tower was above water. Indeed, the tops of the periscope pedestals, being the highest objects, must be about ten feet clear of the surface. The submarine was exposed and stationary, right under the noses of the protecting gun towers, presenting an easy target. The priority was to get *E57* afloat again. As the motors thrummed away at full power with little effect thus far, everyone looked for clues of any movement. In a drill they had practised often, the first lieutenant blew the forward ballast tank and trimmed water from forward to aft to lighten the bow and give the propellers more purchase.

"Standby bearings for a fix on either side of the Narrows," the captain warned his team. "Up periscope! That bearing and . . . that!" Involuntarily, Ted winced and jerked his head back away from the rubber eyepiece. Regaining his composure, he indicated for the periscope to be lowered. On taking the second bearing, Ted had been looking directly at Hamidieh Fort. He saw a spout of flame aimed directly at him as a colossal gun fired, causing his natural reaction. Expecting an explosion any second, he fought to concentrate on the problem at hand.

"Ship's head is paying off slowly to port, Captain," Hackett-Jones announced.

"We're less than three cables south of Chanak on the Asian shore, Captain," Hardacre took his turn to report.

"Very good." The captain endeavoured to sound calm. "We're pinned to the shore by the bow and the current is catching the stern. We don't want it to push us parallel to the shore or we'll have the dickens of a job to get off. Helm, hard a'starboard!"

Slowly, slowly the gyro repeater steadied and, imperceptibly, the motors were having some success, no doubt their wash breaking up the mud and sand holding the bow and marking their position even more clearly to outside observers.

Ted raised the periscope again. Ready this time, he held his gaze on the nearest fort, registering shot after shot. He spun the periscope around; there were still no contacts close, but he saw plumes of spray away from the submarine on the disengaged side. He could also see *E57* gaining sternway. "Steady, Chaps," he tried to settle his crew's nerves. "It's working! Just get me back under the water as soon as you can!"

The top of the submarine had been exposed for at most five minutes before she slid back under the surface, but it had seemed an eternity, and they were still in danger. Ted tried to make light of their predicament, "Well, we were so near that fort that they couldn't train their gun down sufficiently to hit us and all their shots passed overhead! I can only suppose too that we were so far inshore next to Chanak town that guns on the European shore opposite didn't want to risk shooting at their own civilians. But," he warned, "everyone will know we're here now." The submarine was diving ever deeper as *E57* came away from the shore stern first. She hardly seemed under control. Worse, the stream caught the bow and spun the boat quickly to starboard – the opposite direction they needed to go – heading into the bay with the current behind willing them onto the shore again. The crew was still fighting to get back into the correct dived trim, with the new danger of racing propellers crisscrossing just above them. Their desperate situation was exacerbated by the need to use full ahead and astern power to get *E57* back on a northerly course, towards the Narrows and out of the bay.

It worried Ted that they had to use so much power to pull themselves off and get back on track, seriously depleting the battery. He had to make progress as quickly as possible. He allowed another ten minutes before bringing the submarine back to PD. A good fix was crucial to get them through the tightest part of the Narrows. Unsurprisingly, the periscope was welcomed by gunfire immediately after it broke the surface. In addition, a few gunboats and fast patrol boats could be seen to be closing rapidly. With the sea around him a tumult of gunshots, splashes and spray, any observation was difficult. Trusting he was in the centre of the channel, he hurried to get the boat deep again, this time to seventy feet. He increased speed for a dash through to less constrained water on the other side of the Narrows.

Hardly settled at depth, when – bump! – again, the submarine slid relentlessly upwards. How could that be? Where were they now? Ted was straight on the periscope as it passed twenty-five feet and was ready to assess their situation. Absurdly, he found himself on the opposite, European shore, at the very end of the Kilid Bahr promontory at a depth of just eight feet! The now-alerted gunboats and a destroyer raced towards them, firing for all they were worth. This time, the stern started to swing rapidly to port under the influence of the current, pointing the submarine past the Narrows towards their intended course. *E57* was grounded more at the stern than the bow, inclining the boat slightly head-down. The thuds of shots falling around the hull could be felt throughout the submarine, with a hailstorm of shrapnel striking the casing and drowning out other sounds. There was no time to lose. The captain must take drastic action; otherwise, all would be lost. "Full ahead together!" he bellowed.

Ominous noises from aft caused him to fear that the propellers were being smashed against the shore. Then, after one shudder and another, *E57* shook herself free from the beach and was on the move again, slithering down to thirty feet. As soon as the first lieutenant had a modicum of control over the submarine's trim, Ted ordered her back down to seventy feet and increased speed.

Concerned about damage and leaks caused by the second grounding, Chief Bowers raced aft and then forward to conduct a quick check throughout the boat before reporting that all appeared well. They were in relatively clear water at last, with the noise of pursuing ships gradually receding. However, the second, near-ninety-degree dog leg was only a few miles ahead, altering to starboard around Nagara Point. There would be inevitable eddies and cross-currents. *E57* had already progressed further than any submarine before. However, the most difficult challenges might still await her, now against an alerted enemy.

2

"Well, Navigator," Ted smiled at Hardacre. "I got you that good fix you wanted. We were on the shore *here* at Kilid Bahr – 'The Key of the Sea'," he added, stabbing a finger at the chart. "Perhaps we've now unlocked our safe passage through!" Pleased with his little joke, the captain then moved in a clockwise circle around the control room, checking for himself the position of switches and valves, the pressures in the air and hydraulic systems, the voltages and currents on the electrical panel, the movement of the hydroplanes, rudder, inclinometers and depth gauges, pointing to each one in turn to ensure he registered every reading. He prided himself that no one knew more about his submarine. Specifically, the captain was the only one with detailed knowledge of this complex machine's various 'gears' - people and equipment - and how they meshed together to make the boat run smoothly. After all, he was there when *E57* first came out of the building yard in 1914. Rather than being out on the golf course like so many of his colleagues, he had worked alongside his technicians, repairing defects and fine-tuning equipment. Ted had also taken the time to train his people. He nodded to himself, content that all readings were as expected, before returning to the chart table.

"I suggest we plan to come up to PD for a fix here, Captain, about five cables short of Nagara," proposed Hardacre, "in about fifteen minutes."

The bubble was manoeuvred forward at the appointed time, and the submarine rose steadily to PD. As usual, the periscope was raised with the captain pressed against the eyepiece before it broke the surface, swinging left and right to check for anything right ahead with which they might collide.

"Helm Hard a'port!" came the command in the same instant they reached twenty feet. The captain spun the periscope around once and then a second time, calling out the bearings for a fix. "Steer zero-seven-five! Down periscope. Keep thirty feet."

"Nagara's already on our starboard quarter, together with a host of patrol boats waiting for us in the centre of the channel," Ted announced. "We were almost on the northern shore: where do those bearings put us, Navigator?"

Hardacre showed him on the chart. Assured that *E57* was safe and moving into deeper water on the course ordered, the captain took the submarine back down to seventy feet. He tried to keep his crew informed. "It's damnably calm up there, and I feel sure the patrol boats would have seen us. But that's the second turn completed. Now it's a fairly straight run until we're abeam Gallipoli and into the Marmara. Another ten minutes, and you can take turns to stand down and have a cup of tea."

With little enough sleep the night before as they made final preparations, no one had left their posts for over three hours since diving. Anxieties had mounted through frenetic periods of activity and – for the crew – past many unseen dangers. They had to trust implicitly in the captain's ability to keep them safe. The air was already stale and sweaty, condensation was dripping around them, and the inevitable headaches were beginning to pinch at their temples. This welcome announcement helped them to relax a little and shake the tension from their shoulders. That said, the sound of gurgling wakes above them reminded everyone that the Turkish Navy wasn't finished with them yet.

E57 had proven the existence of a saline counter-current helping them on their way, stronger too at seventy feet than at sixty. Nonetheless, there were still more than twenty miles to go along the channel before them, which was a little over a mile wide at a couple of pinch points. They must then pass the town of

Gallipoli on the northern shore before being released into the much broader waters of the Sea of Marmara. Although the information on the chart was sparse, a deeper trench took a direct line up the straits. Hardacre contended that *E57* should remain within this central channel, clear of any surging currents in and out of the bays on either shore. Ted was keen to leave pursuing forces well astern, so he kept the submarine down for another full hour before returning to PD for the next observation. This was an unusually long time to run fast and deep within constrained waters whilst relying solely on the Sperry gyro to keep them on the desired heading.

An all-round look showed no contacts close, and a navigational fix put them just past Gocuk Point and roughly at the mid-position between Nagara and Gallipoli town. Positioned in the middle of a choke point and despite the surface remaining glassy calm, Ted decided to take a prolonged look to check what was in the channel ahead. There he could see three rugged, tug-like boats in line abreast, approaching them from the east at a slow speed. He couldn't tell for sure, but Ted suspected they might be dragging wire cables or even a net between them to snag submarines. He inspected the detail on the chart close to the fix.

The seabed on the European side was steep, plunging down precipitously close to the shoreline. Alternatively, the southern, Asiatic side offered a more gently shelving bottom. Not risking another look, the captain ordered the submarine deep to seventy feet again and altered the heading to starboard, announcing his intention to bottom the boat at that depth. Proceeding at slow ahead on the outboard port shaft, it was another ten minutes before a rasping noise forward announced their bow's arrival on a sandy bottom. Way was immediately taken off the submarine, four tons of water was flooded into a forward tank, and more water was trimmed from aft to forward. These actions served to 'anchor' the bow in position whilst keeping the propellers clear.

It was not long before they could hear the steady, pulsing beat of the nearest tug's propeller as it crept past them, seeming to be directly overhead as best they could tell. A dangling cable scratched and scrabbled over the upper works of the boat like a demented insect, seeking out some little nook or cranny into which it could inject one of its deadly claws. The cowls over the planes and the jumping wires were effective against the taut wires of buoyant mines but no good against a pendulous grappling hook. The first pass was the closest but, not so obligingly to be deprived of their prey, the tugs proceeded to transit back up the channel. They crept past the boat for a second time and, even now, were turning yet again to investigate the submarine's position. This was a grave menace in such constrained waters and the first one Ted had encountered that could present a genuine danger to them whilst dived. The tugs were literally searching in the dark – they could not know *E57*'s location – but, if lucky, their antics could be deadly. Ted decided they couldn't just remain there and hope for the best. He told the crew that they would wait until the tugs had passed on their southwest passage before getting underway again, leaving them behind.

Again, the submariners monitored the movement of the nearest tug past them, thankfully without any contact with *E57* this time. Wasting no time in case their opponents turned quickly, the first lieutenant put the submarine back into diving trim and commenced propelling slowly astern on both main motors. At first, there was no movement, but then *E57* levelled off and started to sink even deeper . . . eighty feet . . . ninety feet . . . one hundred feet. Whether it was mud clinging to the bow or some damage to the ballast tanks sustained during the grounding incidents, they couldn't tell. It was clear even so that more extreme measures would be required for *E57* to wrench herself free of the bottom, including blowing main ballast tanks. Such radical action might result in the unintentional surfacing of the boat in full sight of all, rendering her defenceless. Consequently, propelling ahead again, the submarine was re-anchored by the bow and driven back up the slope to a more comfortable eighty feet. They had no option other than to wait for the cover of night.

Resecured to the bottom and remembering that it was Sunday, the captain summoned the crew for prayers to be read, which had never been so earnest for many. As had become routine in his various commands, Ted ended the impromptu worship by reciting the remembered inscription below the cross at home. In their situation, citing *"ye dragons and all deeps"* seemed wholly appropriate. The submarine's crew simply had to sit it out and pray that the continual backwards-and-forwards patrols above them failed to find their target.

It was quarter-to-seven that evening before the tugs eventually completed their last pass. Having waited for total darkness, Ted surfaced *E57* two hours later. The night was crystal clear and the surface was still mirror-like. Finding no contacts in their vicinity and with not a single shore light around, the captain ordered both diesels to commence the charge. The submarine had been dived for sixteen hours, and the crew swarmed beneath the conning tower hatch, gulping deep lungfuls of the fresh night air.

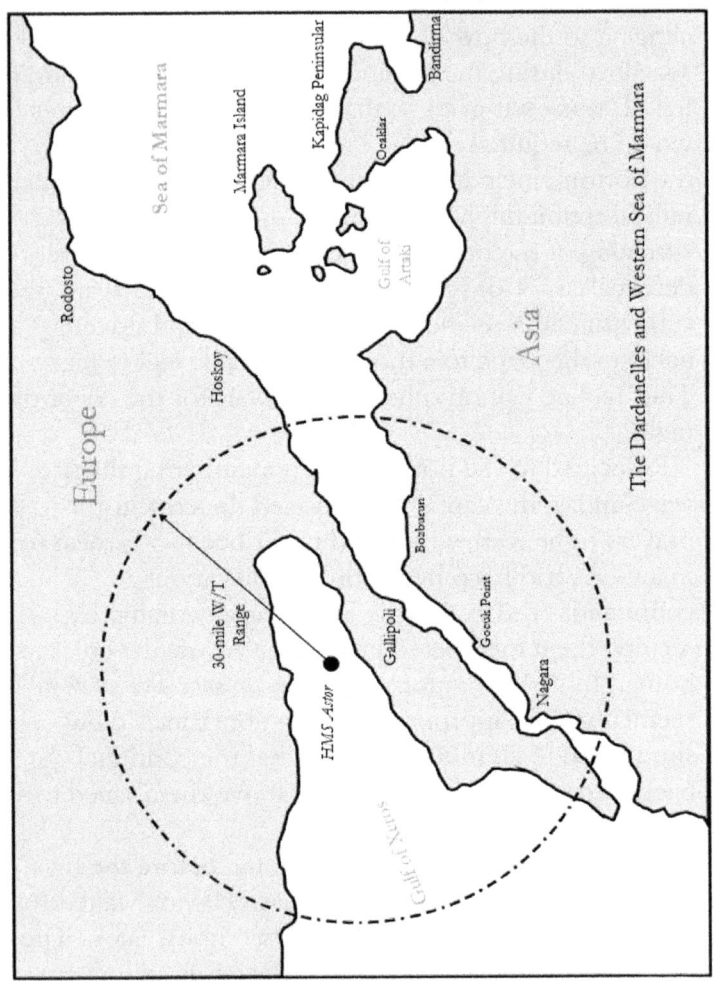

The captain gave himself an hour to charge the battery to a moderate degree before undertaking his next essential task, which might result in him being detected. Keyes needed the vitally important information that *E57* had progressed so far, with the worst behind, knowing that the decision to let other boats follow depended on this. The mast and wire aerials were rigged before the night sky lit up with vivid blue flashes as the Morse signals were sent into the ether. Time and time again, Andrews, the wireless operator, sent out their callsign, but no acknowledgement ever came back. Ted ordered that the signal be sent anyway and repeated twice: they just had to trust that their transmitting equipment was operational and the message was getting through. Hopefully, it was only their receiver that wasn't working. The captain was frustrated: he didn't know how this new radio worked, and there was no operator's manual. In addition, he needed to find out the worth of his replacement telegraphist. Ted pestered him with questions to which the sailor had few satisfactory answers. The telegraphists were an elite branch, recruited from the better-educated sailors on entry and given long technical training. Many still failed the final examinations. Approximately only twenty years old, Andrews had obviously done exceptionally well to be rated Leading Telegraphist already, but with no results to show, this counted little to his current commanding officer. Andrew's feverous efforts continued for an anxious two hours as the submarine lay undisturbed and the battery charge continued. Just after midnight, the weather changed, and drizzle obscured everything beyond a few feet, providing an added layer of security. It was never in the plan, but here was *E57* deep within enemy territory and just half a mile from the shore, unmolested and completing a charge at her leisure.

A light easterly wind dispersed the rain at about three o'clock on Monday morning. The moon had long since set, leaving the submarine in darkness. Hence, the captain decided to continue his passage slowly on the surface, hoping to close the distance towards Gallipoli before first light. The last bottleneck in the channel was there, and, once safely passed, they could range freely into the Sea of Marmara. As soon as the grey of dawn gave any chance of being seen from the shore, *E57* dived and caught a trim before dipping once more to seventy feet to cover the remaining five miles to the end of the Dardanelles.

Able now to judge better the strength of the current at depth and, therefore, the boat's speed over the ground, *E57* was brought to PD about a mile due south from Gallipoli town. A fix confirmed their position but across the channel, extending from shore to shore, bobbed many small vessels. They looked like fishermen, but Ted needed to be more confident, especially given their experiences with the tugs the previous day. There was no obvious way past them except underneath. He dipped the submarine to thirty feet before coming up again when he had closed the range by half to have a better look. Still unsure but without any alternative, Ted made up his mind.

"Six down . . . . keep one hundred and twenty feet. Revolutions for seven knots!"

That certainly grabbed the attention of his crew. This was deeper than they habitually operated, although well within their operational range: *E57's* designed deep diving depth was two hundred feet. "If they have cables or nets down to catch us," their captain explained, "I'm hoping to pass under them. But, if they do hook us, at this speed they'll find they have a mighty big fish to reel in! We'll either part their lines or rip their gear from its fittings."

E57 ran in this way for twice the time necessary to clear the choke point and put the hindering vessels well astern, becoming aware of nothing untoward during the whole time. Returning to periscope depth, Ted first satisfied himself there had been no reaction to their passage before proceeding to take bearings for a fix.

He went over to a grinning Hardacre, indicating their position on the chart.

"Gentlemen," the captain announced to his people. "You have the honour of being the first submarine crew to transit through the Dardanelle Straits. Many thought it was a forlorn hope that this could ever be achieved – but we have done it and others will follow! Very well done, all of you. Now it's time to join the war against the Turks and Germans: we have some serious work to do!"

4

By early afternoon *E57* was patrolling in a deep-water area ten miles east of Gallipoli in the centre of the topographical funnel through which all west-bound traffic must pass. Morale was high. Everyone was elated from completing a near-impossible feat, and they felt more relaxed now that they had sea room and could manoeuvre as desired. They could not yet be sure whether the Turks were aware of their success – there was no evidence that they had been counter-detected since Nagara, thirty miles to the west. Ted decided to continue the patrol dived. He still had to confirm that HQ was aware of *E57*'s position. His problem was that his paltry one-kilowatt Type Ten 'wireless' set's range was so limited that the destroyer HMS *Astor* had been assigned radio relay duties. She would have to operate close to the shore within the Gulf of Xeros, across the narrow Bulair isthmus from Gallipoli, awaiting *E57*'s signals and passing on commands from HQ. *E57* had to remain in an area to the extreme west of the Sea of Marmara to remain within range, and Ted didn't want to wander too far away.

The captain and first lieutenant were taking turns to keep watch on the periscope.

"Captain, Sir, I have some smoke to the northeast," Hackett-Jones reported.

True enough, two Turkish Navy auxiliaries duly appeared on the horizon in close line astern, seemingly keeping a straight track towards them. Ted estimated that they would pass about a thousand yards away. The captain was in two minds. He must get that signal away to HQ and wanted to remain undetected until that had been done. On the other hand, he had been ordered to disrupt the Turkish supply lines, so he couldn't just watch and do nothing, allowing these ships to pass. "Port twenty. Half ahead together," he manoeuvred to close the distance. "Action Stations, Number One. Bring bow tubes to the ready state."

Hackett-Jones disappeared forward. "Flood the tubes!" he ordered on arrival in the fore-ends. "Open the drains and vents! Open air to the for'd trim line!" The loud hissing of air told him that water was being forced from the trim tank into the space around the loaded torpedoes. On receipt of the report, "Tubes full, Sir!" the first lieutenant turned the wheels that released the two bow caps before operating the respective levers to throw them open. "Charge the firing banks!" came next, and he monitored the rising pressure on the relevant gauge. Returning to the control room, he reported to his captain, "Both bow tubes ready, Sir!"

"Very good. Bring both beam tubes to the ready state. Time is tight but I want a shot at both these targets."

Oblivious to anything untoward, the Turkish ships continued steadily on their track without a sharp lookout for that stick-like object appearing fleetingly on their starboard bow.

The range was now six hundred yards. "Standby Number Two tube!" The submarine captain set the periscope on the deflection angle ahead of the target. This is calculated to ensure the torpedo and the target arrive at the same point simultaneously. The bridge of the leading ship crept into his eyepiece.

"FIRE!"

The submarine shuddered as the fish left the port bow tube, and the planesmen fought to keep the bow down and the boat under control.

"Hard a'starboard. Standby starboard beam tube!" Ted wanted to maintain the same distance from the second target by paralleling their course, deciding to use one of his torpedo beam tubes.

As the submarine's heading clicked around, everyone awaited the gratifying explosion from the first weapon. None came. Ted risked another look at the following ship. There was no reaction, and it remained steady on course. Waiting until the last moment, he ordered the periscope up and trained it immediately onto the firing bearing.

"FIRE!"

E57 moved bodily to port on the discharge of the torpedo. "ten seconds," called out the first lieutenant. "twenty seconds . . . thirty seconds . . . forty sec..." A huge explosion rattled the submarine, interrupting Hackett-Jones' countdown, followed by a cheer from the submarine's crew. The captain waited a little longer before raising the periscope again. The leading ship had initially continued on its way, oblivious of the first attack, but now it was altering course rapidly to port to go to the aid of her sister. The stricken vessel was already down by the bow and taking on an exaggerated list to starboard. A pall of smoke enshrouded the entire bridge structure, and the propeller materialised out of the water, still thrashing away.

The submarine's captain had seen enough, and the casualty was dropping astern on his starboard quarter. "Six down . . . keep seventy feet. Revolutions for seven knots." He waited until the boat was steady on depth and safely opening from the attack datum. He had no idea how the Turks would react. "Clearly, the first was *another* duff torpedo," their captain couldn't disguise his frustration, "but *E57* has claimed its first successful attack of the war. The Turks have received our calling card!"

After they had opened the range to about ten miles, the submarine returned to PD. Finding nothing about, Ted surfaced the boat to assess the forces ranged against him. He could just make out some activity on or just over the horizon, which was surprisingly light. For over an hour, the other auxiliary loitered in the area, presumably rescuing survivors, aided eventually by smaller vessels. Then nothing more. As evening turned to dusk, the sea all around remained empty, which augured well for their repeated attempt to signal HQ. The diesel engines were run to charge the battery whilst the submarine edged slowly westwards, back towards her signalling billet. With deep water available into which *E57* could escape if necessary, Ted closed the distance to HMS *Astor's* assigned position as much as he dared. His signal had to get through, and he was prepared to risk the brilliant flashing lights of his transmissions being seen from ashore. Before the pyrotechnic radio show could begin, the mast and aerials had to be rigged, which was no straightforward matter. The thirty-five-foot telescopic mast was hinged at the rear of the submarine's fin, being secured in a narrow channel along the after casing. Four wire aerials had to be attached to the cross tree at the top before the main wireless mast could be erected. The aerials were then attached to two further folding stanchions, one forward and one right aft. The wires were pulled taut and kept separate by spreaders at both ends. Finally, a lead from each wire was led through a deck tube to copper connections with the wireless equipment inside the pressure hull.

The regular use of radios by submarines was a recent innovation that had been introduced only since the beginning of the war. At the start, boats had been free to operate in the Heligoland Bight and The Skaw, attacking any viable targets as opportunities arose. They reported whatever intelligence they had gathered only after they had returned to port. By operating within the egress routes of the High Seas Fleet, they had proved their ability to maintain a close blockade. As a result of such success, their primary mission was amended.

All submarines were now required to *report* – not attack – when the heavy ships of their German opponents ventured out into open water. This was designed to encourage von Hipper and his admirals to believe their departure had been undetected, leaving them to be intercepted by the Grand Fleet. The submariners were permitted to attack only *inbound* ships, which caused considerable ill will. Submarine captains saw their vital role as indispensable offensive units, taking the battle to the enemy, being reduced to radio scouts for those grand gentlemen holed up in the safety of Scapa Flow. Furthermore, the rigmarole of surfacing and making all the preparations to transmit only increased the vulnerability of the boats already in a precarious situation in Germany's backyard. If necessary, the submarines could dive with aerials rigged – as many were forced to do – but this carried the risk of wires becoming detached and fouling the boat's propellors. Many simply took the option of releasing the homing pigeons, which were carried as a backup. That wasn't an option available here in the Marmara!

This resentment remained with *E57*'s captain because his freedom of action was again curtailed by the need to report back to HQ instead of being left free to wage war. He was the only person on the spot and able to assess the actual tactical situation. Another matter gnawed away at him too. An expert in the engines, mechanical apparatus, electrical power generation, torpedoes and all other equipment aboard, he still needed to learn about the new science of radios. He understood nothing of his wireless equipment, which added to his exasperation. It never occurred to him that it might be *Astor's* own circumstances causing the problems. Perhaps enemy action had prevented her approach to the confined waters close to the Turkish coast, or it might be her defective equipment. As a result, Ted was forever at Andrews' shoulder as he attempted to establish communications, seemingly blaming him by overseeing and questioning his every move and venting his frustrations onto the poor sailor. His telegraphist was supposed to operate his equipment within the so-called 'Silent Cabinet', designed to allow faint transmissions to be received without interference from outside noise or vibrations. His commanding officer only made matters worse by insisting that the shielded and padded door remain open so he could supervise what was happening.

A good-looking, intelligent lad, Andrews was of slight build, with dimpled cheeks and fair curly hair, making him look much younger than his twenty-four years of age. Telegraphists received only rudimentary submarine training and didn't remain long with any particular boat. Instead, they were moved around owing to the low numbers available in their branch and according to operational needs. As a result, it was difficult for them to fully integrate into a crew. In ordinary course, Andrews might have discussed his problems with the coxswain. Since his arrival in Malta, Prescott had done his best to welcome the new telegraphist and see he had everything he needed. Nevertheless, Andrews was intelligent enough to realise he couldn't possibly raise concerns about a captain who was clearly held in the highest regard by the entire crew. Who was *he* to complain? He just had to keep his head down, trawl through his memory of everything he had been taught, and check and double-check every element of the communications system.

5

At the exact moment when *E57* saw the searchlights in the Straits being doused on the morning of 25th April, whistles were being blown up and down the western side of the Gallipoli Peninsular. It signalled thousands upon thousands of brave men to be thrown upon various beaches. Poorly controlled and coordinated, early gains were not capitalised upon, with available reserves not deployed to punch their way into good holding positions. With the combined HQ aboard, HMS *Queen Elizabeth* spent much of the day off V Beach and witnessed a stream of hopeless frontal attacks, one after the other. No one thought to order them to desist, with the consequent loss of many of the Army's best leaders. To add to the general misery, Andrina brought Commodore Keyes the news that Turkish authorities had announced that a submarine had been attacked and sunk at Kilid Bahr. After such a depressing day, matters became even worse when a high-level ANZAC delegation arrived onboard after midnight with a message from General Birdwood.

"Both my Divisional Generals and Brigadiers have represented to me that they fear their men are thoroughly demoralised by shrapnel fire, to which they have been subjected all day after exhausting and gallant work in the morning. Numbers have dribbled back from the firing line and cannot be collected in this difficult country. Even New Zealand Brigade, which has only recently engaged, lost heavily and is to some extent demoralised. If troops are subjected to shell fire tomorrow morning, there is likely to be a fiasco, as I have no fresh troops with which to replace those in the firing line. I know my representation is most serious, but if we are to re-embark it must be at once."

The C-in-C, General Sir Ian Hamilton, was roused. He called an immediate conference of his most senior commanders, with all smaller-fry staff officers excluded. Admiral De Robeck was there, of course, together with his Chief of Staff at his side. Charles Brodie had helped Keyes set up the conference room – the same one that had hosted all the submarine captains – and had gained from him the gist of Birdwood's message. Now he waited anxiously in the passageway outside the meeting room. He was in the company of officers sporting a variety of uniforms, all waiting to discover what had been decided. The yeoman of signals pushed through this crowded assembly, seeking out Brodie.

The senior rating approached the staff officer, quite out of breath, pushing a piece of paper towards him. He caught Brodie's eye, and the latter detected a glint that told him this was important news. "From *E57* for C-in-C, Sir!" he just managed to breathe out. The message was garbled, but it was clear that the submarine was past Nagara and safe. Crockford had done it!

Taking a pause and a deep breath to build his courage, Brodie knocked on the conference room door and walked straight in. He was met with immediate silence, with all heads turned crossly in his direction. Brodie looked for his direct superior, to be met by Keyes frostily shaking his head, clearly dismissing him. But the staff officer held his ground. Reluctantly the Chief of Staff came over to the door to be shown the message. Keyes' understanding of its significance was immediate. He smiled at Brodie, now nodding. "Thank you," he mouthed and only then did his staff officer take leave of the august company.

Keyes was elated: his trust in submariners had been rewarded. Obviously, something was up, and all eyes turned to him as he retook his place at the conference table. He cleared his throat and spoke up, "Tell the men this. It is an omen – one of our submarines has done the finest feat in submarine history and is going to torpedo all the ships bringing reinforcements, supplies and ammunition into Gallipoli."

Keyes' interpretation was a little over-optimistic. Still, for Hamilton, it was sufficient to confirm his decision to continue the fight. Indeed, the spreading news that an Allied submarine was in the Sea of Marmara cheered the

Army and the Navy alike. The C-in-C signalled widely to his command his intention to remain ashore, adding the rider, *"You have got through the difficult business. Now you have only to dig, dig, dig until you are safe."*

6

A nervous hour passed without success as *E57* lit her surroundings brightly with the long blue sparks of her transmissions. Now firmly in enemy territory with three lookouts doing their best, the fireworks crackling from the aerial kept destroying their night vision.

Trusting the bridge watch to his first lieutenant, the captain, as ever, loitered close to the radio operator, who suddenly held his headphones closer to his ears.

"It's the *Astor*, Captain . . . acknowledging our callsign. Wait, Sir . . ." he said, holding an earpiece with one hand and writing with the other. After an interminable sixty seconds, he spoke again, "She confirms receipt of the signal we sent *yesterday*. Standby message from HQ . . ." This time, the wait was much shorter for a signal of just eight words.

"FROM KEYES STOP BZ[1] STOP RUN AMOK ENDS"

Ted thanked his lucky stars for sending Keyes to the Dardanelles because no one in higher commands understood the submariners' needs better. *E57*'s mission was clear; she had to do everything possible to disrupt the flow of enemy reinforcements and supplies to the land battle raging on the Peninsular. Here was his authority – Run Amok! – to take the battle to the enemy as he saw fit. Everything else was subordinate to that objective!

[1] Bravo Zulu is the Naval signal code meaning "Very Well Done".

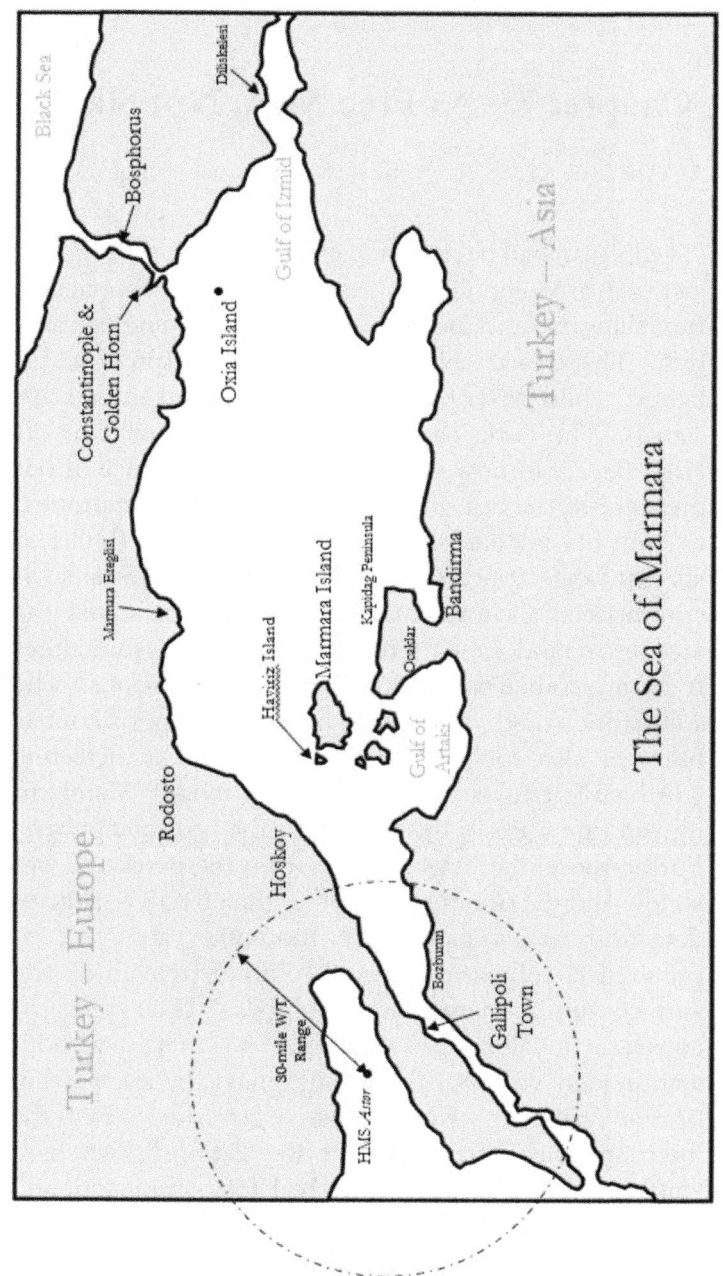

The Sea of Marmara

Chapter 7 – As Free Men, Not Slaves

1

Ted's plan had been to remain in the same general area just east of Gallipoli town, which had the advantage of funnelling westbound reinforcement shipping towards him. This would save chasing targets and preserve his battery whilst never having far to go to send and receive signals. The Turks had thought *E57* had been sunk off Kilid Bahr, but now with unmistakable evidence of her presence in the Sea of Marmara, the enemy determined to hunt her relentlessly. The following day a flotilla of six fast boats appeared from the Dardanelle Straits. It commenced a coordinated movement east across the area in a random pattern, zigzagging and sometimes reversing course to check on anything suspicious. The submarine could avoid them by going deep, of course, but that also robbed her of any chance of detecting worthwhile targets that came within range. Merely to remain safe was not the reason for the boat being there. Furthermore, the height of eye from the periscope was so low and the optics so poor that the effective range of detection was a paltry five thousand yards, so, by preference, submarines would routinely remain on the surface until a target was sighted. Their rules of engagement allowed submarines to attack without warning any vessel of the enemy's navy, be it a warship or auxiliary. Nonetheless, governed by the internationally-accepted "Prize Regulations", merchant ships had to be stopped, searched for contraband, and the crew permitted to disembark. Only then could a vessel be destroyed, by an explosive charge, being set on fire or – for the largest – despatched by a torpedo. Accordingly, a submarine's standard *modus operandi* once in a patrol area would be as a submersible. Thus, operating on the surface to detect targets, they would have good speed available to intercept and challenge merchant shipping. Submarines would dive solely to attack men of war and their support ships.

E57's minimal profile above the surface allowed her to monitor the patrol ships without being counter-detected. Regardless, their activities served to push the submarine further and further east, preventing her from conducting her own search for reinforcement traffic. Rather than remain thus constrained, the captain decided to move twenty miles further east to the intersection of three possible routes westbound ships might take. Their passage could follow the European coast, be along the Asiatic coast from the railhead at Bandirma, or between the islands in the centre. Once there, they found a procession of dhows moving southwest whilst hugging the northern shore.

The captain called for the first lieutenant to prepare his casing and boarding parties and closed in on the largest dhow. As *E57* approached, Ted could see the pandemonium on the deck as the crew frantically dashed about, clearly terrified. With rifles trained on them and orders shouted through a megaphone for them to stop, the sail was dropped, and the submarine manoeuvred alongside. Shaking with fear and believing his entire crew was to be shot, the merchant captain could not understand Hackett-Jones' charades-like instructions to get his men into a life raft. When it eventually dawned on him what was being asked, the Turk's smile was immense, joined by many others once he had explained the situation to his people. With many salaams, they joyfully manned their craft and pushed off, waving at the submariners and laughing as if they were departing on holiday.

The search of the dhow found the hold full of low-grade spares and other equipment but intended for the battlefront nonetheless. The LTO set a charge of gun cotton, and the first lieutenant ushered the boarding party back aboard the submarine, some proudly carrying fresh provisions pilfered from the dhow's galley. *E57* was just pulling astern away from the dhow when there was a shout from the lookout, "Captain, Sir! Red one-zero-five – two patrol vessels!" Sure enough, two of the ships they had spotted previously were at high speed heading towards them: but how on earth had they reacted so quickly? Then, Ted noted smoke rising vertically in the still air from a headland. Was this just a coincidence, or was it possible the Turks had posted lookouts along the shore?

Ted put these thoughts to one side while he dealt with the matters at hand. The captain checked that the casing was secured correctly with his men below before manoeuvring towards the east. He set off at moderate speed, leaving astern the dhow now engulfed in flames. Ten minutes later, *E57* slid below the surface in a controlled dive, leaving the enemy patrol helpless and unable to harass her more. Once dived and in trim, Ted ordered a new course of south to clear from the datum and determined to investigate the southern, Asiatic coast. There was undoubtedly less traffic there, but still, a few ships ploughed their way towards the Dardanelles.

Getting his people fully prepared, the captain paralleled the course of the nearest dhow and surfaced the submarine at a range of just fifty yards directly on her starboard beam. Besides the same terror displayed, the crew's reaction was quite different: the sail was dropped instantly. Everyone stood stock-still with their hands raised without a single order being given. With a wary eye kept to the north, the boarding party were more business-like than before and wasted no time in hurrying the crew onto a small tender before casting them off. The LTO had only just reappeared back on deck, having set his charge, before the two gunboats were seen again approaching from the north. This time, they were joined by two others from the west. Ted checked the coastline. There was another column of smoke from a cliff above a spit of land to the southwest. Closer this time, the patrol ships managed to get two shots away before the submarine escaped undamaged.

2

E57's captain decided that there had been enough action for the day. He cleared away into the very centre of his chosen area, just west of Marmara Island, as far away as possible from each shore. He waited until dusk before surfacing to check around whilst there was some light and, finding nothing, started his generators to commence the charge. The electric oven was switched on, and preparations were made for their only hot meal of the day, supplemented on this occasion with a few fresh provisions courtesy of the Turks. The dinner plates had just been cleared away from the officers' table when the captain was called to the bridge.

It was a calm but cloudy night. The moon was risen, giving just a minimum of light through the thick cover. The lookout could not be sure but thought he had seen something.

"Take the generators off load," Ted ordered down the voice pipe as a precaution while scanning the horizon through his binoculars where the lookout had indicated. At that moment, the clouds parted, and a brilliant moon lit up the scene as if daylight. There was a patrol boat about a thousand yards away where they were looking, but another one was only six hundred yards on the opposite side.

"PRESS THE KLAXON TWICE!"

Amid controlled pandemonium below, with mess tins, cutlery and plates scattered in all directions, the submarine obeyed the alarm and was passing twenty feet before two minutes had passed. The patrol boats had been caught similarly unprepared, but before the guns could be manned appropriately and brought to bear, they had wound on their speed. They turned instantly to try to ram the boat. Passing thirty feet, the submariners could hear the rush of the ship passing just feet above them, and the whole boat was buffeted in its wake. A lucky escape.

This set the pattern for the whole night. *E57* moved away ten miles or so before surfacing and recommencing the charge. After an inconveniently short time, the patrol craft would be detected again, requiring the boat to evade once more. So this pattern continued. First light found the boat northeast of Marmara Island with the crew feeling exhausted, and the battery charged to a less-than-optimal level.

Ted called his officers over to the chart table, and together they perused the mapped detail of the area. Where they were positioned still seemed best to intercept reinforcement shipping, but the captain was concerned about the excellent visibility and flat-calm seas. Ted also raised his uneasiness about the possibility of lookouts along the shore to alert defending forces of the submarine's presence. "We need some bracken to hide amongst," he declared to a mystified Hardacre and Hackett-Jones. He explained his plan to them both before allowing the first lieutenant to go off to brief his team of seamen.

3

Keeping well out from the shore and remaining low in the water, the submarine remained surfaced whilst the bridge watchkeepers sought an ideal target. They were looking for a smaller dhow operating further out from the coast than the main flow of traffic. Having spotted a suitable candidate, *E57* dived and cautiously approached her port quarter. Ted brought the boat just yards off the dhow's beam before giving the order, "Surface!" The defenceless merchantman had no time to react, and within very few minutes, the submarine was secured fast alongside. Ushering the entire dhow's crew down into the hold, the submariners took control of the vessel. The intention was to use the dhow as cover, with the submarine hidden from the shore, without any apparent signs of her presence. The sail was therefore left rigged but poorly trimmed to deliberately spill the wind, the submarine using her engines to propel the two of them. A lookout was placed high in the mast to achieve the best all-around view possible, both searching for more targets and alert to the possible approach of the marauding patrol ships.

Despite the steady stream of small dhows passing slowly down the coast, the morning passed without any significant activity in the sea around *E57*. In early afternoon, however, the lookout called down that he could see patrol ships. More than the original six were sweeping backwards and forwards across the channel north of Marmara Island. Ted climbed up the dhow's mast to see for himself. Sure enough, the patrol craft were in the area they had been in overnight but feverishly zigzagging for no obvious reason. Perhaps they had been spooked by a log in the water or some such. They were not getting any closer to the submarine, so the lookout was left alone again to monitor their movements carefully.

It was not until late afternoon that the captain was called again: Ted grabbed his binoculars and climbed into the rigging. Two larger ships had been spotted to the northeast and were closing. The captain scanned the horizon. The newcomers were still hull-down but moving quite rapidly and putting up a lot of smoke as a result. "I think they might be destroyers," he said to himself. "Now, what are they up to?" Just a few minutes later, he thought he could see another smudge on the horizon. In time, this smoky wraith solidified into the form of a large transport ship which the destroyers were probably escorting. This could explain, too, why the patrol ships to the southwest were in an increased state of alert.

The submarine captain descended and briefed his key personnel on what he intended. He wanted the boat to be prepared to dive in an instant, with just a single line continuing to hold *E57* firmly alongside the dhow. He intended to use her to disguise his approach to an ideal attacking position. Ted gave his instructions. One sailor was to be on the casing to cast the dhow off when ordered, Hardacre was to take up his position on the bridge to relay the captain's orders, and Hackett-Jones was to be below checking all systems were ready. That done, Ted remounted the mast and relieved the lookout who was sent below.

"The destroyers are already at five thousand yards," the captain shouted across to his navigator. "Bring her slowly round four points to starboard to keep us roughly beam-on and to close our distance off track."

The guardian warships kept closing whilst sweeping their sectors. They took little notice of the small, poorly-handled dhow with flapping sail edging in on the port bow of their charge but still far enough away to cause them no concern.

"The first lieutenant reports that the submarine is at action stations, all tubes are flooded and the submarine is in all respects ready to dive, Sir!" Hardacre called across.

"Very good," came the response. "No more than five minutes before the destroyers pass us, and we must be down by then." With that, the captain climbed down, continuing to survey the antics of the enemy ships from the dhow's deck.

Only two minutes passed before Ted had boarded his submarine and was climbing up to the bridge. "Cast off all lines. Carry on below!" he yelled to the leading hand left in sole charge of the casing. Nodding at Hardacre to proceed down the conning tower, the captain took a final look around before following his navigator below.

The destroyers failed to comprehend the significance of the puff of mist coming from the far side of the dhow as the submarine's main vents were opened. A minute or two later, they were past the dhow, and nothing unusual was to be seen. The strange absence of anyone on the deck of the merchantman went unnoticed.

Aboard E57, there was no time to waste. Diving without headway is a ticklish procedure because there is no flow over the hydroplanes to control the submarine. Ted waited until the boat was at thirty feet before propelling ahead, so the wash of her propellers as they stirred up the motionless water didn't alert those on the surface. The boat continued to sink until she was at fifty feet before beginning to answer the cajoling of her operators. Hackett-Jones, with his captain at his elbow, was frantically pumping out water, then flooding it back in again. He trimmed forward to aft and back again, trying every trick he knew to capture that ever-elusive neutral buoyancy.

"Happy, Number One?" The first lieutenant grimaced but followed with a curt nod.

"Six up . . . kept twenty feet! Standby Number One Tube!"

As the water cleared from the top lens, Ted spun around. "Down periscope!" he ordered. "Helm to port. Come one point to starboard." After checking the boat was steady on depth, he briefed his team, "We are astern of the destroyers and the target appears to be keeping a steady course. Standby final target set-up . . . up periscope!"

That observation completed, Ted checked his calculations and then raised the periscope for a final time.

"FIRE!"

The large troopship was now only four hundred yards away. Every member of *E57*'s crew could hear the relentless thumping of the target's powerful engines. "ten seconds . . . twenty seconds . . . thirty seconds . . . forty seconds . . . fifty seconds . . "

"Helm hard a'starboard . . . come two points to port! Standby Number Two Tube."

Ted watched the gyro shudder agonisingly slowly onto the new course. "Up periscope!"

"FIRE!"

The target had spotted the wake of the first torpedo. Panic was followed by much relief as the weapon passed harmlessly beneath the keel directly below the bridge.

Such was the relief that the ship's captain took no action at all, thinking that danger had passed. Less than three minutes later, a brilliant flash of yellow flame on his port quarter opened his engine room like a tin can, with thousands of gallons of water flooding in.

Ted was concerned about being caught under the sinking ship. "Helm hard a'port. Six down, keep ninety feet."

The tension in the control room evaporated, and there were smiles all around. To warrant the protection of two destroyers – not that they were of any use! – everyone knew this must have been a worthwhile target. *E57* had stalked her like a stag and delivered the mortal blow.

A report from the first lieutenant broke their celebrations, "Captain, Sir, I'm having to flood in a lot to get her down. We're stuck at seventy-five feet."

The captain came over to him, "How much have you flooded so far?" he asked.

"Four tons, Sir."

"Very good. Don't flood any more. Keep seventy-five feet."

The submarine remained deep for an hour before venturing to return to PD. It was already dusk, and nothing could be seen through the periscope. Surfacing the boat, there was still no sign of the large transport, and the two destroyers were away to the northeast, returning whence they came. The submarine was directed towards the very middle of the Sea of Marmara, where Ted hoped they would be most difficult to find, with no passing traffic to concern him while he recharged his battery. He was particularly aware that his crew were both tense and exhausted after four days of nearly non-stop action. They had enjoyed extraordinarily little uninterrupted sleep during that time. By midnight, his people had had a hot meal, the atmosphere in the boat had been refreshed, and the charge was complete. The crew was both surprised and not a little disgruntled when they were ordered to take up their diving stations.

"Keep seventy-five feet," came the order when they were again underwater.

E57 stopped short at seventy feet this time and could not be persuaded to pass that depth.

"Stop together," the captain instructed: the hum of the motors ceased and the propeller shafts wound to a halt. "We know that there is a saltwater counter-current under the fresh outflow and I think that's where we are – on the exact boundary between the two," he explained. "As the Straits weave to and fro, in and out of bays and past headlands, the two layers become more mixed without such well-defined limits, but here in the middle of the sea it's probably different. How's it looking, Number One?"

"Speed is less than one knot, Sir, and she seems very steady."

"Very good. Flood two tons to ensure she stays down. We'll wait another five minutes to ensure all is well and then you can stand down to a single watchkeeper as if we were anchored on the bottom." The crew made faces at one another – this was strange indeed, like being stopped in mid-air – but no one was in any mood to complain too loudly if their captain's crazy notion meant more sleep.

Just as Ted had predicted, *E57* sat there on the saltwater layer with all but one person able to get some proper rest. The boat resurfaced the next morning at five o'clock and started a top-up charge whilst the captain permitted the hands to bathe. He had decided they needed some time off, not least to wash themselves and the few clothes they had with them. To maintain the fighting platform, it was also requisite to substantially tidy up the boat, square away loose gear, and attend to those inevitable minor defects that accumulate. It gave Ted the opportunity to take stock of their situation and confer with his section leaders about his future intentions.

It was expected that the patrol would last for about three weeks, that being the maximum endurance of the crew and the submarine in such harsh conditions. It had to be that long to allow other boats to join them too. The three officers, coxswain and senior engineer designed a programme where they would investigate several likely embarkation ports and small harbours. The boat would crisscross the sea as randomly as possible to keep the defending forces guessing where they would pop up next. They also addressed the status of their consumable supplies of diesel, lubricating and hydraulic oil and essential stores. Of most significant concern to Ted was the expenditure of torpedoes.

"We've been out for only four complete days and have already fired four fish; two good ones and two duds that have gone under the target." Turning to Hardacre, he explained, "I'm afraid this is not an unusual situation. Fewer than fifty per cent of all torpedoes run true. We call them "mouldies" for this reason. At this rate, we'll have none left after ten to twelve days, leaving an early return to Mudros our only option. We'll have to use charges wherever and whenever we can, provided this doesn't put us at risk. Is there anything else we can do?"

"I have an idea, Captain," sparked up his first lieutenant. "When a warshot torpedo reaches the end of its run, it is set to sink. That's all well and good in peacetime when you don't want anyone accidentally bumping into a live torpedo bobbing around; but we needn't worry about that here in confined enemy waters." He plucked up his courage before making his proposal. "Why don't we set them to float – it's so easy to change the setting, as you know – so we can go back and try to find any that don't run properly?"

His captain was quiet for a while, thinking the matter through. This suggestion was undoubtedly contrary to regulations, so Ted's immediate by-the-book reaction was to discount it out of hand. All well and good in peacetime . . . but they were now at war! *E57* had a job to do, and they needed as many weapons as they could muster. He fixed his gaze on Hackett-Jones before breaking into a wide grin, "That's a brilliant idea: why not? Even if we fail to find them, what's to be lost?"

4

Their routine after that followed a similar pattern day by day. They would close the westbound sea transportation routes each morning to investigate what traffic might be passing. Nonetheless, the boat's previous antics and successes had dramatically reduced the number of substantial targets. Accordingly, the main work was stopping and boarding dhows and other sailing vessels to check them for contraband. This also enabled them to obtain fresh produce, for which Hackett-Jones always offered some recompense. Many of the Turkish captains thought of this as some kind of trick and, particularly when looking at the strange British coins in the lieutenant's hand, refused payment. This was an unusual treat for the British crew: they were used to patrols in the North Sea when food quality would deteriorate throughout the patrol, becoming almost inedible. Some vessels would indeed be carrying items clearly designed for the frontline but stopping this was meagre pickings for any submarine. Towards dusk, they would travel to the west of the Sea of Marmara to report their activities or receive radioed orders. On every occasion, this took much, much longer than it should have, during which time they could be discovered and attacked by enemy craft. Andrews was spending all his time off-watch tweaking and tuning his equipment. Sometimes, even when his crew mates were sleeping, he would be found either within the tiny wireless space or checking the various outboard fittings leading to the aerial. Nothing he did brought any improvements. His captain grew increasingly frustrated and perpetually quizzed Andrews about the problem. From this interrogation, Ted discovered that the technical staff aboard *Adamant* had fitted some newly-designed parts during *E57*'s time in Mudros. However, they had failed to pass on any documentation about the design or purpose of the changed items. Accustomed to knowing how every little mechanism aboard the submarine worked and was operated, Ted was infuriated with this situation, making his displeasure quite clear to Andrews. To this commanding officer, lack of detailed knowledge of your equipment and inability to complete assigned tasks were the ultimate sins. On completion of the protracted communications ritual, the submarine would return to the centre of their captive lake, charge the batteries whilst cooking a hot meal, and then dive to settle on the saline layer.

Shifting across to the southwest of the Sea of Marmara, on the fifth day, they broke this routine, eventually detecting a medium-sized merchantman heading for Gallipoli. Confident that the submarine had not torpedoed anything in recent days and identifying that those dhows which had been attacked were all towards the north coast, the vessel's captain seemed unperturbed, steering a straight course towards the entrance to the Dardanelles channel. Ted manoeuvred *E57* into a good firing position inshore of his target and released a torpedo at an optimal six hundred yards. Despite seeing and hearing the weapon fire up and leaving the usual bubbling wake behind it, disappointingly, it again seemed to pass under the target. Whatever, the merchantman seemed blissfully unaware and continued his passage. Ted remained dived and waited for twenty minutes before rising to periscope depth. He took a good look around before surfacing the boat. Starting at the point marked on the chart where they had fired the weapon, they carefully tracked along its intended course. Sure enough, they could see the bobbing head of the miscreant torpedo about two thousand yards further on. Following the routine that the first lieutenant had devised, the submarine was trimmed down forward, bringing the cap of the stern tube level with the waterline. Despite Hackett-Jones' objections, Ted stripped off himself, attached a lifeline and entered the water to retrieve the torpedo, carrying with him the tools he would need in a bag secured around his waist. Luckily, the sea was flat calm, and the weapon bobbed only as he approached it as his movements stirred up the water. This was the tricky part: he had to remove a blank and insert a screwdriver to rewind the range to render the pistol safe. Any untoward motion or jolting of the torpedo could bring oblivion. Struggling to keep himself afloat, manage the tools and control the weapon's position so he could gain access, he was breathing hard. Even with the range rewound to zero, it could never be sure that the pistol would not trigger the two-hundred-pound charge of wet guncotton. This was sufficient to open the side of a ship but was now only inches from his face. Again, with extreme care, he had to reach up to the top of the torpedo and use a wrench to extract the initiating mechanism. When done, a ring bolt was screwed into the hole that was left. With almost all his energy expended, Ted untied his lifeline and attached it to the now-inert weapon. Signalling to his casing party, they started to heave in the metal fish. They brought it around the stern of the submarine where two sailors were waiting in the water, ready to guide the torpedo headfirst into the rear tube under the directions of their first lieutenant.

The submarine dived as soon as this was completed and started a slow passage towards the radio reception position. The exacting process of bringing the errant weapon back into use was then undertaken. The stern tube was drained down. The torpedo then had to be extracted and transferred onto rails. These had been rigged all the way through the submarine, through the motor room, the engine room, the control room, the crew space and finally to the weapon stowage space forward. It was to be dismantled there, washed down with precious freshwater and rebuilt, ready for use.

As soon as it was dark, *E57* rose to the surface, and the agonising communication process commenced. After about ninety minutes, contact had been made with HMS *Astor*, but there was no new signal traffic for them. After that, the submarine remained on the surface and headed slowly towards its accustomed night-time location, with one diesel driving the boat along and the other charging the batteries. On arrival at their chosen position, both diesel engines generated on full load and the crew settled down to the evening meal.

Ted was feeling quite chipper about the successful recycling of the torpedo and was trying to chat amiably with Hackett-Jones over dinner. It was evident that something was troubling his first lieutenant, who replied only in monosyllables instead of his usual flamboyant storytelling and joke-making. After the meal had been cleared away, Ted didn't feel like reading. Rather than sit in silence, the captain climbed up to the bridge to join Hardacre, who was on watch. The night was balmy with little wind and remaining at a comfortable temperature.

Ted stood down the lookout and sent him off to get a cup of tea. The captain and navigator stood back-to-back as usual for the watch officer and lookout. With binoculars still to his eyes, scanning the indistinct horizon, Ted spoke over his shoulder, "I've noticed that you have been spending a lot of time in the various areas of the boat, getting to know the equipment and my people. How do you think you're getting on?"

"It's quite surprising how much I'm enjoying the experience," came the reply. "In the capital ships which I'm used to, you just leave it to the engineers and technicians to keep all the equipment running. From the bridge, there's little understanding of how everything works or how best to use it. I find that all the senior rates and even the sailors aboard *E57* are happy to take the time to explain the equipment to me, as well as the procedures for its operation. Perhaps what I find most remarkable is their knowledge of the whole submarine, where their role fits in and even about what is going on operationally. I'm sure the stokers in *Queen Elizabeth* have absolutely no idea at all what the battleship is doing from day to day. I certainly don't miss the constant change of uniforms and those damned stiff collars, but an occasional hot bath and shave would make me feel more human!" Hardacre ended with a laugh.

"Living conditions aside, it is often the way with small ships and why many prefer them. I certainly do," asserted Ted. "Everyone aboard has a role to play and, with such few numbers available, you have to trust people to get on with their job without supervision. Any one of *E57*'s crew could send us to the bottom if they make a mistake. That's also why I always make sure the coxswain and senior engineer know what's going on because they spread the word."

They maintained their vigil without conversation for a few minutes before Ted broke the silence. "You certainly seemed to have risen to a significant challenge. I think you're doing extremely well; the sailors wouldn't have accepted you if you weren't." Ted had indeed watched him closely and noted his interactions with crew members. Brought up innately of an elevated class, with a crisp accent and aristocratic bearing, Hardacre had nothing to prove to the sailors. He could converse easily with all the ratings whilst maintaining that class distinction without effort. Surprisingly, sailors often enjoy talking and joking with their superiors, especially those of the higher echelons. This seemed to be their reaction to Hardacre, which, in truth, Ted envied. Their captain always held the ratings at some distance in case they uncovered his humble beginnings and realised that he was, in fact, no better than them. Furthermore, Hardacre was becoming more familiar by the day with the operation of equipment and routines to be followed. "We'll make a submariner of you yet!" Ted joked.

"I don't know what's wrong with Hackett-Jones this evening." Ted continued after a short break. "He hardly said a word over dinner. Do you know what's troubling him? Does he have a problem?"

"Umm . . . Might I speak freely?"

"Yes, of course."

"Who is normally responsible for all aspects of preparation of the weapons we carry?" the navigator started rhetorically. "It's the first lieutenant. So, perhaps it is understandable that he feels somewhat aggrieved that it was not him who went out to recover the torpedo this afternoon. After all, it was *his* idea. By not letting him do that, it could be interpreted that you are questioning his competence, which I'm sure was not your intention." Hardacre stopped. He was not sure how far he should take this but decided he should answer the question put to him. "I know I'm not a submariner, but he seems to be a very competent officer and an able second-in-command to you. He must be seen to be respected by his captain."

Hardacre paused again, asking himself if he should say more and deciding he must. "Besides Hackett-Jones' hurt feelings, something else occurs to me. You are the one with all the experience of different classes of submarines, various operations in different theatres and attacking. You are too important to the success of *E57* to risk yourself unnecessarily: what would have happened to the submarine if that torpedo had exploded?"

Ted was quiet for a long while, busying himself with playing with his binoculars and scanning his sector. Initially, it was clear he was bristling with indignation. Still, his own logical brain could not discount the sense of what Hardacre had pointed out.

"You could be right," he eventually conceded. "I suppose there is a thin line between doing perilous things yourself or ordering someone else to put themselves in danger. After all, I put the whole crew in danger every time we leave harbour."

"Captain, Sir. Battery charge complete!" came the shout up the conning tower.

"Good," the captain replied, relieved by the distraction ending this conversation. "All that swimming about has made me very tired. Let's get underwater."

With a final sweep around the whole horizon, Ted went below and made his way towards the wardroom area. The first lieutenant came through from the forends, where he had been checking and rechecking the recovered torpedo.

"Right, Number One. You dive the submarine, get a trim and then settle us on the layer for the night. I've had enough for the day and I'm going to my bunk to read my book. You have the ship."

This was the first time his captain had allowed him to dive the boat without supervision, so Hackett-Jones immediately perked up. He took those few steps into the control room, taking charge directly and getting the process underway.

5

Once 'anchored' on the layer and without the throb of diesel engines, the murmur of the electric motors, or even the perpetual banter of the crew, the boat grew increasingly silent. The accommodation spaces dimmed as torches used for reading were extinguished one by one.

It was about three in the morning when Ted started emerging from an uneasy sleep. He half opened his eyes and saw the dimmed pendant light over the wardroom table gently swinging. He shut his eyes again, but his unconscious brain registered that something was not quite right. Suddenly understanding the situation, the captain was instantly wide-awake and swinging his legs out from the bunk. He hurried into the control room and looked at the depth gauge. Sure enough, the boat was at a depth of only fifteen feet and rolling gently in the long swell above. The watchkeeper he saw was Andrews, who was fast asleep.

"DIVING STATIONS!" Ted bellowed.

Unexpected and recognising their captain's voice, *E57*'s officers and crew roused themselves and hurried into their allocated positions.

"Group up. Half ahead together. Six down. Keep forty feet." The submarine obeyed its commander's wishes. "Stop together. Group down. Half ahead together. Speed for trimming, Number One," came the following orders in unusually quick succession. "Relieve the Cox'n on the after planes. Cox'n, you are to place Andrews under arrest for sleeping on watch. We will conduct Defaulters at my table in thirty minutes."

The defaulters' party mustered at the specified time: the captain, the first lieutenant, the coxswain and Andrews. Having all retrieved their caps from the various hiding places around the boat, Andrews had been ordered to remove his. He was now standing in front of his commanding officer. Because the captain was the one who discovered the crime and there were no other witnesses, the documented procedure could not be followed. Undeterred, Ted proceeded with his own truncated version of events.

"Read out the charge, Cox'n," commanded the captain.

"Leading Telegraphist Andrews is accused of sleeping on watch, Sir."

"How do you plead, Andrews?" the captain demanded.

"Guilty, Sir." Everyone noted that Andrews was standing perfectly to attention and answered forthrightly.

"Your plea is noted. Do you have anything to say in mitigation?" The captain continued the interrogation.

"No, Sir," the accused answered.

"Very well. This is a most serious offence. Knowing you were the only person on watch in a dived submarine, you fell asleep. It must have been perfectly clear that your duty was to ensure that the submarine maintained its depth, neither sinking nor rising. There can therefore be no question that your orders might have been misunderstood. If *E57* had sunk, she could have been crushed like a tin can. In the event, she rose and remained just beneath the surface but with periscope standards showing. The submarine could easily have been detected and then rammed by enemy forces. This whole situation could have been catastrophic for *E57* and her entire ship's company. I can hardly think of any more heinous crime in wartime whilst in enemy territory." The submarine's captain was incandescent. His eyes bored into the man in front of him.

With hardly a moment's pause, he continued, "In accordance with the King's Regulations, I sentence you to death. The sentence will be carried out at eight o'clock."

Both the first lieutenant and coxswain started at this announcement, not expecting this harshest of punishments. The latter was just about able to stutter, "The . . . the . . sentence is . . . death. Recorded, Sir. Leading Telegraphist Andrews, on cap! Salute. About turn. Quick march." Prescott led Andrews forward to the crew accommodation space, ordering all others to leave.

In a submarine, there was no other place to hold such proceedings except in the control room. There was no lectern to act as a "table" and only the chart table on which the commanding officer could rest his reference papers. Accordingly, all the watchkeepers had listened intently to what was going on. There was an audible intake of breath throughout the submarine on hearing the punishment. It was not yet four-thirty, leaving Andrews such a short time to live.

"First Lieutenant," the captain announced, "we will remain in this position and surface at seven o'clock. I will carry out the sentence myself on the casing. Make all the necessary arrangements." After that, Ted walked over to his chair, sat down and picked up his book to begin reading. He was trying to act as if this was a regular, everyday event, knowing that his crew were watching him intently. "Aye, aye, Sir," was the muted response.

6

Coxswain Albert Prescott sat disconsolately with Andrews in the torpedo space, having ordered two cups of tea. Hearing the death sentence had been like a direct blow to his solar plexus, knocking all the wind from him. He felt he had failed. After all, it was his job to look after 'the lads', no matter what trouble they got into, typically after too much drink ashore. This time, however, he was at a complete loss about what to do. He could not even find any words of comfort for the condemned man sitting beside him. The charge was irrefutable, and the sentence was only to be expected in the circumstances. But he had got to know this young man slightly, recognised his qualities and seen him work so hard. It was only bad luck, he was sure, that the wireless gear wasn't working. He wasn't technically minded himself, but *he* knew that salt water and electrics do not mix, and this was probably just a case of that. Andrews said nothing and simply sat with his elbows on his knees and head in his hands. The tea arrived, and the coxswain encouraged his young charge to drink it. The kindly senior rating also called for a pencil and some paper for Andrews to write any final letters home.

Bloody war! Bloody Fritzes! Albert Prescott made up his mind and determined he needed to talk to the first lieutenant.

7

When the boat was safely on the surface with the motors stopped, Hardacre took the watch and, as arranged with Hackett-Jones, stood down the lookout so that no one would hear the intended discussion. Down below, the first lieutenant approached his captain with much trepidation. "Excuse me, Sir. Would it be possible for the coxswain and I to confer with you on the bridge?" he started in whispered tones. "We have no experience of what the procedure should be." A curt nod was the only response. When this small party of three had mustered at the after end of the bridge platform, Hackett-Jones took a deep breath and addressed his commanding officer.

"Sir, the coxswain has reported to me some aspects of mitigation which I believe you should hear."

Very tight-lipped, he held his first lieutenant firmly in his gaze, not looking at the senior rate, "Well, what have you got to say, Cox'n?"

"He is guilty of being asleep on watch, of course, but I don't believe that Andrews should take all the blame for this terrible event. The whole crew is aware of how hard he has been working, day and night, to try to get his communications equipment working correctly. He is fully aware of the frustration that you have felt about the poor radio reception on board and Andrews has truly been doing everything within his capabilities to improve the situation." The coxswain stopped, controlling his emotions, before continuing. "I knew he was dog-tired, but still it was _me_ who placed him on watch last night. It is my job to get to know and manage the crew on your behalf and I failed to do so correctly. This incident is as much my fault as it is Andrews'. Forgive me, Sir, I certainly don't want to be impertinent, but I believe this should be taken into account." His captain said nothing but just turned and looked sternly at him.

"Captain, Sir, similarly I feel some responsibility," Hackett-Jones backed up the most senior rating aboard. "Although I followed the procedures we have employed on previous nights, it might have been necessary to take in more water last night to keep the submarine sitting firmly on the layer. Clearly, the boat did become light and came shallow. Yes, Andrews was there to report if this occurred, but it may have been _my_ error of judgement that caused the problem." He paused and took a deep breath before continuing. "Respectfully, Sir, I would also like to point out that no one else can take on Andrews' role should he . . . er . . . become unavailable. We must be able to remain in some contact with HQ – no matter how poor the communications – for the remainder of our patrol."

Ted nodded almost imperceptibly. "You're both dismissed: carry on below."

When they had disappeared down the conning tower, he turned to Hardacre, "Did you hear that? I seem to have made the wrong decision again." More to himself than to the other officer, he shook his head and questioned, "How on earth am I to extricate myself from this mess without seeming indecisive and totally irresponsible? There's no correct procedure to deal with any of this."

"No," his navigator agreed. "Sometimes you simply have to trust yourself to do what you believe is right."

Hardacre stopped, thinking he might have implied some blame or identified a character weakness. Nonetheless, the captain had taken him into his confidence, and Hardacre was left wondering how their relationship now stood. Was he still a subordinate, even though a senior one? Or a brother officer whom he was asking for advice? Or possibly even a friend? He bit the bullet and spoke candidly. "I think you underestimate the loyalty and high regard in which your people hold you. They know you have high standards, and everyone works so hard to meet them. After all, keeping the submarine and them safe is ultimately down to you. You must appreciate that the first lieutenant and cox'n showed real courage to bring these issues to you, and it is of enormous credit *to them* that they did. But they knew you would be approachable and listen to what they had to say, which reflects very well on *your* leadership style. I have seen too many captains who are absolute Tartars, with their crews simply living in fear and never daring to cross them, right or wrong. What about the collision between *Camperdown* and *Victoria*; no one was willing to stand up to that bully, Tryon. And look what happened! Over three hundred sailors died when *Victoria* went down. Had Tryon listened for *just one second* to his staff commander and flag lieutenant, that disaster would have been averted." Hardacre knew he was sailing close to the wind but decided to push his luck. "Listen," he persisted. "Your crew will continue to follow you no matter what you decide. You have made it perfectly clear that you'll stand no truck with anything less than the highest standards. If you give anyone responsibility, you expect them to do their duty." He could see that his remarks were hitting home, so he concluded, "Let's face it, you need Andrews; so why not 'stand over' to await a proper trial when we're back safely?" After a pregnant pause, Hardacre added, "There was a just 'stand over' once before and you were given a second chance."

With unwelcome and near-forgotten memories flooding back into his brain, Ted swung around with eyes blazing. Hardacre thought he was about to be hit. "Don't . . *you* . . *dare* . . lecture me about that!" the captain spat out before disappearing down the conning tower.

8

Just before eight o'clock, the coxswain mustered the other senior rates and some leading hands on the for'd casing, towards the bow and facing aft. He then brought up Andrews. The first lieutenant followed and stopped immediately below the bridge structure, facing forward. When he saw that all was prepared, Hackett-Jones shouted up to the bridge that they were ready for the captain. *E57*'s commanding officer duly appeared with a pistol strapped around his waist, swinging himself over the bridge surround and down the ladder onto the casing.

"Leading Telegraphist Andrews for punishment, Sir," reported the first lieutenant, standing to attention and saluting smartly. He turned about before taking up his previous position.

Their captain positioned himself about six feet in front of the telegraphist. He addressed the assembled ship's company in level, unemotional tones. "We are here deep within enemy territory and we have no one other than ourselves on whom we can rely. It takes only one foolish act by any one of us — me included — to cause our mission to fail. We might yet have to give up our lives to do our duty – I cannot promise that we won't – but I will *not* allow us to be sacrificed on account of some avoidable error or simple negligence. *I* require you all to perform your duties to the *absolute best* of your abilities, and neither do your crew mates all around you deserve anything less. You'll understand, therefore, that Andrews' crime is *unforgivable*, resulting in the sentence awarded."

Ted stopped to allow his statement to sink in. Unintentionally, his own words took him back to years before, listening to *Britannia's* commander before being birched. He understood only now, at this instant, why he *had* to be punished despite the whole situation being so *unfair*. The senior officer's words came back to him about how some crimes can n*ever* be excused – no matter what the circumstances. Ted consoled himself with the thought that Andrews had admitted his offence and, accordingly, must bear the consequences. Surely, all Ted had done had been to award the proper, authorised punishment? But was *he* being fair? Was *he* being just? Hardacre's observation that Ted himself had been given a second chance cut him to the bone.

He looked at Andrews' young face, grey with the discomforts they had all endured. His eyes were tiny and deeply sunk from the few opportunities for sleep he had had since they sailed. His shoulders sagged, and his posture was one of total hopelessness. His hair was lank from no washing, and his clothes were bedraggled. All these were effects of his service to his country, which now demanded revenge. But for what? In front of him was a defeated, if not destroyed, man and – with a jolt – it suddenly occurred to Ted that *he* was responsible. Had he been bullying the man, simply empowered by his position as captain? More starkly and unexpectedly, he saw the same despair marked in the whole countenance and bearing of his coxswain. He had relied on this man for many years, in the certain knowledge that Prescott would never let him down. Ted had to look away. He could not show weakness. His mind raced before deciding how to proceed.

"Just as we all need each other to carry out our assigned duties," the captain explained to his crew, "so we also need Andrews to be able to continue our mission. Accordingly, his crime is not forgotten but I have decided to commute his sentence to one of remaining onboard until his case can be properly reconsidered when safely alongside. I do not have a copy of King's Regulations to hand and, in view of the most serious nature of this offence and appropriate punishment, I need to be certain that their terms are met exactly." Not waiting to judge the reaction, he ordered, "First Lieutenant, carry on."

As their captain turned to climb back up to the bridge, Coxswain Prescott immediately stepped forward to support Andrews, whom he could see was about to collapse.

To a man, the whole crew felt much relief, and the depression everyone had experienced lifted rapidly. Perhaps illogically, this tightly-knit band of men believed they had *all* let their captain down to some extent. Not a single one of them questioned a commanding officer's right to execute anyone guilty of a serious enough charge, despite what he had claimed about King's Regulations. After such a shock, some of them realised too that they hadn't been particularly friendly to the newcomer and made efforts to bring Andrews into conversations and hear what he had to say. As must be expected amongst sailors, there was even a growing amount of light banter about Andrews being required 'to remain onboard' – a sentence they were all sharing! The dark mood aboard lifted as the day progressed. The dramatic events of the early morning were put aside – but hardly forgotten – with the usual routine being resumed.

Patrolling again off the north coast, there was little evidence of reinforcement traffic, and available targets were reduced to the normal dhows and fishing vessels. Three of these were set alight when contraband was discovered onboard, but only after seeing their crews safely away in their tenders. Smoke signals were observed emanating from the high points along the coast, but these invitations to come and play were not taken up by patrol boats as before.

Ted was not content. Without targets, they were achieving nothing and time was passing. *E57* had *not* been sent here to kick her heels as she was.

Chapter 8 – If They Won't Fight Us

1

To complete a dramatic day, *E57* transited towards her communications billet to check in with HQ. This operation lasted more than three hours – as now anticipated – taking an hour to get only four words exchanged. The aerial was sparking badly and kept the crew on tenterhooks throughout. The only difference was that the captain left Andrews alone to his duties. No new helpful information was received, so the submarine headed back north-eastwards. Instead of turning southeast towards their normal overnight position in the centre of their captive sea, she held her course. Ted called his officers, coxswain and senior engineer to the bridge to appraise them of his future requirements.

"The original purpose of attacking the forts at the entrance to the Dardanelles was to allow a fleet to sail safely through the Straits. The idea was for the ships to stand off Constantinople to hold the Turks' capital at risk," he reminded them. "Well, of course, we are not a fleet, but I think we should give more attention to the Ottoman's major city as was originally intended. I will attempt to enter the Golden Horn tomorrow." This was a gutsy move: the others looked at one another with wide eyes.

Giving no chance for comment, Ted continued, "The other matter I want to discuss concerns conditions on board. By diving overnight and resting on the saline layer, the atmosphere is becoming increasingly dank and foul during the day. It's unavoidable, I know, but everywhere there are piles of sodden linen and everything is dripping with sweat before the evening. I need everybody to be at the top of their game tomorrow, so we should give the boat a good blow-through overnight tonight. We will not dive but will head directly towards Constantinople. Get everyone to try and clear up as best they can, Coxswain, and you too, of course, Chief. Nonetheless, I also want the crew to be as rested as possible. If you would kindly take the watch, Number One, the navigator and I will work on a plan. I intend to dive at about six o'clock in the morning, just as Oxia Island becomes visible. Is that all clear? Good: we will carry on below."

It was a typically balmy night. Despite the clearing up, additional watch-keeping requirements and thumping engines, most of the crew achieved sufficient respite and more restful sleep on account of the fresh air in the submarine. With no clear horizon visible, the bridge watchkeepers strained their eyes to maintain a good lookout. By quarter to six, they could smell the approaching dawn, and the barely lighter sky towards the east revealed the faint tops of Oxia, standing two hundred feet high. Without further ado, the captain was called, and the submarine dived in a controlled manner. They could both fix their position and assess the local currents more accurately as they passed the island. With propeller revolutions for five knots rung on, they were making no better than two-and-a-half knots against the current syphoning out of the Bosphorus. Ted prepared to take the boat deep to make his approach to the harbour and was taking a last all-round look.

"That bearing!" was the sudden cry as the captain flipped up the periscope handles. "There's a warship at green one-zero-zero at a range of about three thousand yards. Get me the silhouette book."

Hardacre already had the recognition book of Ottoman warships open on the chart table, and he passed it to the captain. The latter flicked through the pages before finally stopping on one. "It's a Peik-i-Shevket class torpedo cruiser. Standby Number One and Two tubes. Up periscope!

"Bearing . . . . that!" He paused for a few seconds more before lowering the periscope.

"His range is two thousand five hundred yards but we are well abaft his starboard beam. Stand down the torpedo tubes - we'll hope for bigger targets in the harbour. Mark his position on the chart in case he becomes a problem in our exit," he instructed his navigator. "Half ahead together. Six down. Keep sixty feet. Set revolutions for seven knots," Ted ordered. "We'll run like this for twenty minutes."

He was surprised to find himself so far north when he next raised the periscope. *E57* was almost abeam Seraglio Point, marking the entrance to the harbour on the port side and already well within the Bosporus Straits. The saline counter-current had done its work again, and Ted was disappointed with himself that he hadn't anticipated this. After all, it was right here that the caliph of yore had consigned his wife to the deep, only to have her body returned a couple of days later. Nonetheless, they were in the centre of the channel and navigationally safe, with his oversight helpfully reducing the time in the danger zone. He hoped his luck would hold.

He pointed carefully at the chart to inform Hardacre of the position of the boat; there was no need to be more accurate at this stage. Fighting against a racing stream, Ted was only too aware that every time he took an observation, it would create a significant white 'feather' of spray and a noticeable wake. He waited a full ten minutes before raising the periscope again, hoping to have a good look west into the harbour to see what targets might be lurking. The scene that met him was mesmerising. Compared with the drab interior of the submarine, the morning sun now picked out every colour of the mosques, palaces and other grand houses, greenery, flowers and trees that lined the waterfront. He could look several miles up into the Golden Horn harbour from his new location. This most natural and protected haven stretched five miles northwest away from the Bosporus. It had been used as a refuge from bad weather since before Byzantine times until it fell into the Ottomans' hands in 1453.

Ted could see one or two possible targets berthed alongside but no obvious patrolling warships or other defences. With the current trying ever to carry him southward, he decided to continue on his northerly course for another ten minutes before turning in to attack. All torpedo tubes were prepared for action. From his position in the control room, the first lieutenant turned his head fore and aft to order, "*E57* is about to enter Constantinople harbour. Everyone is to remain alert and silent, moving around as little as possible. Pass the word." The resulting whisper hushed as it searched out people in hidden places in the furthest reaches of the vessel until disappearing altogether. The submarine and her people merged into a single entity.

The boat started the long turn to port to head southwest at the appointed time. Ted identified two large transport ships tied up at the Arsenal Wharf and altered his heading slightly to bring them right ahead. He had little time to waste as the current was carrying him down rapidly, so he decided to attack both targets simultaneously. He raised the periscope when steady on course.

"FIRE NUMBER ONE TUBE!"

"FIRE NUMBER TWO TUBE!"

He was disappointed to see no indication that the port tube had fired correctly. Nevertheless, the starboard torpedo could be seen speeding on its way as intended. There was no time to reload and fire again. "Down periscope. Port twenty."

At the same instant, everyone could suddenly hear the loud noise of a racing propeller, with its volume increasing by the second. The periscope had reached only deck level before being ordered up again. Ted frantically searched left and right, before stopping on the port beam.

"Full ahead together. Midships. Six down. Keep forty feet." When the boat was descending as ordered, he continued, "Helm hard a'port."

No sooner had the submarine reached its ordered depth than the racket passed ahead and just above them before heading off somewhere to the north. Then there was a loud explosion on the port side.

The captain briefed his crew, "We must have been spotted from the shore and they fired a torpedo at us. Never mind," he added with a smile, "they missed and it seems we hit one target. Navigator, give me a good course to steer to get us out of the harbour."

Before Hardacre could reply, unwelcome scraping could be heard from for'd. The bow started to come up rapidly, and the submarine rose bodily.

"Full astern together! First Lieutenant, flood in everything you can. We must not expose ourselves here." As if to reinforce the captain's words, fall of shot began to be heard all around them, with shrapnel tinkling down onto the casing: the Turks had joined the action with surprising alacrity. There broke out onboard a pandemonium of shouted orders and activity: some valves were opened, others were shut. High-pressure air was vented rapidly inboard, dulling people's hearing, and sailors rushed aft to lighten the bows. Amid this ordered chaos, all eyes in the control room were focused on the depth gauge.

The long black needle of the depth gauge was winding its way inexorably counter-clockwise. Thirty feet. Slowing now but still passing twenty feet. Nineteen feet. Nineteen feet. Eighteen feet. Eighteen feet. Eighteen feet. Nineteen feet. Nineteen feet. Twenty feet. The propellers were digging into the water with all their might and beginning to drag the submarine astern. In the same manner, however, Ted thought he must be creating a colossal backwash that would reveal the submarine's position to its pursuers. The bow was scraping back down the slope, and the boat was gaining depth slowly whilst still pinned by the bow to the shore. Everyone aboard could now hear ships' propellers circling overhead and knew they were still in danger of having the bridge rammed. Ted allowed the submarine to descend to forty feet before stopping the motors. He stepped across to the chart table to assess *E57*'s situation.

"Where do you think we are, Navigator? It makes no sense. Could there be an uncharted shallow patch in the centre of the harbour?"

"I think that's unlikely, Sir; this harbour is used all the time and, no matter how poor our charts, such an obstruction would have been recorded. All I can surmise is that there might be a strong back-eddy swirling around towards the north shore, perhaps aided by the saline current beneath it. If we were being washed down southwards by the main current, we wouldn't have gone aground at the bow with the ship's head northwest." Hardacre's reasoning seemed totally logical, and Ted started nodding.

"We're going to stay here," he announced. "Let's see if the current can give us a clue about where we are."

So, they remained, with all eyes shifted from the depth gauge to the gyro repeater. It stubbornly remained stock still. After five minutes, the ship's head had moved only a degree or two to starboard, failing to guarantee the submarine's movement. Nevertheless, a further five minutes allowed the boat to swing another three or four degrees, indicating a definite trend, particularly because *E57* was so firmly anchored at the bow. This hiatus led their pursuers to believe that the submarine had already escaped its previous position, and they seemed to have moved away to continue their hunt.

Ted ordered Hackett-Jones to start getting *E57* back in trim as he began to propel astern with the helm hard over to starboard. As a result, the boat continued bumping down the bank until, at last, at about fifty feet, she floated clear. The captain allowed the ship's head to swing to the east before propelling ahead.

"Well done; you seem to have been right, Navigator. We submariners call this navigating 'by guess and by God'," he informed Hardacre whilst also trying to relieve some of the tension in the control room. "We will estimate when we are back in the centre of the channel by looking at how much helm has to be applied to keep the ordered course. Then we will turn southwards and expect the current to carry us out."

They could hear the propellers of several ships crisscrossing overhead, but Ted held his nerve and resisted the temptation to have a look. After thirty minutes and when the sounds of their pursuers had grown faint, *E57* returned to periscope depth. The submarine was in clear water with the closest land five thousand yards to the northwest, and he could make out Oxia about eight thousand yards a little east of south. Satisfied that they were in a safe position, Ted took a final all-round look to ensure there were no enemy warships to the southwest that might impede their passage. He was about to lower the periscope when he spotted a shape coming clear of the left side of the island. He paused just a moment.

"Standby. Bearing . . . . that!" The periscope handles clicked up. The captain, checking his watch, announced to his crew, "It's the torpedo cruiser I saw earlier. She must have been summoned to help with the search for us. The range is one thousand eight hundred yards and I am thirty degrees on her port bow. Standby Number One and Two tubes. Full ahead starboard; half ahead port; starboard thirty. Six degrees bow down; keep thirty feet. Steer east. I need to close the distance off track."

The LTO came rushing aft from the torpedo stowage compartment.

"Captain, Sir. We have only two reloads available in the forends: one's nearly been loaded into the port tube," he reported.

"Very good," his commanding officer replied. "Get on with it; we cannot delay! Standby Number Two tube as soon as it's ready. Standby the port beam tube."

With the minimum time available to get into an attacking position, after only two minutes Ted ordered the motors to be stopped and the submarine to return to periscope depth. Checking and rechecking his calculations in his head, he stood in the correct position to train the periscope immediately onto the deflection angle, constantly monitoring the depth, trim and rapidly slowing speed. He again looked at his watch.

"Number two tube loaded, Captain!" came the shout from the fore-ends.

"Up periscope. Standby Number Two tube." A few seconds later, he would have missed his chance: the vertical hairline in the centre of his view was already on the target's forward gun. He waited until it aligned with the bridge.

"Fire! Down periscope." The periscope eyepiece had hardly gone down two feet before it was ordered back up. "Torpedo running true," the captain informed his crew whilst continuing to watch events unfold. "Wait! He's under wheel to port." The periscope handles clicked up. "Full ahead together; Port Thirty; standby Port Beam Tube; steer southeast!" He watched the gyro repeat as it clicked tormentingly slowly clockwise. The instant he was on course, he shouted, "Fire! ten degrees bow down; keep sixty feet." All Ted hoped to achieve with this second torpedo was to distract his attacker and allow *E57* to get deep before being rammed.

Fifteen seconds later, the boat was rocked by a vast explosion, putting out lights and causing many sparks as electrical breakers jumped. Everybody aboard thought they had been attacked by some new fiendish anti-submarine device. They visibly cowered, expecting a second detonation to send them to oblivion. It didn't come, and nor did the sound of propellers announce their pursuer's arrival directly overhead. Instead, they were greeted by a clamour of grating metal as it twisted and turned. Having opened two hundred yards or so, *E57* returned to periscope depth. It transpired that their captain had achieved a miraculous shot at a fast warship coming directly towards them, presenting the minimum target for the torpedo, which successfully detonated at minimum range. The bow of the ship had been blown off. Together with her momentum, the damage had caused the vessel to sheer around to be lying beam onto the submarine, listing heavily to starboard.

As he was taking in the scene, trying to fathom what had occurred, Ted's peripheral vision caught the flash of a gun. The gun crew had remained at its post on the deck aft, laying down remarkably accurate fire on his periscope. As he swung round to look directly at them, there was a clearly audible "clang", severe vibration on the periscope and the eyepiece, knocking Ted backwards. The view went blank. Holding his eye, he indicated the periscope to be lowered, but it went down only two or three feet before grinding to a stop. The captain waited to open the distance further from the stricken vessel before raising his after periscope. The torpedo cruiser was settling rapidly by the bow, but *E57* was immediately spotted, and the staunch gun crew re-engaged. But, as Ted watched, they managed to get away only two further rounds before the warship rolled rapidly to starboard, turned turtle and disappeared beneath the waves. Mentally, he saluted those gallant warriors who stood their ground in defending their ship, giving no thought to their own safety.

Word went around the boat about what had been achieved. Morale was sky-high as *E57* opened to the southwest. But there was important work to be done. The torpedo in the stern tube had to be unloaded and manhandled forward as one of the only two remaining weapons. There was no question of returning to recover the first torpedo fired at the warship, located just outside their enemy's front door. When the weapon had been moved and the transfer rails unrigged, the submarine surfaced and continued slowly westwards. Inspection of the foremost periscope showed that it had indeed been hit, with the shot passing clean through the tube. Chief Bowers couldn't remove the damaged section by simply unbolting it because it was sealed with lead to make the joint watertight.

2

That evening communications with *Astor* took nearly twice as long. Ted briefed HQ as concisely as possible on *E57*'s achievements that day and reported that he had only two torpedoes remaining. He knew this information would be necessary to plan for the next boat to transit the Dardanelles and relieve him to maintain a continuous patrol in the Sea of Marmara. He was ordered to wait for a response. Eventually, letter by letter, his future instructions arrived.

"NO RELIEF READY STOP TORGUT REIS TO
BOMBARD ALLIED FORCES FROM
GALLIPOLI AREA AT TIME UNKNOWN STOP
IMPERATIVE TO INTERCEPT ENDS"

Whilst this signalling saga continued, the senior engineer's team had lit a fire around the junction of the lower and upper halves of the periscope to melt the sealing lead. Only after two hours' struggle did they manage to remove the top section, which was about six feet six inches long. Bowers could see that only the glass of the bottom lens had kept the sea from flooding in. So, the senior engineer rendered what remained of the forward periscope watertight with a wooden bung covered with a canvas square tied down securely. He reported his success to the first lieutenant, who informed his captain down by the radio gear.

Despite the additional time it would take, Ted sent another message to inform his superiors that he had a single, functioning periscope. He required a new top section if any method at all could be found to deliver it to the submarine. An unlikely expectation, he thought, but it was worth asking. A second periscope would improve his chances of a successful attack on the pre-dreadnought battleship assigned as his priority target.

A simple "- R -" meaning "Received" was his only reply. It had been a long day for everybody. Because the submarine had been surfaced with the diesels pulling fresh air through the boat for most of the afternoon and evening, Ted decided that everyone would be better rested if they dived overnight and settled on the saline layer.

3

The next morning, Ted summoned his officers and senior rates. Now on Day Twelve of the patrol, he informed them of the last evening's exchanges with HQ and the resultant tasking. So that he could make a proper plan for the remaining time, he again ordered a full stocktake of all consumable stores: diesel fuel; lubricating oil; hydraulic oil; fresh water; dried and fresh victuals; gun cotton; rifle bullets; et cetera, et cetera. Dismissing the senior ratings to undertake the necessary investigations, he opened the discussion with his officers. "We must obviously set aside our two remaining torpedoes for the expected encounter with the *Torgut Reis*, so I've been thinking hard about how we should spend our time waiting for her to appear. We should have plenty of diesel fuel – the petty officer stoker will confirm that – and I believe we should make as much of a nuisance of ourselves as we can in all key areas of the Marmara." He outlined his intentions, "I want us to make *E57*'s presence felt and to keep reinforcement traffic to a minimum. We will have the torpedoes for self-defence *in extremis*, but we should try to keep clear of enemy warships. We must not prejudice our readiness for our number one task. Other than that,

I'd be grateful if you'd give the matter some thought and let me know if you have any ideas."

The stocktake results were much as expected, and the submarine's status was assessed as tolerable for two more weeks on patrol. The fresh provisions purloined from the small craft had certainly served to eke out their victuals, and this situation was likely to continue in their amended *modus operandi*. On patrols in the North Sea, not only was it the rancid food that determined the end of the operation. The persistent tiredness of everyone aboard, particularly the stress on commanding officers, was a significant factor. Poor visibility, rough weather, never-ending rolling and vertical 'pumping' of the boat through several feet, together with constant anxiety when operating within minefields and in areas of determined enemy patrols, all took a severe toll. Despite being deep within enemy territory and with no direct route back to friendly harbours, their situation was now different. Ted was confident his submarine could remain on patrol until the job had been done or *E57*'s relief had arrived.

They started as they meant to go on and stopped two dhows that day, both of which were set ablaze after the crews had left, with the submarine not even bothering to tie up alongside one to disguise her presence. The usual smoke signals duly appeared along the high cliffs, but no patrol vessels ventured out to interrupt their operations.

As they were completing their evening meal, Hackett-Jones put down his cutlery and addressed his captain. "I've been thinking about what you said this morning, Sir," he started. "Our campaign to reduce reinforcement by sea seems to have been relatively successful – even just by our presence here – but the Turks must still be receiving support via other overland routes, and I've been thinking about what we can do on that front. No doubt you heard about Captain Larken in the *Doris* and her disruption of the railways at Alexandretta. Well, we don't have a gun, but we have plenty of gun cotton and could land a small shore party to blow up some track. That would certainly help the cause and attract Johnny Turk's attention."

"That's certainly a novel concept," responded his superior, "but we really don't have the manpower to spare, let alone a party of marines. Each Man Jack aboard has a role to play, and we couldn't risk losing a single one of them." Being careful not to discount his second-in-command's suggestion again, he added, "I'm not dismissing the idea out of hand, but I can't see how it could be practicable."

That evening before turning in, the first lieutenant pored over the chart to see how his innovative scheme might be achieved. In the morning, he approached Ted again, inviting him over to the chart table.

"You see the railway line is a very short distance inland here, Sir." Hackett-Jones indicated the northern shore of the Gulf of Izmid with his index finger. "Just inside the Gulf, there is plenty of deep water, and the boat should be able to approach close inshore without danger. Also, you said you want to be as much of a nuisance as possible: well, this is in an area we haven't visited before. It's still only about twenty miles east of Oxia Island, so we could get back to Constantinople quickly if needed. In addition, this is the famous Baghdad Railway that serves the east of the Ottoman Empire. Attacking that would undoubtedly be something of a coup!

"Your point about not being able to spare any men is of course most important," the first lieutenant conceded. "But what if just one man took on this task? What I mean to say is . . . *I* could do it, Sir, as possibly the most redundant person aboard."

Ted had to smile. This was typical Hackett-Jones: amusing, energetic, brave, but, this time, unusually self-deprecating. Nonetheless, *E57* must remain in the west, on the other side of the Sea of Marmara, where possible routes for his target coalesce to pass Gallipoli, where the likelihood of interception would be greatest. Thus, he still believed the whole concept was a non-starter. He was pleased his first lieutenant had thought this idea through, presented his case well and addressed the concerns raised. "We'll see," is all the captain committed himself to.

Communicating again with HQ that evening, they received more information.

"TARGET DELAYED SEVEN DAYS STOP
PERISCOPE DELIVERY VIA BANDIRMA STOP
DETAILS IN THREE DAYS ENDS"

This cast a different light on Hackett-Jones' plan: they now had time to carry out a shore raid without prejudicing their prime objective.

4

To lay a false trail, first light the following morning found *E57* off Marmara Ereglisi on the north coast, harrying the fishing vessels that operated from that small harbour. Then she dived and continued twenty or so miles, doing the same off Rodosto to give indication of a westwards drift. Waiting for the smoke to rise from the high cliffs, confirming she had been spotted, the submarine again submerged. The submarine had eighty miles to the target area, so they continued dived to a position more than ten miles east of Marmara Island and out of sight from any shore. The boat then surfaced to continue her passage to the extreme eastern end of the Sea of Marmara to arrive with full batteries. When not on watch, the first lieutenant had worked with Chief Bowers. Together they built a small floating platform on which Hackett-Jones could put his clothes, gun cotton and revolver to keep them dry whilst he swam ashore. A simple square shape, the corner fixings were not secured fully so that they could squeeze the platform into a diamond shape to manoeuvre it out of the submarine's hatch before tightening it up once outside.

The submarine arrived in the approaches to the Gulf of Izmid in the late afternoon, still with sufficient light for a proper dived reconnaissance of the area. The entrance was only three miles wide, and the boat would have to travel another six miles past this to be off the intended landing area. Interpreting the topography of the shore, they surmised that the railway line must travel across at least one viaduct in that area, and, if so, that would be Hackett-Jones' target. They could detect no patrol craft or any other apparent military activity, so the captain decided they would continue inshore to get a closer look. Remaining in the centre of the channel and without a racing current to contend with, they felt safe to keep the periscope raised whilst surveying the scene. They were far enough offshore not to be spotted. The Gulf narrowed again to less than two miles by Diliskelesi, but they hoped to remain west of that area. *E57* closed the northern shore, with the setting sun conveniently lighting their chosen target area. As if on cue, a moving column of smoke indicated the location of the railway line, with the train eventually coming into view over a latticed viaduct. The submarine's officers all agreed that this was a viable enterprise, and the boat gently backed away into deeper water to await dusk.

Only when it was totally dark did the captain think it was safe to surface. The makeshift raft was manhandled onto the casing just aft of the bridge, and final preparations were completed whilst still away from the shore. Chief Bowers fussed over their invention and ensured it was ready for its purpose before lashing it down lightly.

The captain took his rightful place on the bridge and ordered everyone else below except for a solitary lookout. Checking with the control room that all was ready, he ordered the boat to be trimmed down. He waited until just the conning tower was clear of the water before starting to propel ahead at minimum speed on one shaft. The chart showed the coast shelved steeply into the depths here, but Ted took no chances. He believed a near-dived approach would conceal *E57*'s presence from any eyes on the rocks above whilst also easing their escape should they unexpectedly run aground away from the shore or come under fire. The submarine's bow gently nudged the bottom a matter of yards off the beach, and Hackett-Jones was up to the bridge in a flash.

"Go well, Number One," Ted wished him luck, offering his hand. "You know we have even more important tasks ahead so, remember, I don't want you taking *any* undue risks. I really *do* need you to come back in one piece. We'll be right here in this bay, waiting for your signal."

Without further ado, the brave first lieutenant climbed down from the bridge, loaded up his raft and released its fastenings before launching off the boat.

Holding the raft ahead of him both to steer it and as a buoyancy aid, Hackett-Jones paddled towards the shore, trying not to splash as he kicked his legs. Despite the constraints of submarine living, he kept reasonably fit, and the short swim did not challenge him excessively. Regardless, the beach provided little welcome, armed with sharp stones and slippery rocks. The land rose quickly above it, which at least provided some cover from any searching eyes. The shoreline here was five yards wide at most, however, and Hackett-Jones had difficulty finding somewhere to hide his raft for the return journey. Likewise, there was no obvious path to take him inland. He dressed, hoisted his bag of essentials over his shoulder, and climbed up the slope.

After about fifty yards, the land started to flatten a little. Squinting into the gloom, the railway track was undoubtedly further inland than they had thought. He stumbled on but was suddenly brought to a stop by the frantic barking of dogs. He thought he could just make out the silhouette of a small farm or house to his right. He paused for a few moments, but there seemed to be no reaction to this canine alert. He continued as silently as he could. Eventually, the barking behind him faded before ceasing altogether.

He was breathing quite hard by now after his steady climb, and he checked with his hand-held compass that he was still heading in a northerly direction. He had landed thirty minutes before and was concerned that he had yet to reach the railway line: could it really be this far inland, or had he somehow missed it? As if in answer, he immediately came across a steeper rise and guessed this was part of the supporting embankment. He was right. As he came up to track level, he stopped and looked carefully left and right for any activity. Sensing none, he pulled himself up level with the track, turned left and started off towards the viaduct. His long legs made it easy to progress quietly, stepping from sleeper to sleeper without the crunch of gravel.

He must have progressed some three or four hundred yards in this manner before reaching a curve in the track. Advancing more gingerly, he ascertained that this was the start of the viaduct structure but there, guarding it, were three Turkish soldiers who were relaxing beside a campfire. Cursing his luck but remembering his captain's warning not to take undue risk, he retreated back up the line. He remembered he had passed a culvert under the track not fifty yards further back. If it were impossible to blow up the viaduct without undue risk, he decided that destroying a part of the track would still inconvenience his enemy. He relocated the culvert, finding it to be a brickwork support with a hollow underneath, and commenced his preparations. Five minutes later, he was content that the Ottoman soldiers had made no move. He was ready to trigger the explosion, but there was danger yet. The fuse had to be fired by a pistol: that would cause a loud report, and the night was still. Checking that he was ready to flee, Hackett-Jones gathered up all his accoutrements, tried to muffle the noise by wrapping the pistol with rags and then fired it.

The resulting 'crack' shattered the night's silence. Birds in the woods all around signalled their displeasure at the disturbance to their slumbers. There was no way the guards would not have heard, but rather than starting to escape in the opposite direction, Hackett-Jones rushed a few yards towards them in the time he had. As soon as he saw the soldiers coming around the curve, he fired two shots at them and only then did he dive off to the left and down the side of the embankment. He wanted them to follow him and turn off the track before reaching the culvert and discovering the surprise he had left.

The Turks managed to get away a couple of wild shots at this unexpected interloper and, with their night vision destroyed by the firelight, hardly saw him before he disappeared out of sight. Hackett-Jones slithered down the rough slope, grazing the backs of his legs and arms before regaining an upright stance. He sprinted a considerable distance parallel to the track in an easterly direction, trying to return to a position opposite the bay where *E57* was waiting. He veered off toward the beach when he thought he'd gone far enough. The land was rough with dips and hollows, and he had to take extreme care not to twist an ankle or, worse, break a limb. There were trees ahead of him now, which he hoped would disguise his silhouette as he left the shadow of the embankment. He would have better cover once he had reached them. Shots were beginning to whistle past him, and these few soldiers managed to keep up a surprising rate of fire. It was also clear that they were still in pursuit rather than remaining at their post and guarding the railway. He had just reached the trees when there was a satisfying flash, a rumble and applause from a shower of stone and rock. The sixteen pounds of guncotton had done its work. The rifles were silent for a few seconds before the fusillade was renewed, striking the trees around their target.

Hackett-Jones felt safer in the copse but had now to avoid the branches, twigs and brambles that tore into his face. They ripped the skin on his arms as he raised them to defend himself. He must take even more care not to trip over tree roots. Panting hard now, the noise of his pursuers seemed to quieten, but he dared not slacken his pace. Ten minutes later, the farm dogs re-joined their alert: but these barks were coming from his right, indicating he had overcompensated and was on the other side of the farm. This time, however, lamps were being lit, and Hackett-Jones' ardent wish was that the dogs would not be released to join in the pursuit. Tiring rapidly, his pace was reduced to a fast walk as he sucked in the night air to revive his efforts. After a seeming age, he reached the place where the land fell away steeply towards the unseen beach. Nonetheless, he could not locate his previous – or indeed any – route down as he searched backwards and forwards. Moving a considerable distance towards the east, he finally found a place to descend by sliding down on his bottom. Not before time: he could hear a general hubbub and shouted orders becoming louder and advancing in his direction. Obviously, the guarding party had been joined by reinforcements.

On the beach, Hackett-Jones realised he couldn't bring *E57* in to rescue him because it would place the submarine in too much danger. Instead, he dived directly into the water and decided to get a considerable distance offshore before giving the return signal. Still fully clothed and without his raft for additional buoyancy, his skin abrasions added to his exhaustion. He was hundreds of yards from the beach when he gave the single loud blast on his whistle as the agreed signal that he was ready to return aboard. With no response from the submarine and realising he was in an increasingly fragile state, Hackett-Jones reluctantly paddled back to the shore. Daybreak was rapidly approaching. As the light improved, the young officer could better appreciate the coastline and why the boat might not have heard him. He needed to rest just a few minutes before launching himself back into the water and swimming westwards, dispensing with the superfluous pistol, bayonet and electric torch.

Good to her captain's word, *E57* had remained in the same departure bay. The first lieutenant's success was announced by the roar of the detonation. Small splashes of rock fragments fell around the submarine, even though the explosion had taken place nearly half a mile away, and all the crew had to do now was to get him back aboard. The bridge watchkeepers were on high alert, listening for his signal. Unfortunately, a high rocky headland marked the bay's eastern extent, which blocked the sound of Hackett-Jones' whistle.

The breaking dawn brought no comfort to Ted, knowing *E57* might be discovered if she remained so close inshore. Although desperate to recover his loyal first lieutenant, the possible loss of just one man did not justify risking the submarine. Everyone knew this to be the situation. With a heavy heart, the captain started to back the boat out of the bay.

As he cleared the headland, Hackett-Jones was utterly spent. More in hope than expectation, he mustered his remaining strength to give a final loud blast on the whistle. Suddenly, he saw a shape appear, then another. Believing they were fishing vessels that would pass too close, he started swimming dejectedly back to the shore. Halfway there, with energy reserves exhausted, he turned over to float on his back, allowing him to assess if he had been seen. The reflections and mist can play cruel tricks in the half-light of the morning on those occasions of perfect still when the sea and sky cannot be distinguished. Hackett-Jones suddenly saw the two shapes in the water meld into one, and there, like a phantom, was *E57* rising slowly. She was edging rapidly towards him, with sailors on the saddle tanks ready to retrieve him.

Propelling astern to depart the bay, the whistle signal had been heard. A much-relieved captain started manoeuvring *E57* towards the bobbing head some fifty yards off the headland. But the watchers on the shore heard the whistle too, and light rifle fire opened up on the boat. There was no time to waste before enemy reinforcements arrived. Their adventurer was recovered and guided gently below. Within a short five minutes, the submarine was again safe underwater, heading out of the Gulf towards open water.

E57 had successfully attacked the famous Baghdad Railway. Her first lieutenant was a hero, and morale aboard soared. But the most significant challenge lay ahead.

Chapter 9 – We'll Fight and We'll Conquer

1

With no need for the long trek west to establish communications with *Astor* later that night, *E57* headed southwest to lie off Bandirma, the railhead serving the country's south. This was where they expected the delivery of the replacement periscope section to occur, and Ted was keen to reconnoitre the area. The captain saw the exhausted state of his first lieutenant and told him to rest for the day whilst he and the navigator stood watch and watch about. Nonetheless, the irrepressible Hackett-Jones was up and about after lunch.

The harbour at Bandirma lays within its own enclosed bay. The port was about eight miles from the narrow entrance, only three miles wide, which was overlooked by high ground immediately to the south. There would doubtless be shore observers there. Thus, unable to reach the harbour or observe what might be alongside, Ted ordered the submarine to a position about three thousand yards north of the entrance to the bay whilst remaining dived. Having seen little, it was already five o'clock in the afternoon, and thoughts were turning towards finding a better position to spend the night.

Hardacre was on the periscope and called the captain to look at a new contact. A patrol boat was emerging from the narrows guarding the bay, and as Ted continued to watch, it became clear that the small warship was leading out a merchantman. Such protection would only be offered to such a small vessel if it carried contraband for war. Still, there was nothing

E57 could do without torpedoes to first take on its escort. The transport ship cleared the entrance, following which a puff of smoke from the patrol boat's funnel indicated an increase in speed as it turned back towards the harbour. Only a little over a mile away now, the tramp steamer altered course towards the submarine. She was probably heading eventually towards Gallipoli, Ted assessed, keeping its transit covert by hugging the coast in the fading light. Ted lowered the periscope and brought the submarine's head to the northwest to parallel the merchantman's likely track. The boat's crew could now hear the steady one-two-three-four, one-two-three-four of the ship's propeller as it approached them. Ted was content that he could easily outpace the merchantman after he had surfaced, so he let her pass. When he had achieved that, he raised the periscope again to ensure the warship had indeed opened away. It was nowhere in sight, already hidden by the islands protecting the entrance. Ted gauged that there would be more than enough time to deal with this softer target, even if a call for help was picked up. The captain rapidly briefed the crew on his intentions.

"SURFACE!"

No sooner was the top of the conning tower clear of the water than the hatch flung open. Ted was followed up by Hackett-Jones and his boarding party, who climbed down onto the for'd casing as lithely as they could. Next to the bridge came a team brandishing rifles which went to the rear of the platform. *E57* was one hundred and fifty yards astern and rapidly overhauling her prey. The boat was almost abeam at a range of only thirty yards before the surprised crew of the ship even became aware of the submarine's presence. A few rifle shots were enough for the vessel to signal its surrender, to stop its engine, and for the six crew members to be mustered on the foredeck with hands raised. Grappling hooks brought her alongside, and the first lieutenant was aboard in seconds. In the now-familiar fashion, the steamer's crew was herded aboard her own tender and cast adrift. The LTO reported that the charge was set and requested permission to light the fuse. Hackett-Jones took a slow and deliberate look around to ensure everything necessary had been done. Looking up to the bridge, he gave a thumbs-up sign which was greeted by a firm nod from his captain. The LTO again vanished below deck whilst his first lieutenant sought out the galley, both men reappearing a couple of minutes later. The former with his bag of demolition equipment and the latter with arms full of fresh provisions. All lines to the merchantman were cast off, and the submarine opened from her rapidly. Ten minutes later, an ear-splitting report announced the demise of another Turkish transport ship, marked only by the disappearing periscope four hundred yards away.

Ted was more than pleased with his day's work. He rewarded his crew with a 'hands to bathe' and the opportunity to wash their clothes before a hot dinner with fresh victuals. A good night's sleep was achieved whilst resting on the saline layer.

2

The next day, the submarine continued to make a nuisance of herself at various harbours along the north coast before heading westwards again to her communications billet. The mast and aerial were rigged before the tortuous routine recommenced. Before *E57* could make its routine report of the previous days' activities, the following message was received from HQ:

"TURKS REPORT SIX SMS IN MARMARA STOP
BZ STOP RV 122300Z8MAY15 AT 402650N7
0274550E3 STOP TWO GREEN LIGHTS STOP
RESPONSE SINGLE RED LIGHT AT ONE
MINUTE INTERVAL STOP ACKNOWLEDGE
ENDS"

It was clear that HQ was receiving good intelligence of their operations, which was most satisfying. Receipt of its orders and the submarine's acknowledgement had taken nearly six hours, so Ted decided that was enough for one night.

Hardacre plotted the rendezvous position to discover it was just off Ocaklar at the eastern end of the extensive Gulf of Artaki. This location was ten miles northwest of Bandirma harbour but on the other side of the isthmus out to the towering Kapidag Peninsula. Ted studied the arrangements and was happy HQ had prepared well, probably with Brodie's help. The rendezvous was only twenty-five miles off the central Constantinople-to-Gallipoli passage, so Ted could continue to monitor that route. Furthermore, Artaki Gulf was capacious, with deep water available down to about twenty fathoms, so *E57* couldn't be easily trapped inside. The local time of the rendezvous was two o'clock in the morning, when the world would be in its deepest slumbers. The problem was, therefore, not an excessively challenging navigational exercise. Still, he realised he must recognise the hazards involved in such a clandestine undertaking. Unlike Hackett-Jones' adventure ashore, with *E57* and her ship's company the only participants, he would have to trust those making the delivery. The operation would depend upon their non-discovery to avoid placing his submarine in undue peril. Careful planning was required to cover all possible eventualities.

With two days to go, Ted remained on the north coast, harrying both westbound and eastbound traffic, even exposing the top of his bridge to the larger transports. If he could not attack without torpedoes, he would ensure they would certainly register his presence. First thing in the morning of 12th May, he made a feint westward as far as Gallipoli town, hoping that his enemy might suspect he was returning to Mudros. For the rest of the day, *E57* stayed deep and quiet, avoiding all contact with Turkish forces, as she meandered her way back eastwards towards the entrance of the Gulf of Artaki.

By one o'clock the following morning, the batteries were fully charged, and the submarine was sitting on the surface ready, just five miles from the rendezvous position. The torpedo-handling derrick had been rigged to lift the periscope from a small boat if necessary. If they needed to crash-dive to make an escape, so be it: they would leave it in place. A slight breeze and high clouds dappled the night sky allowing the new moon to provide the minimum light. The conditions were perfect. Hardacre and Ted were on the bridge with two lookouts, all with binoculars firmly clamped to their eyes and scanning left and right. Hackett-Jones kept an eye on the chart below whilst getting his casing party ready for the transfer. With ten minutes to go, there were no lights, headlands or high points that could be used to fix her position and the submarine edged forward at minimum speed towards the beach. The captain checked his watch: only two minutes left. Everyone on board was totally silent.

It was Hardacre who saw them first. "There, Captain! Red three-zero!" Two green lights, separated horizontally, were at a considerable distance off his port bow: the boat was too far to the east by three or four hundred yards. Whilst the captain manoeuvred the submarine, his navigator sent the expected response by uncovering a red light every minute. The submarine had hardly achieved a position between the green lights before a small wooden skiff appeared bobbing by her bow. The first lieutenant was immediately ordered onto the for'd casing with his people. The small wooden craft with its four occupants was brought alongside the port saddle tank, where sailors were waiting to take its lines. Looking down from the bridge, Ted could just make out one person wearing a dark hood stepping across to the submarine and giving inaudible instructions to two more in the boat. They were starting to uncover an object hidden by a tarpaulin whilst a fourth visitor remained by the tiller. The skiff was led forward to be opposite the derrick, which had been swung out, with the block and tackle lowered. Hardly a word was spoken before the person in charge climbed onto the casing and whispered to the first lieutenant. Hackett-Jones didn't need to supervise the LTO, who had done similar operations on many, many occasions. The first lieutenant came to the foot of the bridge and summoned the captain down to the casing.

As Ted approached the leader of the beach party and was just one or two yards short, he realised it wasn't a hood that was being worn but rather a tightly-wrapped scarf.

"Andri . . . Mrs. Kapadoukas?" he corrected himself. "What on earth are you doing here? Surely this is not a safe undertaking for a lady?"

In affronted tones, she admonished him. "Well, who else could do it? Who else could speak Turkish while still having some friends left in Smyrna who could make the necessary arrangements? This is the easy part; remember, my father was a master mariner. I've been messing about in boats since I could walk."

"Of course, . . . of course. I didn't mean to offend. It's just that I'm so surprised."

Clearly not appeased, she continued, "As well as the periscope, I've brought this package which is fragile. It's new parts for your radio receiver. It seems that some defective items had been distributed before proper checks were carried out. Everyone has been suffering with these problems, so Brodie thought it best to bring you the replacement components whether you need them or not."

The first lieutenant appeared from behind her. "The periscope is below, Sir, and the loading hatch is shut and clipped. We are unrigging the derrick now."

"Very good, Number One. As soon as you're done, leave just one hand on the casing to slip the skiff and get everyone else below."

Turning back to his visitor, Ted continued their conversation, holding the precious package. "Do thank Brodie for me: we've been having terrible problems, and I hope these will help. But most of all, thank *you* for all your efforts. You must have faced huge risks to get the periscope and these parts to us." In the dark of the night, he still couldn't make out the details of her face, but he peered at her intently. "I always seem to do or say the wrong thing to you. I'm really sorry. Take great care on your return journey and arrive safely. Tell Brodie to send me a signal: I want to know when you get back to HQ."

These gentle words melted away her anger. She put her hand forward and held Ted's wrist tenderly. "*E57* is in much greater danger than me, with still so much to achieve. It is *you* who must take care. I want to be there when you arrive safely back." At that moment, the cloud moved aside, allowing a slither of the moon to peek through. Her eyes looked straight back at him, and their softness could not be disguised.

Their reverie was disturbed by the sudden silence that had descended around them. They were alone on the casing except for a single sailor holding the lines to the skiff, with its three other occupants already aboard. With a final squeeze of his arm, she removed her hand and climbed down into the boat. Ted nodded to the sailor, and the skiff's lines were thrown back to them. Hardacre was already starting to propel astern to move the submarine away from the beach. Within seconds, the small boat was engulfed in the darkness.

Feeling that same emptiness as on the night before *E57*'s departure from Mudros, but now with her words providing the faintest glimmer of hope, Ted returned to the bridge. Andrina was right: he had much still ahead of him.

3

Ted wanted to get the replacement periscope fitted as soon as possible and decided to remain in the very middle of the Gulf of Artaki for the rest of the night. The chart showed no significant centres of habitation around that stretch of water, and absolutely no lights could be seen on either shore. The northern islands were very rocky and probably too small to support any communities, whilst the mainland to the south looked like uninhabited, marshy ground. The captain and navigator considered the possibility of this area being appropriate for their regular overnight operations. The saline layer would likely be more mixed and less well-defined here, but the gently shelving southern beech still offered the option of a controlled grounding whilst deep. The main advantage, however, would be the short distance back to the main westbound route that their target must follow.

At the first hint of a brightening of the eastern horizon, Chief Bowers was up on the bridge platform, assessing how best to erect and attach the top periscope piece. With his engineers standing ready with bolts and spanners, the LTO and his torpedo men took charge of manoeuvring the heavy item up through the conning tower and into its assigned position. Immense care was required to prevent damage to the tube and the precious lens at the top. Also, everything had to be kept immaculately clean, so no debris entered the lower mechanism. Nonetheless, the new section was in place after an hour, and the captain was invited to check the optics from below. Under the usual procedure, the periscope sections would be assembled in a spotless workshop. The inside of the tube would then be dehumidified before the whole apparatus was craned into the boat in one piece. As a result, the vision of the repaired periscope was not as good as would generally be acceptable. Still, it would be perfectly adequate as a spare *in extremis*. With his commanding officer content, the senior engineer completed his work by again sealing up the joint with molten lead. Everything was complete by eight o'clock, and the submarine dived to check the repair remained watertight.

It remained necessary to plan how to deal with the *Torgut Reis,* and Ted called his officers to the chart table to confer with them. Their assigned target was a whole order of magnitude larger than anything they had tackled so far in the Sea of Marmara. This pre-dreadnought behemoth had previously served in the German Navy as the *Weissenberg* and was the Ottoman fleet's first "modern" battleship. Built in 1890 but modernised in 1904, she and her sister ship, *Barbaros Hayreddin*, were probably already past their prime by 1910 when the Turks bought them. Nonetheless, at over ten thousand tons and armed with guns with a range of fifteen thousand yards, *Torgut Reis* carried much prestige for the Turkish Navy and would likely be accompanied by a sizeable escort. How was *E57* to deal with the destroyers protecting her, even before they could attain an attacking position against this battleship?

The submarine's officers agreed that the best position for an attack was in the principal east-west channel between Hayirsiz Island and the town of Hoskoy to the northwest. This area was within easy reach, just ten miles north of the entrance to the Artaki Gulf. But even here, there were nearly nine miles of open sea, and the target might still escape past them. The three of them stood there quietly, all looking at the chart, pondering the problem and lost in their own thoughts. The captain eventually broke the silence. Seemingly to himself, Ted muttered, "We need some fir cones to distract the dogs."

The first lieutenant and navigator looked sideways at one another with the slightest of shrugs. Hackett-Jones was brave enough to speak. "Pardon, Sir? I didn't quite catch that."

Ted shook his head as he emerged from his reverie. "I was wondering how we could distract any escorts, so we could give ourselves the best chance of getting through to the target. It's a situation we've faced before, of course, but this is different. Let me explain. This attack is unlike any we have attempted before. Many lives – of our soldiers ashore and in the ships supporting them – depend on us destroying this battleship. Compare what we did in the Heligoland Bight. There, we were involved in a navy-to-navy contest, and if we were unsuccessful in one attack, so what? We'd be disappointed, of course, but the strategic situation would hardly change. Here the success of the entire campaign in this theatre of the war might be resting on us alone. Do you see how important it is for us to succeed?

"I've made a decision," the captain continued. "If the intelligence is right, we should have only two or three days more to wait for the *Torgut Reis* to emerge out of Constantinople. I intend *E57* to lie low until she does. The Turks must be anticipating that we will return to Mudros soon and I want to encourage that line of thought, to keep our attack even more unexpected and startling to them. By delaying the attack until the later part of the transit to Gallipoli in the position we have identified, I hope they might have developed a false sense of security by that time, with their lookouts feeling tired. Is this all clear?"

Following her captain's instructions, the submarine's modus operandi was again modified. Rather than the previous belligerent stance of closing and investigating all contacts, the boat was now to avoid and open away from all ships, even small dhows and fishing vessels. Furthermore, *E57* must remain clear of the coast. The enemy must believe she had departed the Sea of Marmara altogether.

That afternoon and early evening, Ted and Hardacre noticed that Hackett-Jones was not sitting reading a book as was customary when off watch. Mysteriously, he was engaged in some project back in the motor room with Chief Bowers. Whilst there was just enough light, with Hardacre on watch on the bridge, Hackett-Jones summoned the captain up to the casing where the object of his attentions was revealed. There, the senior engineer proudly uncovered a wooden structure.

"Captain, Sir. I think we can use this as a . . . umm . . . as a fir cone," the first lieutenant explained bravely. In response to his commanding officer's icy stare, he continued, "Let me show you how it works."

With that, Hackett-Jones and Bowers down climbed onto the saddle tanks and launched a floating platform remarkably like the raft they had made previously. But in this case, it was only an outside framework with the centre left clear. In the middle, however, was a long pole with a hefty weight on one end and a small wooden box at the other. This spar was connected to the corners of the raft by four lengths of rubber. In this configuration, the spar automatically took up a vertical orientation in the water with the box at the top. The outside frame was awash and hardly visible in the prevailing sea conditions, which were calm with little wind, sea or swell. Nevertheless, they were still sufficient to set the platform rocking gently, with the spar in the middle starting to bounce steadily up and down. Hackett-Jones didn't have to explain more: its purpose was instantly clear to his captain.

"That's brilliant!" Ted exclaimed to the evident delight of his subordinates, who smiled at one another. "From a distance that should look exactly like a periscope. This might be just the thing we need to draw off any escorts and possibly even divert the target towards us. Well done you two! All we need now is the target. Hoist 'Son of *E57*' back aboard: we need to establish communications with HQ."

During the day, Andrews had been busy too. He exchanged all the old components in the radio receiver with the new ones delivered. He was as anxious as everybody else to discover whether these alterations improved the communications situation. Arriving at their regular station to contact *Astor*, he was rewarded and much relieved that reception was so much better. He could quickly exchange identities with the picket ship. The actual transmission of the radio signals was still the same and accompanied by much sparking of the aerial. Still, in relatively good time, *E57* had reported the successful periscope repair and requested further instructions. There was no new intelligence on their assigned target, but HQ believed a new anti-submarine net had been installed across the Narrows above Nagara.

Ted never truly trusted intelligence reports – he had been caught out by false ones before. Thus he maintained the next day's patrol in the centre of the channel west of Marmara Island. Without prior warning, he could not deploy his decoy 'periscope' but didn't want to miss a chance if one presented itself. Hackett-Jones continued working with Chief Bowers, refining the design of the top of their masterpiece to look more like a periscope head. They had already asked their captain for another opportunity that evening: they needed to doublecheck the buoyancy and trim of their contraption. In the meantime, Ted and Hardacre made good use of the time by considering plans for their return passage down the Dardanelles. The warning of a possible new net was timely in this regard. For a long time, they discussed their options and the various approaches to this problem. The captain left his navigator at the chart table, recording the plan that they had devised.

In the communications billet that evening, they received the message they had been eagerly awaiting.

"TORGUT REIS SAILS TOMORROW STOP
ETD UNKNOWN STOP GO WELL ENDS"

4

The following dawn broke bright and still – too still for her captain's liking – to find *E57* already dived, leaving Artaki Gulf behind. Having talked through the attack plan time and time again, they realised that they must remain unseen by the watchers ashore if *Torgut Reis* was not to be given any signs warning of their presence. The problem was deploying their decoy in the correct position ahead of the target's track so it could be spotted and allowed to do its work. At the same time, *E57* must remain undetected. They couldn't launch it too early because the raft would be caught by the current running the length of the Sea of Marmara, moving it away from an optimum position. Accordingly, Ted decided to employ their previous tactic to capture and tie up alongside a dhow, but constantly aware that their target could appear on the horizon at any moment.

It was already eight o'clock before they reached a position east of Hoskoy. They knew that smaller reinforcement transports would sometimes make an overnight stop in the small harbour. The waiting seemed interminable as they watched intently for any vessel emerging, but none came. It was half-past eleven before they saw any activity, and this was a sail to the northeast, closing only slowly. The choice seemed clear: either they chase north and capture this vessel for their purposes, or they sit and wait for their target to come to them. Every minute that ticked past could bring their target into view, catching them unprepared if they were focused on some other operation. Ted decided to take a chance and go for the former option. He took a careful look at the potential dhow. He estimated its range as accurately as possible before taking the submarine deep to close the dhow at speed. On regaining periscope depth about fifteen minutes later, he first carefully scanned the northern sector to ensure his target and her escorts were not approaching. Having satisfied himself, he concentrated on the dhow, got his team ready, and positioned *E57* almost abeam the dhow and to seaward from her. From then, the now well-rehearsed operation took less than ten minutes to present the submarine firmly tied up alongside the sailing vessel, with her crew held captive on the foredeck. The risk had been worthwhile, especially because a lookout high on the dhow's mast could see over a much greater range than the submarine's periscope, giving them more time for final preparations. There was nothing else they could do except sit and wait.

It certainly felt like the longest day of the patrol, just wallowing and drifting south slowly in the current. Two o'clock and three o'clock both came and went with no sign of any movements to the northeast in the direction of Constantinople. With their target's previous delays, the crew of *E57* were left wondering if *Torgut Reis* had experienced another breakdown and not sailed at all.

It was past four o'clock when the vaguest smudge of smoke appeared on the horizon. Ted immediately joined his lookout up in the mast. If this was his target, he wanted the earliest possible view of the enemy forces employed and their disposition. Eventually, he could make out two well-handled destroyers zigzagging at regular intervals and closing rapidly. They were already at about fifteen thousand yards, but there was no sign of *E57*'s principal target behind. She had to be there.

Consigning the dhow's crew into their small wooden tender and casting them off, there was no need now to act so elusively from the shore. There would come a time soon when Ted wanted them to believe there was a submarine in the area. Checking his watch, he slipped from the dhow. He steered *E57* quickly out towards the main channel, launching his decoy periscope about a thousand yards later. He dived the submarine well before she came within visible range of the escort ships. Late in the afternoon, he was in an almost perfect attacking position, with his targets to the east and brightly lit. On the other hand, his opponents must search into the glare of the lowering sun, and, common at this time of day, a stiff breeze had arisen, causing a slight chop on the surface. Taking up her chosen position to the southeast of the main channel by Hayirsiz Island, *E57* waited for her playmates to arrive.

At last, Ted could identify the escorts: they were two Samsun-class destroyers, now in full hull-up view at a range of four thousand yards. Needing to keep periscope exposure to a minimum, he could take only furtive searches for the battleship behind. The left-wing escort's track was bringing her directly towards the submarine, which was not the plan. As the seconds ticked by, it seemed as though the decoy had failed in its mission and remained undetected. In a couple of minutes, Ted would need to duck beneath the closing destroyer and hopefully be able to come up again and attain an attacking position. Easily said, but this took time and a significant degree of luck. Memories of being nearly run down by a German battle cruiser were all too raw.

Ted looked at his watch again and questioningly at the man sat by the for'd bulkhead. The LTO also looked at his watch before responding with hands held open and a shrug, that well-known gesture to say, "I don't know."

Suddenly, they could hear a muffled report through the hull. Ted risked raising the periscope for the briefest of looks. He saw the dhow they had captured engulfed in flames, with debris from the explosive they had planted still falling around it. That had caught their attention!

Playfully, Ted turned to his first lieutenant, "In addition to a fir cone, I thought we might need the shrill scream of a buzzard to get our prey running!"

As intended, both the escorts put their wheels hard over to port and raced towards the northern shore to investigate. Hopefully, they would now also detect the decoy, which should keep them busy for a vital couple of minutes. As the destroyers cleared away from the submarine, Ted could conduct a more rigorous search for the battleship.

There she was! There was the target, not six thousand yards away. She had been hidden by the smoke billowing from the old destroyers' funnels. She was positioned in the centre of the channel, already under starboard helm, and heading toward their side. But, as Ted watched, she continued to turn and was now beam on. This could be a disaster. Was she going to return to Constantinople? As best he could tell, her course then seemed to steady, directly towards Marmara Island, and Ted had no clue of her intentions. He took the two paces to the chart table where Hardacre pointed to where they were and the estimated position of the *Torgut Reis*.

"Umm. Perhaps she's closing Marmara Island for safety, before turning north to retrace her steps. Either that or she's going to push on to Gallipoli by navigating *that* gap between Marmara Island and Hayirsiz Island," the captain thought out loud and stabbed his finger at the chart. "If she goes back home, we haven't a chance of catching her. But I really think she's going to continue her passage. We've no time to lose! Helm hard a'port. Stop together. Grouper switch up. Full ahead together!"

There was no question of raising the periscope whilst at high speed, which would reveal their position. The captain and his navigator had again to navigate "by guess and by God". They had to relocate about three miles to the south to have any chance of an attack if and only if the *Torgut Reis* continued her push westwards. During this hiatus, there was the opportunity to check around the boat to ensure everything was functioning correctly. The senior engineer came to the control room. He reported that the use of full power had shown up a serious earth on the port main motor and he was concerned for the safety of his motor room team. He knew there was no option, but his captain had to be informed. Otherwise, *E57* was holding up, even after so many days on unsupported patrol.

Ted was over the chart again and asked Hardacre to draw out possible routes the *Torgut Reis* could take. She would follow a track just west of south to navigate between the two islands and, once through, would revert to a near-westerly course towards the Gallipoli channel. Remaining optimistic that this would be the case, the battleship would have to cover twice the distance as the submarine, which might give *E57* the opportunity she was desperate for. If the target chose to continue down to the southern shore and then follow the Asian coast, the submarine hadn't a hope.

E57 ran for nearly twenty minutes in this most dangerous manner. She could not fix her position and was blind without her periscopes raised. Being shallow, the submarine was vulnerable and could be rammed. Ted stopped the motors and waited until the speed was just two knots before raising the after periscope again. He could see the *Torgut Reis* was clear of the channel, and they were in luck: she was commencing a turn to starboard towards them. But the situation was different from what Ted had visualised. Clearly, the current had carried the boat further south than anticipated. As the target continued to turn, Ted realised he had overrun. She was still five thousand yards away, but he was too fine on her starboard bow, resulting in her passing just two or three hundred yards from them. The torpedoes would not have time to take up their ordered depth at that range and could pass underneath, as had happened too often before.

"Down periscope! Full ahead together. Helm hard a'port," the captain ordered.

They now had this colossal battleship charging at them at full speed, with all her twelve coal-fired boilers feeding the belching smoke. Never mind attaining an attacking position: a very few degrees alteration in their target's course could spell *E57*'s doom as she would be run over.

"Captain, Sir! The port motor is sparking badly," Chief Bowers shouted urgently from the engine room. "One of the men has already been severely burned. We've got to stop it!"

Ted looked at his senior engineer but turned away as if dismissing him, "Steer northwest." The control room team tried to concentrate solely on managing the submarine's movements as ordered. Nonetheless, the pungent smell of electrical arcing was filling the boat, and the crew's eyes were beginning to water. No one except the submarine's captain knew what was going on around their craft and the possible peril that she was in. After three minutes, to his crew's immense relief, he ordered, "Stop port!" To be followed immediately by, "Helm hard a'starboard! Steer south . Standby Number One and Number Two tubes!"

The combined effect of full port rudder and starboard propeller at maximum revolutions compelled the submarine, degree by degree, agonisingly round to its new course.

"Number One and Two tubes ready, Sir. Bow caps open!" came the cry from the forends.

"Very good," the captain acknowledged. "Stop starboard!"

With hope upon hope that the swirling water from their frantic manoeuvres had not been spotted, Ted waited for the submarine's speed to drop before raising the periscope. This Goliath towered above him. It was as if he could reach out to touch that protruding bow designed to spear him. There was no time left to refine any aspect of his attack: it was now or never. Fighting to focus only on the attack, he trained the periscope on the deflection angle. Already on the huge for'd turret, the hairline had only milliseconds to wait for the bridge to line up.

"FIRE NUMBER ONE TUBE!"

"FIRE NUMBER TWO TUBE!"

"Down periscope. Hard a'port!"

Ted waited just ten seconds before raising the periscope again. He could see both torpedoes were running correctly, but as he watched, he saw the first one miss ahead of the target. Perhaps this old lady of a battleship was no longer capable of the speed he had calculated, he pondered, and would the second run the same? The submarine was jarred by an immense explosion just as Ted saw a sheet of flame rise from aft the bridge and engulf the forward funnel.

A cheer went up through the submarine. The captain smiled too, then stopped.

"Quiet! Quiet, everyone! What's that?"

As the crew's clamour died down, they too became aware of a new noise. Racing propellers.

"Up periscope!" As soon as it was raised, Ted spun around but did not complete the full circuit.

"FULL AHEAD TOGETHER!"

"TEN DOWN! KEEP SIXTY FEET!"

He had seen the bow of a torpedo cruiser coming straight towards him at speed and not two hundred yards away.

"Flood in, Number One. A third escort is about to ram. Standby collision!"

"Fire! Fire in the motor room!" was shouted from aft. At the same time, a scream of twisting metal came as *E57* was bowled over to about a fifty-degree angle. There she hung whilst a dreadful high-pitched tumult of scoring, scraping and scratching filled their heads. It continued for an eternity before the racing propellers slowly died into the background. Only reluctantly did the submarine return to an upright position. The captain's warning had come in the nick of time, allowing most to grab whatever they could. Still, some of the crew had been thrown off their feet and slammed against the hull, pipes, or valves and were slowly retaking their assigned positions whilst rubbing sore limbs or heads. Battery acid had slopped out and the acrid smell of chlorine exacerbated the already-choking atmosphere. Even now, the submarine was passing only thirty feet, and Ted ordered the port shaft to be stopped. Hackett-Jones raced aft to check the boat for damage. The coxswain asked to be relieved on the afterplanes. Once done, he grabbed the medical bag and followed his first lieutenant.

Once the port motor had been stopped, the fires were quickly put out. The collision had caused a few minor leaks in the top circumference of the hull above the Engine Room. These were either isolated or plugged with softwood wedges kept ready for such a contingency. In addition to a couple of the crew in the motor room with burns, the only other significant injury was the broken arm of a stoker standing watch by the diesels. The biggest problem was the atmosphere in the submarine, which was almost unbreathable, and many were coughing painfully despite holding wetted cloths to their faces. This experienced crew had suffered foul conditions before, but these were the first to be caused by action damage. Nothing could improve the situation until the submarine could surface and run the diesel engines to suck in fresh air and burn up the corrosive atmosphere. Surfacing was no option with enemy forces all around and no doubt searching hard for them. The submariners now knew to their cost that there were at least three escorts. There could be even more now with additional craft summoned to help. Accordingly, *E57* limped off to the northwest on just one motor to open from the flaming datum they had left. It was already six o'clock, and the fading light might soon bring some relief.

Having just survived the day, Ted took no chances and waited until late evening before returning to periscope depth, checking carefully all around before surfacing the boat. With the atmosphere so foul, the engineers initially turned the diesel engines using the main motors to draw in a stream of fresh air before attempting to start them. Even then, the engines would not fire initially because the air was so contaminated, but at the third attempt, one, then the other, sparked into life with a bang. Everyone off-watch gathered around the bottom of the conning tower to breathe in the fresh air. Knowing that enemy forces would still be in the area, Ted took the bridge watch himself with two lookouts. He was relieved to find the submarine in open water, clear of other vessels. The lookouts could make out some distant lights to the southeast, which might be where their target had been attacked. The captain hoped that their single-weapon attack had been enough to take the battleship down and incapable of being salvaged.

Ted made his plan. His crew needed some rest, and he wanted a full inspection of the submarine and all equipment before committing to the perilous return passage through the Straits. He already knew he had a problem with the port motor, but an initial inspection for damage also found a crack in the starboard intermediate shaft. This was the same problem that had caused them to lie over in Malta. This shaft between the engine and the electric motor was critical, and additional strain risked breaking it at any time. Chief Bowers needed some time to make a proper assessment and see if any amelioration of the defects was possible. Having surfaced, they shone a light down onto the after casing to discover that part of it had gone entirely, carried away by the charging escort. Apparently, they had dived just deep enough before the collision, avoiding the escort's bow and causing the ship's bottom to graze over the after casing. The boat must have dropped further before the destroyer's propellors could inflict severe damage. It was decided they would maintain their current position and charge the batteries. Tomorrow would be used to clean up, rest and make repairs before contacting HQ in the evening to signal their ETA off Cape Helles the following day.

With the charge complete, *E57* dived and made a slow passage south, back to the entrance of Artaki Gulf to lick her wounds. From there, the submarine would retrace her path back through the Dardanelle Straits, where new threats awaited.

Chapter 10 – Steady, Boys, Steady

1

Harry Bowers and his men worked steadily throughout the night. His electricians were busy trying to locate the source of the earth on the port motor, stripping down and cleaning all the associated equipment. At each stage, they repeatedly placed a cable with a light attached between the motor's armature and the submarine's hull to test the electrical insulation. By morning, the test light was still dimly glowing: the earth remained, but no longer at full brilliance as the previous evening. His engineers went through the submarine, checking all valves and connections to check for tightness after the collision, particularly in the deckhead of the Engine Room. Only minor repairs were possible, but thankfully, nothing would stop the diesels from running. The starboard intermediate shaft was another matter. There was nothing that could be done other than treating it gently by not applying rapid changes of power or direction. They just had to pray that it didn't shatter and fail completely.

Albert Prescott completed his own rounds of the boat to assess how the crew was bearing up. *E57*'s success in her priority task of sinking the battleship had helped to buck their morale. Still, it was clear to this experienced coxswain that the length of the patrol and parlous conditions were taking their toll. Even the most robust of the ship's company now looked wan and dog-tired. The collision with the destroyer was by far the worst incident that had ever befallen the submarine, severely shaking up some of the younger men who had previously considered their boat invincible. Although relatively minor, damage was evident all around, only to remind the crew of the frailty of their craft, the ever-dangerous environment in which they operated, and the significant dangers they must face on their return to safety. Prescott stopped to chat with many, cajoling where necessary and joking with others. But there just wasn't the usual banter that would relieve anxieties.

Aware that the radio mast was folded down onto the after casing, Andrews was anxious to check his equipment as soon as possible. Accordingly, at first light, the submarine surfaced, and the telegraphist made his way out to investigate. He found that the top part of the mast had been contorted. So too, were the fastenings that kept the aerial clipped to the casing, leaving the mast loose and flapping about, with the potential for further damage. He disconnected the parts he could, to repair them onboard, and used rope lashings as a temporary measure for keeping the aerial secured. The submarine was then able to dive again.

By late afternoon, the crew had done what they could to prepare *E57* for her hazardous return journey. They were stood down and ordered to rest. Hackett-Jones had done much of the work, supervising and receiving reports from the coxswain and senior engineer whilst the captain and navigator revised their plan for tackling the Narrows. Slowly and taking careful all-round looks whilst the light allowed, the boat edged its way out of its protective gulf and commenced its passage towards its signalling billet.

They were in no rush. The intention was to clear their ETA message with HQ before charging the batteries overnight. The submarine could then approach Gallipoli town on the surface as dawn broke to see what fishing vessels or other activities might be there to obstruct their passage. Ted, therefore, waited until it was fully dark before surfacing and making his way into the small bay east of Bozburun, where the coast seemed to comprise only marshland. Andrews was immediately dispatched onto the after casing with two sailors to help him rig the wireless aerial. The repaired section was attached before the mast was raised into position, after which the radio operator proceeded below and started to call *Astor*.

Vivid blue sparks, lighting up the sky, indicated that transmissions had started. Receiving only a broken acknowledgement from the communications picket, Andrews continued nonetheless, passed *E57*'s ETA message and waited for a response. Nothing came. He transmitted the ETA again, but with the same result. The captain was waiting close by the radio shack, and the wireless operator reported what had happened.

"*Astor* picked up our initial transmission, Sir, but I've received no acknowledgement of the ETA," Andrews explained. "The repair to the comms mast was fairly straightforward and I don't think the problem would be there, but I could check it again if you wish."

Without confirmed receipt of their ETA signal, the submarine's unannounced return amongst friendly forces could be just as dangerous as meeting the enemy. *E57*'s training patrol had demonstrated that adequately. They were at the end of their patrol and, even more than his crew, Ted felt drained by the constant stress on him over the last weeks. He felt inclined not to take any more risks. Accordingly, the captain agreed that Andrews should have a last chance to check for any apparent defect whilst the aerial was lowered and secured. He followed the leading telegraphist and the casing party up to the bridge, joining his navigator on watch. Well used to the routine despite the damage to the casing, the communications mast was quickly lowered and secured. The two sailors returned below whilst Andrews remained on deck, checking the aerial's connections with the aid of a torch.

"Well," Hardacre started. "We've nearly made it. You must be immensely proud of all you have achieved during this patrol. It's been remarkable what a single submarine is capable of. The rest of the Navy, let alone the other forces or civilians, have *no idea!* It's been a great privilege, and to my huge advantage that fate brought us back together again and gave me this opportunity. Thank you so much."

"With a crew like mine, you can achieve anything," Ted explained. "After all the defects and other setbacks we've experienced since emerging from build, I'm just surprised that they keep delivering such splendid results. I trust all my ship's company when we are at sea. Yes," he added, seeing Hardacre turning to look at him, "every single one. I shouldn't have come down so hard on Andrews," the captain admitted. "That's certainly clear now that I know his equipment was defective through no fault of his own. I should have seen how tired he was becoming."

"So, we will be back alongside tomorrow and I will have to rejoin *Queen Elizabeth*," Hardacre continued after a short pause. "Who knows? It might be years before our paths cross again, but I hope not. Before we part, I still want to ask your forgiveness for the inexcusable manner in which I conducted myself at Dartmouth."

"No, that's ridiculous," Ted objected. "We were just boys and it was so long ago; I've hardly given it a second thought . . . unless reminded," he added pointedly with a half-smile.

"Well, _I_ have. I make no excuses but there were reasons. If ever I didn't come out top, I would be beaten by my father. He heard about our climb up the mast and how you outshone me. That was just another excuse for him to take a belt to me. I'm afraid I took all that righteous anger out on you. I was wrong and I was weak. I'm truly sorry."

Before Ted could reply, a brilliant white light on the starboard side blinded all the submarine's watchkeepers, followed by the flash of a gun firing at them. The first shot fell short, but the second hit the after casing a glancing blow, sending up a shower of metal fragments. A cry went up from Andrews as he fell to the deck, clutching his right side.

"Standby to dive," ordered the captain. "Get everyone below. I'll get Andrews."

"No, you mustn't . . . !" His navigator's protest went unheeded as the captain pulled out of his grasp. Ted was over the edge of the bridge in a second and made his way rapidly towards the injured man. Taking one arm over his shoulder, he brought Andrews to the ladder and had to help him up rung by rung. Hardacre had shouted down to the control room to prepare to dive and started to propel ahead. At the same time, he ordered the helm hard to starboard to move away from their attacker and present the minimum target. This successfully disrupted their attacker's aim, but only for a short while. The navigator also knew they could not dive on this course as they would be in danger of running rapidly ashore. So, he waited until Andrews was on the bridge before reversing the helm, altering the ship's head hard to starboard towards the open sea.

Ted was now level with the top of the bridge and was about to swing a leg over the rim when, for Hardacre, everything shifted into slow motion. The searchlight was quivering as it tried to track its jinking target, with the warship rolling and pitching as it raced closer. The reports from the gun were getting louder and the flashes more brilliant. For Hardacre, there was the man he had known in his youth, exposed to the enemy. In what must have been only microseconds, he saw the gun's heavy shot hit his friend square in the centre of his chest. Ted was carried horizontally away from the submarine and into the darkness. His eyes, caught in the spotlight, were the last Hardacre saw of him, staring forward in disbelief.

"PRESS THE KLAXON TWICE!" Hardacre roared, whilst pushing Andrews down the conning tower, none too gently. He managed to pull the upper hatch shut just as the water was beginning to lap over. The advanced warning had allowed the first lieutenant to start flooding in. The thrashing of their attacker's propellers could now be heard by all onboard, as well as the gunshots. Just as the bridge was about to be swamped, a final shot hit the periscope standards, knocking the boat sideways a little. Twenty feet. Thirty feet. They were safe just before the escort raced overhead without contact.

"Investigate damage," the first lieutenant commanded, eliciting shouted reports to come back from both ends of the submarine.

All seemed well. Once again, *E57*'s luck had held out. Despite some knocks and bruises, no additional damage that threatened her operational state had been sustained. As they realised this, the crew could be seen to relax physically. The coxswain was attending Andrews, who had been given morphine for his wound and was comatose. It was Hackett-Jones who noticed first.

"Where's the captain? Is he injured?" the loyal first lieutenant asked as he walked forward to the wardroom area to see if Ted was lying down. Palms open, questioningly, he turned round to look at Hardacre.

"The captain's dead. He received a direct shot from the escort's gun and was carried over the side. There was nothing anyone could do," the navigator reported glumly.

"What? How could you know he was dead? You should have brought him below; the coxswain might have been able to save him," Hackett-Jones retorted angrily, approaching Hardacre threateningly.

"The truth is that he was hit square in the chest by the gun of a patrol craft. It was likely to have been at least a six-pounder – not just a rifle – and swept the captain clean off the bridge! He probably died instantly." As he explained the situation, already upset as he was, Hardacre was now becoming angry by the cruel unfairness of it all. He faced up directly to Hackett-Jones, with arms straight down by his sides and fists tightly clenched. "How could we have stopped? To search for his body in the water? Even if we did find him, how could we have recovered him aboard? Are you forgetting there was a destroyer firing at us and trying to ram us? There would have been no submarine to bring him back to, with everyone here already dead. There was no option: I had to make the decision to dive and save the boat!"

Despite numerous setbacks and difficult circumstances, their captain had brought them through safely ever since *E57* had been on the building blocks. The whole crew mourned his death deeply. To have been suddenly taken away from them with little evidence brought some suspicion upon Hardacre, a person they had known for only a few weeks. He could surely have done more: at least they should have been able to give their skipper a fitting burial. The looks that Hardacre received behind his back showed growing resentment.

2

The first lieutenant would now take command, and the coxswain would oversee ship control, whilst the navigator would continue his regular duties. Accordingly, these three gathered around the chart table to discuss the transit ahead of them through the Straits. Hardacre went through the plan that he and Ted had devised. Despite the navigational challenges, all seemed straightforward, helped as they would be by the following current for most of the passage. "The greatest challenge," the navigator opined, "was the reported presence of an anti-submarine net across the straits by Nagara Point, to be countered by charging it at one hundred and ten feet." Hackett-Jones was bemused. He thought they should be shallow at, say, thirty feet, making the most of the helpful current behind them. Hardacre tried to explain that Ted and the other submarine captains at Mudros had given this matter a lot of thought. Their considered view was that submarines had a greater chance of breaking through whilst deep, with the net's weight helping them. Furthermore, if the boat were shallow, they thought this would give surface forces an earlier indication of their presence.

Hackett-Jones would not be convinced. Either he could not accept the arguments presented, or, as Hardacre came to believe, it was a matter of pride. The erstwhile first lieutenant wanted to make his mark and be seen to make all decisions as the new commanding officer. Hardacre was clearly becoming frustrated by this intransigence, and the discussion was becoming rather heated. Finally, Hackett-Jones decided this conversation must come to an end.

"Well, I have made up my mind, and we will attack any net shallow," adding with a sneer, "should there indeed be one. I'm now the captain, and that is the way it will be."

Years in the Navy had taught Hardacre to obey orders, but now he was torn. Should he allow Hackett-Jones to continue as intended, possibly placing *E57* and her crew in peril? Or should he make a stand for Ted's assessment of the situation and his ultimate wish? He had no option but still had to gamble.

"If you do that you will be in direct contradiction to what Lieutenant Crockford had intended. He was a submarine officer of immense experience and I cannot countenance how you could simply discount his plan, and I would stress that this is *his* plan, not mine. I will ask you again; will you carry out his intentions?"

"No, I won't. How can I be sure that is what he wanted? Again, I have only *your* word for it," bristled Hackett-Jones.

"I had truly hoped it would not come to this, but now you leave me no choice," Hardacre responded, his cheeks reddening. "I am senior to you and *I* will take command, to ensure that Lieutenant Crockford's wishes are carried out."

"What? I am the first lieutenant and second in command. You cannot come along and make yourself the captain, just like that."

"Yes, it would have been different if Lieutenant Buckle, a reservist officer, were still the navigator. But I'm a regular officer in the Royal Navy and senior to you: you know that. In fact, I'm only a couple of weeks junior to the captain. That's how the Senior Service works and has always done for centuries. In such a situation, the next senior officer takes charge as laid down in King's Regulations." Turning to the coxswain, Hardacre continued, "Can you get KRs please, Cox'n, so I can show the right section to Lieutenant Hackett-Jones?"

"Er . . . . We . . . we don't carry them, Sir. As a tender, we depend upon our depot ship to hold all necessary reference books," stuttered the senior rate in reply.

"Well, that's awkward. Nonetheless, you are a coxswain of some experience. Doesn't it occur to you that the next most senior officer should take command if the captain is killed in action?"

"I suppose so, but . . . but it just doesn't seem right," answered the coxswain, whilst turning to his first lieutenant with a look of hopeless defeat.

"Your loyalty is highly praiseworthy, Cox'n, but these are truly exceptional circumstances and we must follow established procedures." Accepting no further debate, Hardacre started to take charge. "Right. We will follow the intended plan. You will take ship control, Coxswain. First Lieutenant, you will be my eyes and man the periscope whilst in the straits, taking observations as I direct. Having been detected here, so far to the west, the Turks can be expected to come to the correct conclusion that we are about to try to get back to Mudros. So, tomorrow is likely to be an exceptionally long day, and everyone should get what rest they can."

In truth, Hackett-Jones felt relieved. He knew what a challenge lay ahead of them, and although a confident officer, he wasn't arrogant enough to believe he could fit easily into Crockford's shoes. After all, he had been a lieutenant for only a year. The division of labour that Hardacre described seemed sensible, and, ultimately, it didn't matter who wore the title 'captain'. Despite the disagreement about how to tackle any net, he had had time to take stock. Hackett-Jones couldn't argue against Hardacre's intentions if these were indeed the same as what the college of captains at Mudros had discussed. He had gotten to know Hardacre well during the patrol and didn't consider him capable of such deceit to make this up. All that mattered was *E57*'s safe passage.

3

The ship's company was roused at four o'clock for a basic breakfast, with just a hot drink. *E57* then surfaced, and the diesels topped up the battery as the submarine started a slow westerly transit to cover the ten miles before entering the Dardanelle Straits. Having navigated past the shallows at the extreme western end of the Sea of Marmara, they were positioned about three miles northeast of the town of Gallipoli. The dark hills on either side indicated the start-line of their challenge.

Usually, the sailors were confident and light-hearted, with banter abounding, but today everyone was in a sombre mood. The loss of their beloved captain was terrible enough, but now, to have this relatively unknown individual placed above them was even worse. For goodness sake, he wasn't even a qualified submariner! Few could understand why their first lieutenant wasn't the natural heir to command. Nonetheless, Hardacre was not without supporters. They had seen how hard he had worked during the patrol to learn their ways and machines, proving he was very able. Whenever those few spoke out, however, they were quickly shouted down. Morale had collapsed. The good fortune the boat had enjoyed at the beginning of this patrol had all run out. The bad luck they had suffered perpetually whilst on patrols in the Heligoland Bight had clearly returned but without Crockford present to keep them safe. The omens were not good, and many held dread misgivings about the return passage.

With the minimum light available, Hardacre took the watch on the bridge and carefully scanned the whole horizon. He could see no other vessels at all: perhaps it was still too early even for the fishermen. But patrol craft could still be sitting and waiting with lights extinguished. Taking a deep breath, he was ready.

Coming below, he commanded the first lieutenant to dive the submarine and then waited for the coxswain to adjust the trim to be the best possible. Once satisfied, he ordered the boat to sixty feet and increased speed to five knots. He dived the boat deeper to eighty feet when they were a mile short of Gallipoli and sped up to overcome the expected counter-current at that depth. This was the position where they had encountered the group of fishing vessels on the way out, and he didn't want to take any chances. After thirty minutes, Hardacre judged they were clear of any vessels which might be patrolling the approaches to that strategic bottleneck. He ordered *E57* up to sixty feet and slowed down again. Fifteen more miles lay between them and the sharp turn to port at Nagara Point, taking them into the Narrows and thence escape. The strait ran almost straight in a south-westerly direction until this turn, without any significant bays or tributaries to cause swirling eddies and currents to knock the submarine off course. Hardacre therefore kept *E57* deep, straight and fast for ninety minutes before coming up to periscope depth. He needed a navigational fix, of course, but he also wanted a better assessment of the current. Their transit in the other direction seemed an age ago.

It was still dark when the submarine dived and went deep, with no opportunity to check the vision through the periscope. When the first lieutenant raised the after periscope to take the intended fix, he couldn't understand why he could not see clearly through it. Then it occurred to him that the final shot from last night's destroyer attack must have knocked the optics out of alignment. It was impossible to orientate himself, let alone take a fix. Ordering the after periscope down and raising the forward one, his hope was that the hit on the periscope standards had not affected both periscopes the same. Luckily, it had not, but this was the one they had repaired at sea, and the vision was cloudy from the unavoidable moisture that had entered the tube during the repair. It would have to do. They were committed.

The first fix was less closely defined than he would have liked, but it was adequate for Hardacre's purposes and showed the boat to be safe and near the centre of the channel. Taking fixes every fifteen minutes thereafter, Hardacre implored Hackett-Jones to keep alert to the possible presence of a net across their path. Whilst continuing the cycle of observations, the first lieutenant suddenly stopped on a bearing to the southwest. Going across to the chart table, he pointed to a small headland just east of Nagara Point.

"There," he said. "It looks like a net coming ashore. I'll look at the other beach. Raise forward periscope!" He scanned the northern side of the channel carefully, then stopped and called Hardacre over. "That bearing! Take a look."

"No, there's no point. I trust your judgement. But can you see any buoys along the water?"

Hackett-Jones scanned the ahead sector again before putting the periscope down. "No, I can't see anything, but I wouldn't expect to until awfully close. I'd be lucky even then with the periscope in such a poor state."

"Very good. Take final bearings as best you can. Then we'll go deep," Hardacre ordered, inviting no further discussion about his future intentions. The new captain could feel the antagonism all around him but couldn't let any such truck interfere. He kept up an imperious stance whilst remaining businesslike and focused only on the matters at hand.

With the fix plotted, *E57* descended to one hundred and ten feet on a south-westerly course and wound up speed to eight knots. This was a novel experience for the crew with a new danger ahead. Such their apprehension, there was silence throughout the boat as they monitored their equipment and panels for anything untoward. Everyone had been aware of the altercation about how to tackle the net, which served to unsettle them further. The hum of the motors was the only noise as the submarine raced on at nearly her full speed.

The collision with the net came without fanfare. Despite the forewarning, many were thrown forward off their feet as the submarine was brought to a near stop. The bow was immediately flung up, and the boat rose to ninety feet. The plan had expected that such a charge would at least have parted enough wires to allow the boat to power through. Hoping this was the case, Hardacre ordered maximum power. "Just give me all you can, Chief," he instructed his senior engineer, who had appeared at his shoulder to remind him about the earth on the port motor. Of more concern, the ship's head started paying off rapidly to starboard. It was vitally important for the submarine to remain as closely perpendicular to the net as possible to cut through. If she were pushed by the current alongside and parallel to the net, *E57* would be doomed.

"HELM HARD A'STARBOARD!" roared the captain.

"FULL ASTERN PORT!"

The clicking of the gyro repeater at first slowed, then held steady before swinging back to port in answer to the steering orders. At the same time, loud cracks could be heard forward. The submarine was picking up headway: *E57* was breaking through! As soon as the submarine was back on a westerly heading, Hardacre ordered, "Stop port. Half ahead port!" to continue the drive through the net. The claws of this menace could now be heard scratching and screeching on both sides of the hull. The boat was picking up speed, and smiles started appearing on the faces of the crew. Then their expressions froze.

"I can't hold her," the foreplanesman cried out, straining. "My planes are jammed . . . I can't move them!" The submarine was sinking steadily and was already back at one hundred and ten feet. The bubble in the inclinometer was creeping determinedly aft, with the bow dropping away.

"Trimming for'd to aft, Captain! Full rise on the afterplanes!" the coxswain reported without waiting for an order. "Forends! All hands aft, at the rush!" As the sailors blundered their way through the control room, the coxswain grabbed two of the strongest hands to help heave away at the substantial brass wheel controlling the foreplanes. With three men sweating away, they were beginning to move them. The foreplanes were still hard to dive, so they had much work to do yet. The afterplanes had no effect at all, and the submarine sank ever faster. The coxswain and first lieutenant exchanged mystified glances: it just made no sense.

Hardacre was the first to guess what was happening. "The noise from the net has stopped. I think we've carried part of it away and it must be jammed around the foreplanes. Its weight is dragging us down. Blow 'A' auxiliary tank . . . immediately, Cox'n, before the outside pressure gets too great. Blow number one and number two main ballast tanks!" As the mind-numbing hiss of the high-pressure air blocked out all other noise, the submarine was already fifteen degrees bow-down. Everyone was hanging on to whatever they could whilst watching the depth gauge as it recorded the relentless plunge into the deep. One hundred and fifty feet. One hundred and eighty feet.

"First Lieutenant, get up into the conning tower," Hardacre ordered. "Look through the conning tower port holes to see what's happening." Swinging off pipes and the ladder, Hackett-Jones reacted instantly, disappearing upwards with extraordinary agility for such a tall man. He peered out. There was just sufficient light for him to make out a section of net streaming astern on both sides, shouting his findings down to the captain below before climbing back down.

"We've got to make the turn soon, and perhaps that will throw the net off. Helm hard a'starboard! Steer south!" Hardacre had little clue about where they were in the channel. He could only hope *E57* wasn't turning too soon to end up on the rocky outcrop extending from Nagara Point. A turn too late would cause the submarine to run aground on the opposite European shore. The boat answered her helm, and the weight of the net did shift slightly, resulting in a list of ten degrees to port as she settled on her new course. A shout from the coxswain dragged Hardacre's mind back from his navigational concerns.

"We're nearly at two hundred feet, Sir! We've never been this deep! We're twenty degrees bow down!"

"Stop together! Full astern together!" In a last-ditch measure, Hardacre was hoping that the powerful electric motors could arrest their downward travel.

"We've got to surface, Captain, and blow all main ballast," Hackett-Jones offered circumspectly into Hardacre's ear. A curt shake of the head was his only response.

Two hundred and ten feet. The whole boat was drumming with the main motors at full power slowing, but not halting, their descent. The unmistakable noxious fumes from the ailing port motor began to fill the control room. Streaming and anxious eyes were fixed on the first lieutenant, desperate for him to do something. Hackett-Jones remained loyal to his new captain and did not react.

Two hundred and twenty feet. Very slowly, the buoyancy in the empty forward ballast tanks at last started to counter the enormous weight of the net and its sinkers and to lift the bows. Fifteen degrees bow down: the bubble was coming off.

Two hundred and thirty feet. Ten degrees down. Every watering eye in the control room was on the depth gauge. Sailors were wincing and expecting the instant collapse of the pressure hull at any second. Others were silently praying. Together with her crew, *E57* was mourning her predicament, joining in with a chilling refrain of groans, creaking fittings and squeaking rivets as the enormous pressures from outside continued to increase.

Two hundred and forty feet. Level bubble. It was time for Hardacre to act again, "Stop together. Full ahead together! Drive her up, Cox'n!"

Three loud cracks in succession deafened the crew. A dense mist filled the control room, and water started pouring down from the conning tower. The air was filled with shouts, prayers and groans. Everyone froze in terror, thinking the end had come. All except one. On his own initiative, the first lieutenant battled against the flow and pulled the conning tower lower hatch shut, clipping it securely. "Some of the windows have shattered," he reported breathlessly. How long had the water ingress been? Ten, maybe fifteen seconds? Already there was about an inch of water surging around their ankles.

A stoker watching from the engine room, with little part to play except to think too much, cracked under the strain of this latest emergency. "We're going down! *He's* done for us," he screamed out, pointing at Hardacre. "We're going to die! It's all *his* fault!"

"Pipe down!" ordered the senior engineer in a loud and most threatening scouse accent, placing a firm and not too gentle hand on the sailor's shoulder. He looked round, daring anyone else to challenge him. "Eyes front and check your panels again. This old girl's not finished yet."

Speed was building, and the stalwarts on the foreplanes had managed to attain a few degrees of rise. The afterplanes were having some noticeable effect but, reacting to this additional weight of flood water, *E57* was down at two hundred and forty-five feet. Rivets began to be fired into the boat like rifle bullets. The senior engineer and first lieutenant immediately marshalled available manpower to pounce on every new leak and hammer home the small wooden dowels carried for precisely this occurrence.

Two hundred and forty feet. Five degrees bow up. The submarine was coming up.

Two hundred and twenty feet. Still five degrees up. *E57* was rising bodily but not really under control. With the immediate situation partially resolved, they could now hear the unwelcome sound of racing propellors above them. Obviously, the boat's altercation with the net had been spotted. Enemy craft were in hot pursuit.

The captain shouted for the first lieutenant to return to the control room. "I need you here, Number One. We've got enemy patrol boats above and we've got to do our damnedest to stop her broaching: that's going to be difficult. If we do, I want you on the periscope to get whatever bearings you can to fix our position." Walking over to the chart table, Hardacre continued, "We seem to have got past Nagara here, but I have absolutely no idea where we are down the strait towards Chanak. The Cox'n and I will look after ship control, you focus on our location."

"Report the foreplanes and depth," ordered the captain.

"Foreplanes are fifteen up, Sir! Depth now ninety feet and coming up."

"Very good, Cox'n. Half ahead together. Flood 'A' tank!"

"Flood 'A' tank, aye, aye, Sir. . . . 'A' tank flooded," came the retort from the panel operator.

"Made any difference, 'Swain?"

"Not enough, Sir. We're coming up too fast. We'll have to flood main ballast and hope the foreplanes can counteract the weight of the net. Foreplanes are now twenty up."

"Thank you, Cox'n, I agree. Flood number one and number two main ballast tanks. Keep working those foreplanes," Hardacre ordered. "Here comes your chance for a fix, First Lieutenant."

The bow started dropping as soon as the forward tanks were flooded, but the boat maintained its upward momentum. Forty feet. Thirty feet. Hackett-Jones indicated for the for'd periscope to be raised and fixed his face against the rubber eyepiece. He then started to walk their single sensor around in a full circle, indicating to Hardacre that the top window was clear of the water. "Eighteen feet. Twenty feet. Twenty-one feet. Twenty-two feet. Going deep," called the afterplanesman. The periscope hissed back down into its well.

"I couldn't see a thing," Hackett-Jones sighed. "There must be at least six patrol boats up there. They all started to fire like crazy as soon as the periscope was seen. There was just spray all around where their shots fell. It was like being in a blizzard."

"Foreplanes aren't holding it, Sir," came the cry from ship control. "Bubble's moving aft and driving us back down."

"Very good. Blow Number One Main Ballast! Leave the foreplanes at full-to-rise and try to get a trim at that. Keep sixty feet. Speed for trimming," Hardacre commanded. He waited a little while to see how the coxswain would manage. After a few deep and shallow depth excursions, the submarine settled on depth by maintaining a five-degree bow-up attitude at about six knots. The captain then indicated for Hackett-Jones to join him at the chart table.

"I cannot estimate by guess or by God or any other method where we are on the chart," he started in muted tones so as not to be overheard. "It's imperative we make that turn around Kilid Bahr because, if we overshoot, we might never get out of Sari Siglar Bay the way we are. Even if we make that call correctly, I cannot think for one minute we'd ever survive going under those minefields with all this debris hanging off us. Do we have any options? Could we manoeuvre aggressively astern to try to shake it off? I suppose a last resort would be to surface and run the gauntlet through the guns and the mines? Do you have any ideas?"

Before the first lieutenant could answer, the two officers were thrown off their feet, as were most of the crew, as the boat was brought up all standing. What was this? Another net? The bow was flung up to about ten degrees, and the boat came up to fifty feet. The captain demanded full power yet again to try to break through. As the boat started to move ahead again, the crew could hear a rasping starting from the bow and moving aft. Whatever was causing this new noise also forced the boat deeper.

Yet another clamour now grabbed their attention, becoming louder and louder. Propellers were racing and fizzing. At that speed, it could mean only one thing – a torpedo! The torpedo's whine was building towards its crescendo on the starboard side. Even the most hardened warriors aboard were waiting for the impending oblivion at any second, quietly praying to themselves and thinking of families with their eyes shut. In a flash, they could hear the harbinger of doom zoom above and behind them to disappear on the other beam.

Having dragged himself to his feet, Hardacre hardly moved from his position between the lowered periscopes nor said a word. But as much to himself as to his crew, he explained, "We thought they might guard any obstruction with torpedoes."

Above, the deadly cable obstructing their passage continued to stroke *E57*'s jumping wire like a violin's bow in a ghastly glissando. Then, reaching the periscope standards, it released its captive with a jolt. Miraculously, it carried away with it the trapped remnants of the anti-submarine net. Liberated from the net's hold, the submarine's list came off, and the foreplanes became free to operate. The boat shot up to fifteen feet with the bow broaching the surface.

"Flood number one main ballast tank! Full ahead together! Full dive on the planes. All hands for'd!" yelled the captain. "Number One, we need those bearings! If nothing else, get Kilid Bahr!"

Once again, the sea around the exposed periscope was stirred up into a violent tumult of boiling water by the falling shot from the pursuing patrol boats. Still, the greater height of eye allowed Hackett-Jones to get the vital bearing he needed. Indeed, he could hardly have failed to see Kilid Bahr fort as it towered massively overhead, no more than five hundred yards away and directly on the starboard beam. There were one or two loud clangs as shots hit home on the conning tower, which would have no effect because it was already flooded. The first lieutenant swung the periscope round to the southwest and glimpsed Kephez Point just as the submarine dipped back down beneath the surface.

"Half ahead together, keep eighty feet, speed for trimming," the captain ordered as the boat passed thirty feet and into safety. The orders were repeated to his back as he turned quickly to the chart table to join Hackett-Jones.

"Good fix. We're here," the latter pointed out with a big grin. "Ready to wheel over in a couple of minutes." They were right in the centre of the narrowest part of the whole transit, where they had run aground *twice* at the start of the patrol. But now, *E57* had only to make this turn and then dip beneath the minefields to safety.

"Helm hard a'port! Steer southwest. Speed five knots," ordered the relieved captain.

Less than five minutes later, loud scrapings of the wires tethering the buoyant charges overhead announced *E57*'s arrival in the minefield. The submarine's passage through this last danger area seemed interminable at her slow speed and head-on to the saline counter-current. Their already-frayed nerves remained on edge as the wires screeched past one after another. Would their luck hold for this final obstacle?

After thirty-five minutes, Hardacre assessed that they must be close to open water beyond Kephez and free of the minefields, and the scratchings of the mine wires had ceased. Then they noticed that these noises had been replaced by another. There was a steady thump, thump, thump at five- or six-second intervals. Hardacre looked at Hackett-Jones for any ideas, to draw only a shaking of his head. The boat seemed to be under control, with no evident defects in equipment operation. Hence, the cause of this new knocking was a mystery. The submarine was ordered back to periscope depth to take a navigational observation.

Believing they were safely past the minefields, the atmosphere in the control room became noticeably more relaxed. The periscope was raised, and the first lieutenant rattled off the bearings to fix their position, pausing briefly to look right ahead before ordering the mast down. With Hardacre busy plotting out the fix, Hackett-Jones joined him in a huddle over the chart table.

"I think we've caught a mine," he said quietly and in a measured tone, not to raise any anxiety with the rest of the ship's company. "You need to have a look."

"Fix on. Puts us safe in the centre of the channel and past the Suandere River. We're safely past the minefields," their commanding officer announced to the control room team. "I'll have a look to see if I can identify our escort ahead. Raise periscope!"

Looking forward, Hardacre could just make out the enormous black shape with its deadly horns occasionally breaking the surface between the bow and the periscope. A second or two after it disappeared, he could hear the ominous boom as the mine hit the for'd casing. While the mine's lead detonators remained undamaged, they would remain safe. However, any unexpected movement could spell disaster.

Keeping up the pretence, Hardacre lowered the periscope and reported, "Nothing in sight," before rejoining Hackett-Jones over the chart to continue their discussion in hushed tones.

"We cannot do anything here. We are still under the guns at Kephez Point, so surfacing is out of the question. In any case, if we surface as normal to free it, there is also the real danger that we set off the explosive. We could move as many people as possible aft and shut the forends bulkhead door to save as many as we can. What do you think, Number One?"

"From the way it is behaving, I believe the wire is trapped somewhere forward with the heavy sinker below and buoyant mine above, keeping it in place," Hackett-Jones opined. "If the thing goes off, the submarine and the crew will be lost - everyone - no matter what precautions we take or where people are positioned on the boat. Therefore, I don't think we need tell them until just before we surface because this might just cause unnecessary anxiety. But I do believe there is a way out. When we are clear of the Straits, we could jolt the boat astern as we surface to try to shake it free."

"Very well. I agree," consented Hardacre after little thought. "You will surface the boat and do what you think is necessary: you know how to trim *E57* better than me. We have the other problem of course. We're not sure whether the ETA signal was ever received and that we are expected. As you bring her up, I will be ready to get to the bridge as soon as possible with two sailors available with White Ensigns. In the meantime, we will keep the speed steady and hope the wire doesn't slip down or jam tighter."

The submarine was almost abeam Cape Helles, close to the agreed rendezvous position by Morto Bay. Still, they did not wish to be detected even by friendly forces. There was a call for quiet. As they listened, they could detect the faint rhythmic beat of a destroyer's propellers as it patrolled slowly north and south, but was this their escort?

Hardacre waited until this vessel had turned and was opening from them when he ordered, "First Lieutenant, surface the submarine!"

"Aye, aye, Sir. Standby to surface." Hackett-Jones addressed the control room team, "Now, I want you all to pay close attention. We have fouled a mine trapped by the foreplanes, so we won't be surfacing in the normal manner. I need you to follow my instructions exactly and immediately." The young lieutenant turned to look aft. "Chief Artificer Bowers," he called to the senior rate stood by the front of the diesels – somewhat formally to broker no dissent. "I really need you to give me *all* you've got despite the defective armature." With a curt nod, *E57*'s senior engineer disappeared aft.

"Stop together! Grouper switch up! Full astern together!" came the command. "Standby the blows!" Having waited for sternway to be firmly established, the submarine was ready.

"BLOW THE AFTER TRIM TANK! BLOW NUMBER FIVE, SIX, SEVEN AND EIGHT MAIN BALLAST TANKS!"

E57 responded to the orders, with the stern rising rapidly as the bow dipped deep into the water. The surge of power from the propellers sent a boiling wash along the entire length of the boat. Checking through the periscope – there was no need now to be circumspect – Hardacre saw the mine's mooring wire freeing itself from the hydroplane. The mine bobbed twice on the surface and then disappeared, dragged down by its heavy sinker into the depths.

He signalled this to the first lieutenant, who surfaced the submarine fully while still going astern to clear away from the mine. Hardacre wasted no time easing open the lower hatch and earned a good soaking as the conning tower emptied. He was followed immediately by the two hands with ensigns ready. Reaching the bridge, he was pleased to identify the destroyer as *Grampus*. She was of the same class of escort that accompanied them on their outward journey, indicating that she had been sent to meet them. She was undoubtedly alert and had started reversing course at the first sign of the submarine, which was now fine on her port bow. Thankfully, she remained at a slow speed, and her guns remained trained fore and aft. It was clear that the ETA signal *had* been received, and they were expected.

More than just expected, word of *E57*'s remarkable exploits had spread even to the troops ashore, and the beaches were lined with cheering soldiers throwing caps in the air. Hardacre called all the submarine's key personnel to the bridge to enjoy the spectacle and accept the adulation. They watched *Grampus* lay a dan buoy to mark the position of the mine to be swept later. Next, the destroyer signalled for the submarine to take station astern and follow them back to Mudros.

Hardacre instructed the first lieutenant to prepare the submarine for the return to harbour because he knew the routine, whereas the new commanding officer did not. Although soaked to the skin, Hardacre was happy to keep the bridge watch. He didn't have to care about navigation, Turkish gunboats or any other stresses of being on patrol in the enemy's backyard. He had been given this unique opportunity in a previously unimaginable environment. Not only had he genuinely enjoyed the whole patrol, but at last felt that he personally had contributed to the war effort. Exhausted but content and with so much to reflect upon, the short journey to Lemnos Island passed in a flash. The submarine was just short of the harbour entrance, and he could already see that the anchored ships had their officers and ratings lining the rails to welcome them home.

Hardacre shouted down the conning tower, "Pass a message to the first lieutenant, coxswain, senior engineer and LTO, that I request the pleasure of their company on the bridge." In short order, the three appeared from the conning tower hatch, looking quite bemused.

"It looks like they're arranging quite a reception for *E57*," he started, pointing out the preparations.

"Captain," interrupted the coxswain. "I thought you'd want to know that Andrews has come round and seems none the worse for wear despite the flesh wound on his side. He remembered exactly what happened and confirmed your opinion that nothing could have been done to save the capt . . . er . . . I mean Lieutenant Crockford."

"But," the coxswain continued, "it does leave the question open about what we're going to do with Andrews as regards the charge against him. Have you any ideas?"

"Umm, tricky," replied Hardacre, scratching his chin in a pantomime gesture. "As *I* remember the incident, however, there was only ever one witness to the *alleged* crime. That witness is no longer available to provide evidence, so it would be rather difficult to prove. Also, I believe the exact sentence awarded has been served. Is that not right, Coxswain?" In a more serious tone, he added, "Struggling with faulty equipment, Andrews went above and beyond his duty. I don't honestly believe that Lieutenant Crockford would want him to suffer more anguish. But it's not up to me.

"You see, I have an admission to make." Hardacre turned to face the others directly. "Indeed, I had no right to assume command. King's Regulations dictate that the next most senior officer appointed to the ship should have that honour. Therein lies the rub. I have never been *appointed* to *E57* but only loaned from my assigned duties in *Queen Elizabeth*. You are right, of course: it *should* have been the first lieutenant who took command. You see, I knew you didn't have a copy of KRs onboard. I won't bore you with the full story, but I had a long-standing debt of honour to repay to Lieutenant Crockford. I needed to ensure that *his* final instructions to get his beloved submarine and crew back safely were followed to the letter. It was a close-run thing, granted," he grinned, "because even *he* didn't account for catching a mine. But we made it!

"It is so fitting that today is a Tuesday when the traditional toast is "Our Men". It's never been about who is the captain of this submarine, and it's probably been simpler for an outsider like me to see that. You –

all of you and the men down below – are *E57*, and all the boat's successes are yours equally.

"I'm just a passenger," he finished with a shrug. "So, I'm going to leave you to enjoy the homecoming. I'm going below. Lieutenant Hackett-Jones, you have the ship."

With that, Hardacre climbed down the conning tower and, ignoring the mystified looks all around him, sat down in the 'wardroom' chair and picked up a book to read.

The cheering in Mudros harbour went around and around as each ship *E57* passed took up the hurrahs and waving of caps. The first lieutenant and senior ratings basked in the glory, grinning like idiots. For the first time, they fully understood what had been achieved and the contribution they had each made to the whole campaign.

The first lieutenant slickly manoeuvred the submarine alongside the depot ship before mooring lines were passed and the light aluminium gangway manhandled into place. Hackett-Jones felt somewhat uncomfortable as, for the first time as the commanding officer of *E57*, he was piped across the brow to report to his flotilla commander. This was indeed a momentous occasion, and Somerville had been joined by Roger Keyes, bringing his own and the commander-in-chief's congratulations. There had been no opportunity to warn HQ of the captain's demise. Hackett-Jones had some rapid explaining to do to quell their initial surprise that it was he who crossed the gangway. This was sad news for them indeed, and there was much other feedback the command group wanted to hear, so they led the young lieutenant away for a full debrief.

4

The usual hubbub resulting from a submarine returning from patrol died down after twenty minutes or so. The sailors were permitted in stages to proceed to their inboard messes, leaving the minimum duty watch aboard.

Hardacre picked up the small grip holding his few personal belongings and climbed up the conning tower ladder only when it was all quiet. The casing sentry saw his arrival on deck and stood smartly to attention at the end of the brow. He saluted this officer, whom the entire ship's company now appreciated was more than worthy of such respect.

Hardacre thought the waists of the depot ship were empty, but as he turned forward in the direction of the wardroom accommodation, he found Andrina standing in the shadows, clearly upset.

"Madam, is there anything I can do for you?" Rupert Hardacre asked tenderly.

She, too, had thought she was on her own and rapidly tried to compose herself as this officer approached. "No, no. It's quite all right. It's just that I was . . . I was a . . . . a . . friend of Lieutenant Crockford and was dreadfully shocked to hear that he had been killed."

She was dressed in her usual, all-black garb whilst on duty in the ships, with a headscarf tied tightly and concealing her hair. Rupert thought there was something familiar about her.

"Aren't you the one who delivered our periscope? All the crew was so surprised that a lady should take such risks to get that to us. You should know it was vital that we had that spare because the other one was damaged. We could not have navigated back safely through the straits if you hadn't done that for us.

"Your friend, Edward, had a magnificent patrol and one that will be commemorated and celebrated for a very long time." He saw that she was trying to be brave but trembling slightly, so he added, "Listen, you've had a terrible shock. Why don't you let me take you to the wardroom, so I can tell you all about it over a drink."

She realised she *was* upset and found this gentleman's kind manner comforting. Unusually, she consented. Together, they turned and walked forward.

Chapter 11 – We Never See Our Foes

The tall, upright officer walked out onto the open quarterdeck, hoping that the shade and afternoon breeze might provide some relief away from the stuffy atmosphere inside the cruiser. His discomfort was not helped by the high, stiff collar and the formal clothing designed for northern latitudes. Following the custom the Kaiser had adopted during his frequent visits to the Ottoman capital, officers were required to wear a Fez. To his mind, this was the most ridiculous headwear, totally unsuitable for duties aboard a warship. In fact, the whole vessel was designed for the open North Sea and the Atlantic Ocean, not for these land-locked waters. It was no better for the Imperial High Seas Fleet, of course, forbidden by the Kaiser to venture out in force to seek offensive action. In effect, the pride of Germany was now blockaded in Kiel by the English submarines and by the brooding, self-styled 'Grand Fleet' of the damned British.

He gazed around at the splendours of the Golden Horn but saw little; he had been trapped here for far too long, and these sights no longer held any attraction or interest. His ship once bore the name of the proud Prussian city of *Breslau* in Silesia but now had been renamed as the almost unpronounceable *Midilli*. Rather than taking on the enemy's might as she should be, his ship's operations had been reduced to laying minefields, bombarding defenceless towns and harbours, or even – the ultimate disgrace – acting as a troop carrier or supply ship. Where was the honour in any of that? Having recently been damaged by a mine, repairs to the cruiser were expected to last at least six months, stranding him here.

Being the signals officer, he had been privy to hearing of the exploits of British submarines in the Sea of Marmara. He privately admired the invention and initiative of those junior officers who were having such an inordinate effect on the resupply of essential men and materiel to the frontline on the Gallipoli Peninsula. The latest sinking of the *Torgut Reis* whilst under heavy escort was a remarkable achievement. Under the dynamic and aggressive leadership of Korvettenkapitän Hermann Bauer, *Führer der Unterseeboote*, he saw that Germany's submarines were having no less impact. They were successfully attacking British warships in the German Ocean and waging an unrestricted *guerre de course* in the North Atlantic.

But here was an ambitious young officer. The accepted route to high office was via the capital ships with their massive guns, and that was how, from a young age, he had always perceived he would manipulate his own career. That had now changed. He would not be promoted to Oberleutnant zur See until March 1916 so, although junior, he must not waste time and could not just stagnate here. The war might be over before he could make his mark. German authorities did not hold their submariners in high regard, so he kept his own counsel in case it counted against him in his current appointment. He had decided to act independently and, some months ago, had written to the personnel division of High Command.

A steward appeared at his elbow, "Leutnant Dönitz, there is a letter for you."

Hardly acknowledging the messenger and seeing the embossed seal on the envelope, he ripped it open and scanned the single-page letter. He punched his two fists to his chest in celebration. Yes, his escape plan had worked. He would be transferred to submarine forces in October 1916. Selfishly, he hoped that Germany would not have won the war by then!

Epilogue – This 'Wonderful' Year

I will not retell here the whole Dardanelles and Gallipoli chronicle, but the reader might appreciate a few vignettes and a chronology to set the historical context for this story.

SMS *Goeben*, a modern battlecruiser, and SMS *Breslau*, a light cruiser, having been on station in the Mediterranean since 1912, had been undergoing repairs in Pola, a harbour to the north of the Adriatic Sea. Convinced that Konteradmiral Wilhelm Souchon of the Imperial German Navy would attempt to break this *Mittelmeerdivision* out via the Gibraltar Straits, all Allied efforts in the Mediterranean were directed towards intercepting and destroying these capable ships. On 4th August 1914, contact was eventually made when the British battlecruisers HMS *Indomitable* and HMS *Indefatigable*, rushing west to reinforce the Gibraltar Straits, passed *Goeben* and *Breslau* heading in the opposite direction. However, it was only nine-thirty in the morning and, unlike France, Britain was not yet formally at war with Germany; that would happen only at eleven o'clock that same evening. London was informed of the location of the German squadron, but without mention by Admiral Milne – Commander-in-Chief Mediterranean – of the key factor that it was *heading east* and not towards Gibraltar. An initial Admiralty order authorising an attack had to be withdrawn because the Cabinet decreed that it wouldn't be honourable to commence hostilities before a formal declaration of war.

Uninhibited by such sentiment, a secret German-Ottoman defence treaty had already been signed on 2nd

August 1914 and, two days later, Souchon had been ordered to proceed at once to Constantinople (present-day Istanbul), the Ottoman capital. By a supreme effort, which included requisitioning coal from every available German merchant ship in Messina harbour, Souchon managed to disguise his intended destination and evaded the battlecruisers of the British Mediterranean Fleet. The German High Command did not help their Admiral's predicament when it signalled on 6th August to inform him that Austria would not provide any naval aid and – a more severe setback – that the Ottoman Empire was still officially neutral. Thus, he should no longer make for Constantinople. Unlike his British counterparts, Milne and Troubridge, Souchon acted with commendable initiative as the military commander on the spot and determined that he *would* continue to Constantinople regardless. With the only other option being a return to Pola where the ships would probably be interred for the duration, his grasp of the strategic situation was exceptional, stating his intention as being, "to force the Ottoman Empire, even against its will, to spread the war to the Black Sea against its ancient enemy, Russia." *Goeben* and *Breslau* entered the Dardanelle Straits without hindrance on 10th August, being granted access by Enver Pasha, Minister of War and leader of the 'Young Turks'.

With the growing importance of the Dardanelles zone, the next issue for the Allies was the selection of a suitable leader. Rear Admiral Ernest Charles Thomas Troubridge had been in command of the battlecruisers that failed to engage *Goeben* and *Breslau* off Cape Matapan. He meekly followed them east and had initially remained in command of forces on station off the Dardanelles. Troubridge had then been recalled to the UK to be court-martialled, facing the blame for the escape of the German warships. Churchill had wished to appoint Rear Admiral Arthur Henry Limpus as Troubridge's replacement; Limpus had been the head of the British naval mission to the Ottoman Empire since May 1912, so knew the Turks and the theatre of operations well. Nevertheless, the Foreign Office – still desperately hoping the Ottomans would remain neutral – thought that Limpus' appointment to such a role would be "unduly provocative". Again, 'gentlemanly behaviour' was considered by politicians to be more important than pursuing the Country's objectives in war. Promoted to Vice-Admiral on 14th September 1914, Limpus replaced Carden as the Superintendent of Malta Dockyard. The ensuing selection of Vice-Admiral Sir Sackville Hamilton Carden to take command of the burgeoning Dardanelles fleet certainly came as a shock to many. Already fifty-seven, Carden had been promoted to Rear Admiral in 1908, but had flown his flag at sea for just one year, but only as the second-in-command to then-Vice-Admiral Jellicoe. Clearly unhappy to have Carden in command of his all-important project, in January 1915 the First Lord, Winston Churchill, offered Vice-Admiral Sir Percy Scott command of the fleet tasked with forcing the Dardanelles. Although Scott had retired from the Navy in 1913, he was a gunnery expert and still actively involved with the Service in connection with the development of director firing. Scott refused, "I could not accept the offer as I knew it was an impossible task . . ." When Carden later fell ill and had to withdraw, another opportunity to employ Limpus' talents was missed – understandably perhaps – because de Robeck had a better detailed knowledge of the well-developed plans for the impending operations.

This is a classic "what if?" Had *Indomitable* and *Indefatigable* been permitted to engage, or Troubridge had not followed his Flag Captain's faint-hearted advice, such forces should have been more than a match for the two German ships and the whole Gallipoli story might have unfolded quite differently, if at all.

Stuck in an impasse, having already tested the shore and minefield defences on several occasions, the whole plan for the Royal Navy's bombardment of the forts on 18th March 1915 depended on either the enemy being hopelessly inefficient as gunners or their moral fibre being unable to withstand the terrifying onslaught to be unleashed upon them. As had been demonstrated previously, neither presumption could be supported. Furthermore, there was ample evidence that these stone redoubts enjoyed relative impunity from naval shells fired on a flat trajectory. In addition, little attention seems to have been afforded to the vulnerability of the Allies' own units from the moveable howitzers ashore, which delivered their payload in a high trajectory down onto the unarmoured decks of the mighty British and French warships. The only surprise was that the defeat of the Allies on this occasion was brought about by an undetected minefield. In the event, the defenders fought on effectively and gallantly despite losing more than two hundred men. This lesson seems to have been missed in future planning too, with the mainly-conscripted Turkish soldiers proving to be doughty fighters and very well directed by their German leaders. The Dardanelles Commission came to the same conclusion: "*At the outset all decisions were taken and all provisions based on the assumption that, if a landing were effected, the resistance would be slight and the advancement rapid. We can see no sufficient ground for this assumption.*"

Once committed to the land campaign on the Gallipoli Peninsular, the Navy played a key role by landing soldiers ashore, in providing gunfire support and by maintaining the constant supply of ammunition, provisions and water. But after 25th May, when HMS *Triumph* was sunk by *U21*, who struck again two days later by torpedoing HMS *Majestic*, the heavy ships were withdrawn leaving the donkey work to be carried out by vessels of lesser worth; torpedo boat destroyers and smaller units. The presence of a single German submarine had therefore been able to completely disrupt the operational plan. Despite submarines having been a reality for more than a decade and the presence of German boats being suspected, no anti-submarine measures appear to have been in place other than ineffective, self-defence nets rigged from the major warships, supposedly to block torpedoes. Later-to-become-Admiral of the Fleet Andrew Browne Cunningham was in command of HMS *Scorpion* and later reflected on the limited anti-submarine measures available at the time. Mourning the absence of asdic and depth charges, he related that one idea, "was for an armed whaler to be kept in readiness. In it were a few elongated canvas bags, and the blacksmith with his forty-pound sledgehammer. On a periscope being sighted the whaler went off in chase, and a man in her bows slipped a bag over the top of the periscope, thus blinding the German gentleman with his eye glued to the eyepiece below. If the bag project failed, believe it or not, the blacksmith was directed to smash the top of the instrument with his hammer... we laughed and laughed!"

Having set the scene, the chronology of the campaign principally from a submarine and theatre perspective follows.

1914

2nd August
: Ottoman Empire signs a secret Treaty of [defensive] Alliance with Germany against Russia. Despite weasel words, it confers "chief command" over Turkish forces to the German military mission in the event of war.

4th August
: At 11 pm, Great Britain declares war on Germany.

5th August
: Churchill requisitions the Turkish warships that are building in Great Britain. *Sultan Osman I* and *Reshadieh*, become HMS *Agincourt* and HMS *Erin* respectively. These ships had been funded by Ottoman public subscription, so the 'Young Turks' Government used this situation to stir up anti-British feelings.

10th August
: *Goeben* and *Breslau* arrive at the Dardanelles.

18th August
: Ottoman Notification of Neutrality.

27th September
: Turkish Straits closed to maritime traffic.

19th October
: *Goeben* and *Breslau* gifted to the Ottomans by Germany, being renamed *Yavuz Sultan Selim* and *Midilli*, respectively.

31st October
: Admiralty authorises hostilities against the Ottoman Empire.

2nd November Russia declares war on Turkey.

5th November Great Britain and France declare war on The Ottoman Empire.

14th November Ottoman Empire's formal declaration of war on the Triple Alliance. The Sultan declares *'jihad'*.

22nd November The Turks launch an offensive against Russian positions in the Caucasus.

13th December *B11* (Holbrook) torpedoes *Mesûdiye* in Sari Siglar Bay. Holbrook awarded the first Royal Navy VC of the War. In a letter to Roger Keyes, Holbrook described the extreme difficulty in maintaining trim whilst manoeuvring within the Straits.

1915

2nd January The Tsar requests the Allies to attack the Ottomans to prevent the Russians having to fight on two fronts; the Turks in the Caucasus and the Germans in the west.

4th January The Russians defeat a large Ottoman army in the Caucasus at Sarikamish. The battle was fought in a temperature of -30°C and more than 30,000 Turks froze to death.

5th January Exceeding her orders, FS *Saphir* (de Fournier) attempts to repeat *B11*'s exploits and go further, only to develop a leak and suffer grounding off Chanak. Forced to surface, and coming under shellfire, she is scuttled by her crew. 15 perish (including the CO) and 14 are rescued by Turks and made POWs.

1st February | *AE2* (Stoker) arrives in theatre.

4th February | The declaration of unrestricted submarine warfare. Merchant ships having been sunk without warning, German atrocities had already been committed by *U20* (Droescher), contrary to International Law and Germany's own Prize Regulations. Admiral von Pohl, on assuming command of the High Seas Fleet, now formally declares that, after 17th February, "every merchant ship in this War Zone [around Great Britain and Ireland] will be destroyed, nor will it always be possible to obviate the danger with which the crews and passengers are thereby threatened."

8th February | Roger Keyes superseded by Sydney Hall as Commodore (S) and Arthur Waistell replaces him as Captain (S) in command of HMS *Maidstone* and of all submarines of the Harwich Striking Force.

6th March | Undetected, the Turkish minelayer *Nusrat* lays twenty mines in Erenkoy Bay. Rather than being in a line *across* the Straits, these mines were positioned *parallel* and close to the Asian side where it had been seen that Allied warships had a habit of turning to exit the Dardanelles. It was these – and not the floating mines suspected — that were responsible for damaging British and French ships during the naval bombardment on 18th March.

11th March	General Sir Ian Hamilton is appointed to command a proposed Constantinople Expeditionary Force (later changed to Mediterranean Expeditionary Force).
18th March	Failed all-out Naval attack on the forts in the Dardanelles, involving 16 heavy ships.
9th April	*Adamant*, *E14* and *E15* arrive at Mudros.
14th April	Conference of submarine COs. When briefing, C G Brodie used most of the details he had worked out previously with Stoker. As described, "No, No, No" went round the table in answer to Keyes' question, "Do you think an E-Boat can make it?" It was T S Brodie (*E15*) who gave the answer Keyes really wanted, "Yes!" So, it was decided that *E15* would be the first to attempt the transit.

To T S Brodie must be accorded the credit, therefore, for accepting the challenge the Hellespont represented. Had Stoker not been stuck in Malta, there is no doubt that he too would have supported the attempt and probably would have strenuously volunteered to be the first to try.

16th April	*E15* (T S Brodie) fails the first attempt to transit the Dardanelles and runs aground west of Kephez. The CO and two others are killed with the rest taken as POWs. The submarine was destroyed by torpedoes launched from *Triumph's* and *Majestic's* picket boats. T S Brodie might have been in some hurry to get away before Nasmith arrived, expecting him to be the favourite for the first attempt.
18th April	*E11* (Nasmith) arrives at Mudros from Malta. Alongside the repair ship *Reliance* (Eng. Captain Humphries) to effect repairs to the intermediate shaft, it was necessary to take off the after superstructure and remove plates from her hull over the engine room, work expected to take three weeks.
21st April	*AE2* (Stoker) arrives at Mudros after repairs in Malta.
23rd April	The poet, Rupert Brooke, who was a member of the Royal Naval Division bound for Gallipoli, dies on the Greek island of Skyros from an infected mosquito bite.
	His most quoted lines are: *"If I should die think only this of me; that there's a corner of some foreign field that is forever England."* Brooke was a friend of General Hamilton who, much to the annoyance of *Queen Elizabeth's* communications staff, spent much time in composing

long, 'priority' messages to him whilst the battle was raging. He clearly wasn't aware that Brooke had already died.

25th April 1915 After a false start the previous day owing to a faulty foreplanes mechanism, *AE2* (Stoker) executes the first successful submarine transit of the Dardanelles. Underplaying the navigational difficulties, Keyes had encouraged Stoker to attack anything that looked capable of laying mines as he passed through, in part as a measure to protect the warships and troop transports engaged that same day in conducting the amphibious assault.

Accordingly, Stoker sinks a Turkish gun boat off Chanak and this additional objective was probably the main reason for *AE2* running aground twice as described. It would be difficult to identify a more challenging location to carry out a submarine attack, with so little sea room in which to manoeuvre, together with unknown currents, whorls and eddies.

Whilst nominally still in command of the B-boats and smaller French submarines, Lt Cdr George Harley Pownall is killed whilst acting as Assistant Beach Master in the leading boat arriving on V Beach. Previously, that role had been assigned to Lt Cdr C G Brodie who was engaged in *E15*'s destruction.

25th April (Cont.)	At the command conference that evening, having read *AE2*'s signal, Keyes' true words were:

"Tell them this. It is an omen — an Australian submarine has done the finest feat in submarine history and is going to torpedo all the ships bringing reinforcements, supplies and ammunition into Gallipoli."

Another splendid reason for celebrating ANZAC day on 25th April.

Having been the first submarine to sink a warship — HMS *Pathfinder* on 5th September 1914 — German submarine *U21* (Hersing) departs Wilhelmshaven for the Dardanelles.

27th April	*E14* (Boyle) successful transit of Straits.
29th April	*E14* (Boyle) and *AE2* (Stoker) rendezvous inside the Sea of Marmara and arrange to do so again the next day.
30th April	*AE2* (Stoker) suffers severe loss of trim, is spotted by Turkish gun boat *Sultanhisar* and holed by shell fire. The submarine is scuttled and the entire crew taken as POWs.

The cause of the extreme loss of trim is unknown. This might have been the mixing of saline and freshwater layers, or perhaps the serious grounding off Kilid Bahr was responsible, resulting in some undetected damage. Extremes of trim had been reported previously: by *B11* when in Sari Siglar Bay; and by *E11* in 1914 when off Heligoland.

FS *Joule* (du Petit-Thouars) attempts the transit. She is assumed to have hit a mine and lost with all thirty-one hands.

13th May	The battleship *Goliath* is sunk by three torpedoes from the Turkish destroyer *Muavenet-I Millet*. The British CO, Captain T Lowrie-Shelford, and five hundred and seventy of his crew were lost.
15th May	Lord Jackie Fisher resigns as First Sea Lord as result of disagreements with Churchill concerning handling of the Dardanelles expedition.
18th May	*E14* (Boyle) returns safely from the Sea of Marmara – the first to do so. A most successful patrol, Boyle is awarded the VC.
19th May	*E11* (Nasmith) successful transit of the Straits.
23rd May	Off Constantinople, *E11* (Nasmith) attacks the Turkish Torpedo Gunboat *Peleng-I Derya* with single torpedo. Before sinking, a shot from the warship's six-pounder deck gun hits *E11's* for'd periscope putting it completely out of action.

E11's damaged periscope after it was hit.
By kind permission of IWM. © Imperial War Museums (Q13268)

25th May   *E11* (Nasmith) attacks *Stamboul* alongside Constantinople's Arsenal Wharf. As observed from *USS Scorpion* at anchor, the torpedo thought to have been fired from the shore was in fact Nasmith's first torpedo, running rogue and circling the submarine. The second torpedo passed *Scorpion* at a range of only thirty yards, before blowing up lighters moored alongside *Stamboul*, and tearing a large hole in the steamer's starboard quarter.

25th May
(Cont.)

E11's attack on Constantinople, the first by an enemy vessel in over a hundred years, has an enormous impact on Turkish morale, causing a panic in the city and compelling *Goeben* to shift to a safer mooring.

Battleship HMS *Triumph* is torpedoed by German submarine *U21* (Hersing). As a result, the theatre is thought too dangerous for HMS *Queen Elizabeth*, which is sent back to the Grand Fleet. The other large ships are withdrawn to Mudros with the consequent loss of heavy gunfire support to the troops ashore.

27th May

Battleship HMS *Majestic* is torpedoed by German submarine *U21 (Hersing)*.

7th June

E11 (Nasmith) completes her first patrol. Having been disappointed that there were no enemy warships in the Nagara anchorage, Nasmith returned to the Mussa Bank area (about 5 miles back) where he had seen a large troop ship. Sinking the vessel with the single torpedo he had left, he continued his safe exit from the Dardanelles. By propelling full speed astern and surfacing stern first, he shook free a large mine which had been caught by his port foreplane. Nasmith was awarded a VC. His First Lieutenant Guy D'Oyly Hughes RN and Navigator Robert Brown RNR both received a DSC and every other crew member a DSM.

10th June	*E14* (Boyle) successful transit to commence her second patrol, this time armed with a three-pounder gun.
18th June	*E12* (Bruce) enters the Sea of Marmara, having fought through a net which causes damage to her main motors.
28th June	*E12* (Bruce) completes her foreshortened patrol.
30th June	*E7* (Cochrane) successful transit of the Straits to relieve *E14*.
3rd July	*E14* (Boyle) completes her second patrol in the Sea of Marmara.
20th July	*E14* (Boyle) successful transit to commence her third patrol.
24th July	*E7* (Cochrane) completes her twenty-four-day patrol in the Sea of Marmara, sinking thirteen ships.
27th July	FS *Mariotte* (Fabre) is caught in an anti-submarine net at Nagara and forced to surface. The boat is scuttled and crew taken as POWs.
5th August	*E11* (Nasmith), transiting the Straits, is caught in a net beyond Nagara Point and snags its 5-inch wire foot-rope. The submarine was lifted from one hundred and ten to ninety feet, before a crack was heard and *E11* freed. *E11* torpedoed a three-masted transport ship even before passing Gallipoli to commence her second patrol, now armed with a twelve-pounder gun.

6th August	During the late evening, British units begin landing at Suvla Bay.
8th August	*E11* (Nasmith) sinks *Barbaros Hayreddin* (sister ship to *Torgut Reis*) to prevent that battleship countering the new British landing at Suvla (near Bulair) by shelling the Allied positions.
12th August	*E14* (Boyle) completes her third patrol of twenty-four days in the Sea of Marmara, but not without having to break through an anti-submarine net off Nagara. A total of seventy days had been spent in the Marmara during her three patrols.
13th August	*E2* (Stocks) enters the Sea of Marmara, taking ten minutes to fight through the net at Nagara and plunging to one hundred and forty feet having broken through.
15th August	*E11* (Nasmith) torpedoes *Isfahan* berthed alongside Haidar Pasha Railway Pier, on the east side of the entrance into Constantinople. This was a collier and a great loss to the energy-strapped capital city.
20th-21st August	Overnight, *E11's* First Lieutenant, Guy D'Oyly-Hughes, swam ashore and blew up a section of the Constantinople–Baghdad railway line, a feat for which he was awarded the Distinguished Service Order (having been recommended for a VC by VAdm de Robeck).

3rd September   *E11* (Nasmith) returns from her second patrol. The submarine was propelling at eight knots and at eighty feet to encounter the net, being brought up to sixty feet but holding her course before breaking through.   D'Oyly-Hughes observed the net through the conning tower portholes to assess its construction.   As a result, Nasmith advised that it should be attempted to pass under a net at one hundred and twenty feet or more.

4th September   *E7* (Cochrane) attempts the transit for her second patrol when her starboard propeller becomes entangled in an anti-submarine net. Battling for twelve hours to free her, Cochrane scuttled *E7* after she was badly damaged by a depth charge.

8th September   *E2* (Stocks) lands her First Lieutenant, Harold Vernon Lyon, with intention to emulate D'Oyly-Hughes' feat but, although a loud explosion was heard, Lyon was never heard of again.

14th September   *E2* (Stocks) returns from patrol.

16th September   *E12* (Bruce) enters the Sea of Marmara, the first boat to be equipped with a 4-inch gun.

2nd October   *H1* (Pirie) commences her patrol in the Sea of Marmara. A US-designed and built boat, she was much smaller than the E Class; she nonetheless achieved a good 'score'.

| 15th October | General Sir Ian Hamilton relieved of his command. |

| 22nd October | FS *Turquoise* (Ravenel) is the first French submarine to successfully penetrate through to the Sea of Marmara but, having run aground twice during the passage, she experiences lasting damage. |

| 23rd October | *E20* (Warren) completes successful transit of the Straits, having torpedoed two steamers en route. |

| 25th October | *E12* (Bruce), exiting the Dardanelles after a forty-day patrol, snagged and carried away part of an anti-submarine net, severely affecting the trim as described. The nets were made from nine-to-twelve feet squares of heavy wire, eventually extending to two hundred and thirty feet deep, held down by two-thousand-pound sinkers and held up by large buoys. |

| 30th October | Forced by defects to exit after only a week, FS *Turquoise* (Ravenel) ran aground near Nagara, came under fire, surrendered, with the crew taken as POWs. *Turquoise's* CO failed both to scuttle her and to destroy classified information aboard, which included details of a planned rendezvous with British submarine *E20* on 6 November. When *E20* showed up on the surface, she was torpedoed and sunk by *UB14* with only nine of the crew surviving. |

30th October (Cont.)	*Turquoise* was recommissioned and entered the Ottoman fleet, named *Müstecip Onbaşı*. On release in 1918, *Turquoise's* CO and XO were appointed as Knights of the Legion of Honour.

30th October (Cont.)

Turquoise was recommissioned and entered the Ottoman fleet, named *Müstecip Onbaşı*. On release in 1918, *Turquoise's* CO and XO were appointed as Knights of the Legion of Honour.

31st October

H1 (Pirie) completes her 29-day patrol.

6th November

E20 (Warren) is sunk by *UB14* [see entry for 30 October].

E11 (Nasmith) embarks on her third patrol, now with a larger 4-inch gun.

9th December

E2 (Stocks) enters the Dardanelles for her second patrol.

13th November

First Lord of the Admiralty – Winston Churchill – resigns. Excluded from the new War Committee of the Cabinet, Churchill believes he is being censured for the Dardanelles expedition.

18th-19th December

Evacuation of troops from Anzac Cove and Suvla Bay.

23rd December

E11 (Nasmith) completes her third patrol, having broken through the net with a special net-cutting arrangement that Nasmith had devised himself. This patrol was for a record 47 days, completing 96 or 97 days in total over her three patrols.

1916

3rd January

E2 (Stocks) exits the Dardanelles as the last transit of the campaign.

8th-9th January   The last seventeen thousand soldiers and forty guns were evacuated from Cape Helles, with the loss of just one sailor. Thirty-to-forty per cent losses had been anticipated.

Postscript – two years later – January **1918**

It was known that the defences of the Dardanelles had been strengthened since the end of the Allied land campaign in January 1916. More mines had been laid, including across the entrance to the Dardanelles between Cape Helles and Kum Kale. All the gun positions were also back in Turkish / German possession. Nonetheless, *E14* (White) was ordered to penetrate the Narrows to sink *Goeben* which had been damaged by mines in the Battle of Imbros (*Breslau* had sunk) and reportedly run aground off Nagara. The battlecruiser had been refloated and had left the scene by the time *E14* arrived, so Lt G S White attacked another ship, only for his own torpedo to explode prematurely and dramatically, possibly having hit a mine, severely damaging the submarine. Faced with severe flooding, White decided to try to exit the Straits on the surface, only to come under fire from all the forts. Sustaining yet more damage, *E14* was in a parlous state and White tried to run the submarine ashore to save the lives of his crew. The CO and Navigator on the bridge were both killed by a shell, and the First Lt died below. Nine crew, led by the Coxswain, survived and were taken as PoWs. White was awarded a posthumous VC.

E14 is the only submarine to have two of its Commanding Officers awarded the Victoria Cross.

Endpiece

Of the fourteen submarines that took part in the Dardanelles campaign (including *B11*), eight were sunk – three British, four French and one Australian (not including *E14* in 1918). Nine submarines undertook fifteen patrols in the Sea of Marmara and, between them, they accounted for the following Turkish losses:

- One battleship – *Barbaros Heyreddin*.
- One coastal defence ship – *Mesûdiye*.
- One destroyer.
- Five Gunboats.
- Eleven transports.
- Forty-four steamers.
- One hundred & forty-eight sailing craft.

In addition to this dramatic disruption to the sea lines of communication and seaborne support, significant damage was also inflicted upon railways and overland reinforcement routes. With some justification, Vice-Admiral de Robeck told Vice-Admiral Limpus in a letter dated 16th May 1915,

". . a submarine in the Marmara now is worth an Army Corps."

On 3rd June he wrote to him again,

"Our submarines in the Marmora (sic) are the most valuable weapon that the Navy has at present."

The Admiralty was also aware. On 9th June, the First Sea Lord, Admiral Jackson, wrote to de Robeck,

"Your submarines have done wonders . . ."

Endpiece

As far as my research has revealed, all merchant vessels were stopped, or ordered to heave to, prior to search, with only those found to be carrying war materiel being destroyed. In this case, the crew and passengers were disembarked, either into their own tenders or by taking them aboard the submarines, despite the cramped space available. Such conduct is in marked contrast to the unrestricted submarine warfare sanctioned by the Kaiser, announced by Admiral von Pohl on 4th February 1915. This is intimated by Winston Churchill in the continuation of the quotation on the front cover.

"Their exploits constitute in daring, in skill, in endurance, in risk, the finest examples of submarine action in the whole of the Great War, and were, moreover, marked by a strict observance of the recognised rules of warfare[2]."

Four Victoria Crosses were won by submariners in this theatre and it is these and the other COs' names that are remembered – Holbrook *(B11)*, Brodie T S *(E15)*, Stoker *(AE2)*, Boyle *(E14)*, Nasmith *(E11)*, Cochrane *(E7)*, Bruce *(E12)*, White *(E14)* amongst others. However, in '*Seven Pillars of Wisdom*', T E Lawrence writes,

"It is still less fair, of course, like all war-stories, to the un-named rank and file: who miss their share of the credit, as they must do, until they can write the despatches."

Glorious stories of derring do are mostly credited to the leaders, whereas anyone with any military nous knows that it is usually only truly cohesive *teams* that earn success. Nowhere is this truer than in submarines where the actions of just one man – officer or rating – could bring glory. But the same individual could equally court

---

[2] Churchill W S – The World Crisis 1915 p422

disaster. Perhaps it is most appropriate, therefore, that this story *is* told as fiction with an unknown submarine and her crew representing all those courageous men who achieved the most remarkable results. Accordingly, the reader is invited to consider the lowliest crew member. His actions remain unrecorded but were no less vital to his boat's survival and achievements.

Furthermore, in the Dardanelles submarine campaign, it was the entire cadre of boats working as a team that brought eventual success. Individual fortitude was necessary, of course, but together they encouraged one another to overcome the hazards they faced: navigation in poorly-charted waters, with ever-changing salinity, whorls and currents; the incalculable menace of a host of mines (three thousand were swept at the end of the war); the unavoidable, heavy nets strung across their paths; and not forgetting the stout-hearted Turks whose forces always put up a fight when possible.

In his book, "Forlorn Hope 1915: The Submarine Passage of the Dardanelles", C G Brodie – Keyes' staff officer – identifies the team up to the initial defeat of Hellespont.

"Nasmith, the captain, whose mastery of the game made him, though off the field, an example and a spur to the side. Stoker rather as a brilliant amateur, who stole the show from the professionals, but missed the limelight. Boyle the centre forward who scored the winning goal and got well-earned applause from the public and the team. T.S. [Brodie, his twin brother killed in *E15*] *I like to think of as "the little cherub, sitting aloft," doing his best to look after the side. I can fancy him gently plucking the sleeve of the helmsman as E14 skirted shoals and mine moorings on her passage, less gently jogging the elbows of the Turkish gunners firing at AE2, aground. Yes, a team, and a good one."*

Endpiece

Kipling finishes his poem 'The Trade' with this final verse:

> *Their feats, their fortunes and their fames*
> *Are hidden from their nearest kin;*
> *No eager public backs or blames,*
> *No journal prints the yarn they spin*
> *(The Censor would not let it in!)*
> *When they return from run or raid.*
> *Unheard they work, unseen they win.*
> *That is the custom of "The Trade."*

The rest of the Royal Navy and families at home were left significantly uninformed of the remarkable achievements of the Submarine Service in the Dardanelles, in the Baltic, in the Heligoland Bight, in the Skaw and elsewhere because, as Kipling implies, their operations were considered too secret. Arthur Balfour who had been Prime Minister (1901-1905) and was First Lord of the Admiralty from May 1915 until November 1916, having read *E11*'s patrol reports, minuted,

"It is worth considering whether some episodes of this remarkable story might not be published verbatim . . ."

It never happened. But perhaps the most incredulous example of such unawareness is when Admiral David Beatty, in the command of the Grand Fleet since November 1916, wrote to the Admiralty on 18th January 1917 concerning the disposition of submarines around the coast. He opined,

"It would appear that nine-tenths of these valuable craft have been used entirely for defensive purposes, and consequently have not been in a position to enable them to do anything during the 2½ years we have been at war."

In their response, the Lords of the Admiralty – graciously interpreting his comments to refer only to the D- and C-Classes – pointed out that the former were employed in overseas work. In addition and despite the small craft being unsuitable for off-shore employment, the C-Class had nonetheless been so tasked when appropriate. Feeling the need to explain to the Commander-in-Chief that units of his own Grand Fleet in Scapa were unable to respond with sufficient rapidity, their response of 30th January stated,

". . Submarines constitute our principal defence against raids of all kinds . . ,"

In August 1916, Commodore (S) had previously reported,

"The percentage of losses of our overseas submarines has been 33%, probably heavier than in any other of H.M. Forces."

Twenty-two boats had already been lost at this early stage in the war – fifteen of these with all hands – and Commodore Hall concludes,

"These losses . . . bear out my contention that the overseas submarines . . . are always in action when in enemy waters, though actions have not been made the subject of despatches and the losses have not been announced."

By November 1918, fifty-eight submarines and 1,174 officers and men had been lost, but with little celebration of their strategic contribution to the winning of the war, which was out of all proportion to the numbers deployed.

It is hard for us in the 21st Century ever to conceive what life was like in WW1 submarines: no sonar; no radar; unreliable gyro compasses; inaccurate distance measurement; no echo sounder; poor periscope optics;

radio of pathetically short range; no air purification or resupply; and certainly no ability to charge batteries whilst dived. All these elements rendered the fragile craft truly vulnerable both to enemy action and to the exceptionally hostile natural environment. Perhaps the best analogy available today is to consider the astronauts in those space probes bound for the moon in the late 1960s: cramped; trapped within their vehicle in an unforgiving environment; subject to system failures; and with less computing capacity aboard than a modern 'smart' phone. We look back speechless with wonder at, and with huge admiration for, the courage of those pioneers. Now take those thoughts back to the technology of fifty years before that. We should hold early submariners in no less regard, even before pitching them against a determined enemy.

Again, it is Churchill who sums it up best, completing his previous quote:

"When one thinks of these officers and men, penned together amid the intricate machinery which crammed their steel, cigar-shaped vessels; groping, butting, charging far below the surface at unmeasured, unknown obstructions; surrounded by explosive engines [mines]*, any one of which might destroy them at a touch; the target of guns and torpedoes if they rose for an instant to the light of day; harried by depth charges, hunted by gunboats and destroyers, stalked by the German U-boat; expecting every moment to be shattered, stifled, or hopelessly starved at the bottom of the sea; and yet in spite of all, enduring cheerfully such ordeals for weeks at a time; returning unflinchingly again and again through the Jaws of Death"*

HELLESPONT!

Acknowledgements

Bibliography

Ashmead-Bartlett E	The Uncensored Dardanelles
Aspinall-Oglander C	Roger Keys
Basarin V & H H	Beneath the Dardanelles – The Australian SM at Gallipoli
Benbow T	Naval Warfare 1914-1918: From Coronel to Zeebrugge
Bennett G	Naval Battles of First World War
Blackburn J A & Watkins K	The British Submarine in Being
Brenchley F	Stoker's Submarine - Australia's Daring Raid
Brodie C G	Forlorn Hope 1915 - The Submarine Passage of the Dardanelles
Bush E	Gallipoli
Carr W G	By Guess and By God: The Story of the British Submarines in the War
Carr W G	Hell's Angels of the Deep
Chatterton E K	Dardanelles Dilemma: The Story of Naval Operations
Chatterton E K	Gallant Gentlemen
Churchill W S	The World Crisis 1915
Compton-Hall R	SMs and the War at Sea 1914-1918
Compton-Hall R	The First Submarines – The Beginnings of Underwater Warfare
Crossley F J	Churchill's Admiral in Two World Wars

Bibliography

Cunningham AoF Viscount A B	A Sailor's Odyssey
de Bernières L	Birds Without Wings
Domville-Fife C W	Submarines and Sea Power
Domville-Fife C W	Submarines, Mines and Torpedoes in the War
Downer B (Ed)	Barrow Built Submarines
Edmonds M (Ed)	100 Years of the Trade
Edwards Lt Cdr K	We Dive at Dawn
'Etienne' [King-Hall S]	A Naval Lieutenant 1914-1918
Evans A S	Beneath the Waves - A History of HM Submarine Losses 1904-1971
Fleet Admiral H L	My Life and a Few Yarns
Forester W B C W	From Dartmouth to the Dardanelles
Forrest M	The Defence of the Dardanelles – From Bombards to Battleships
Gough B	Churchill and Fisher - Titans at the Admiralty
Gray E	British Submarines in the Great War
Gray E	Damned Un-English Weapon: Story of SM Warfare
Harris M	Harwich SMs in the Great War – The First SM Campaign of the RN in 1914
Hough R	The Great War at Sea 1914-1918
Jameson W	Submariners VC
Johnson S	Enemy of All Mankind
Keyes AoF R	The Naval Memoires of AoF Sir Roger Keyes
Kipling R	Sea Warfare (includes the Poem 'The Trade')

'Klaxon' [Bower J G]   Dead Reckoning - The Story of Our Submarines

'Klaxon'   The British Submarine Service: the RN & the Submersible War 1914-1918

Lambert N (Ed)   The Submarine Service 1900-1918

Lawrence P   A Century of Submarines

Lipscombe Cdr FW   The British Submarine

MacKay R   A Precarious Existence – British Submariners in World War One

MacKay R   Damned Un-English Sailors – British Submariners 1901-1945

Masters D   "I.D." New Tales of the Submarine War

McCartney I   British Submarines of World War One

National Archives   Dardanelles Commission Report: Conclusions (Website)

Newbolt H   Submarine and Anti-Submarine

Noppen RK   Ottoman Navy Warships 1914-18

Parker J   Illustrated History 1900-1950: Guide to development of underwater vessels

Parker J   The Silent Service - The Inside Story of the RN's Submarine Heroes

Preston A   RN SM Service: a Centennial History

Rudenno V   Gallipoli - Attack from the Sea

Shankland P & Hunter A   Dardanelles Patrol

Snelling S   VCs of WW1 – Gallipoli

Snow P & MacMillan A   War Stories

Stoker Cdr H G   Straws in the Wind

Taylor S   Commander - Biography of Edward Pellew

Bibliography

Usborne C V   Smoke on the Horizon –
Mediterranean Fighting 1914-1918

Vicary A   The Royal Navy 1914-1918:
A Photographic Record

Welch I   Great War - The Countdown to
Global Conflict

Wilson M I & Kemp P   Mediterranean SMs in World War One

Wilson M   Destination Dardanelles –
The Story of E7

Acknowledgements

Many kind people have provided rock-solid support to me throughout this enterprise and I hope to name them all. If I have unintentionally missed anyone, please let me know and I will correct the mistake in the second edition! At the outset was my long-term friend and the other survivor of my half of Perisher 1/84, Rear Admiral David Cooke CB MBE. Having discussed my ideas with him, he spotted Usborne's '*Smoke on the Horizon*' when we were together in a second-hand bookshop, which was the first of the yards of books I have acquired since. David also introduced me to George Malcomson, then-Curator of the RN Submarine Museum, who opened up some of its treasures for me. David, an officer of great integrity and a superb submariner, sadly died at age fifty-nine in December 2014.

The writing started properly when a friend, Celia Andrew – herself a published author – introduced me to a US scheme called the National Novel Writing Month (NaNoWriMo). I recommend it to any budding author as a great challenge to start getting words down on paper. Celia also read through an earlier draft and offered extensive, priceless comment.

In addition, I've imposed on many relatives, friends and colleagues, by seeking advice or by sending them drafts to read and requesting feedback. I thank each one for their brilliant work: Richard Raggett; Jack Pizzey; Barry Coward; Paddy Melhuish; David Southcott; Neil Avery; Iain Ballantyne, Paul Barrett; Ian Whitehouse; Jason Phillips; Tim Wills; and Barbara Thwaites. Andy Benford – inventor of the submarine board game '*We Come Unseen*' – also provided useful resource material. Friend and author of over fifty novels and books, Peter Clover, gave me some of his valuable time, advising on the mysteries of submissions to editors, synopses, and 'elevator pitches'.

I'm grateful to Tom Witcomb of The Literary Consultancy for his detailed and thoughtful input. Thanks also to the staff of IWM, NMRN and NASA for providing cover and internal photography. Tim Brown of Avery and Brown (averyandbrown.com) produced and polished the cover design, logo and internal maps.

Author 'Swan Morrison', more usually known as Brian Huggett, directed me towards self-publishing and suggested the use of Lulu.com with which I started. Such print-on-demand is a more sustainable option than normal publishing and I was keen to pursue this eco-friendly line wherever possible. Avery and Brown is a 'B Corp' company and so is Krystal (krystal.io) through which I acquired the byrneavery.com website domain. 'B Corp' companies – Certified B Corporations – are businesses that meet the highest standards of verified social and environmental performance, public transparency, and legal accountability to balance profit and purpose.

This project has been too long in the making and possible only then owing to the encouragement of my family, for whom 'The Book' has become something of a standing joke. Huge thanks to sons Alex and Russ for their practical support and occasional not-too-gentle nudge for me to get on with it. But it is my long-suffering wife, Sarah, who deserves most praise. This book could not have been written and produced without her.

So, it took quite a number of people to produce this tome and, borrowing C G Brodie's remark, "*Yes, a team, and a good one.*"

Printed in Dunstable, United Kingdom

70359861R00201